MW00626539

ArtScroll® Series

Rabbi Nosson Scherman / Rabbi Gedaliah Zlotowitz

General Editors

Rabbi Meir Zlotowitz ז״ל, *Founder and President*

אמונה

Published by

ARTSCROLL
Mesorah Publications, ltd

Just One Word

EMUNAH

Heartwarming and inspiring
stories and words of chizuk
to strengthen our faith

Esther Stern

FIRST EDITION
First Impression … January 2018

Published and Distributed by
MESORAH PUBLICATIONS, LTD.
4401 Second Avenue / Brooklyn, N.Y 11232

Distributed in Europe by
LEHMANNS
Unit E, Viking Business Park
Rolling Mill Road
Jarow, Tyne & Wear, NE32 3DP
England

Distributed in Australia and New Zealand
by **GOLDS WORLDS OF JUDAICA**
3-13 William Street
Balaclava, Melbourne 3183
Victoria, Australia

Distributed in Israel by
SIFRIATI / A. GITLER — BOOKS
POB 2351
Bnei Brak 51122

Distributed in South Africa by
KOLLEL BOOKSHOP
Northfield Centre, 17 Northfield Avenue
Glenhazel 2192, Johannesburg, South Africa

ARTSCROLL® SERIES
JUST ONE WORD: EMUNAH
© Copyright 2018, by MESORAH PUBLICATIONS, Ltd.
4401 Second Avenue / Brooklyn, N.Y. 11232 / (718) 921-9000 / www.artscroll.com

ALL RIGHTS RESERVED
The text, prefatory and associated textual contents and introductions
— including the typographic layout, cover artwork and ornamental graphics —
have been designed, edited and revised as to content, form and style.

No part of this book may be reproduced
IN ANY FORM, PHOTOCOPYING, DIGITAL, OR COMPUTER RETRIEVAL SYSTEMS
— even for personal use without written permission from
the copyright holder, Mesorah Publications Ltd.
except by a reviewer who wishes to quote brief passages
in connection with a review written for inclusion in magazines or newspapers.

THE RIGHTS OF THE COPYRIGHT HOLDER WILL BE STRICTLY ENFORCED.

ISBN 10: 1-4226-1982-6 / ISBN 13: 978-1-4226-1982-7

Typography by CompuScribe at ArtScroll Studios, Ltd.
Printed in the United States of America by Noble Book Press Corp.
Bound by Sefercraft, Quality Bookbinders, Ltd., Brooklyn N.Y. 11232

We are privileged to dedicate this volume on Emunah in memory of our beloved husband and father, who personified Emunah

Rabbi Moshe Alon ז״ל
הרב משה בן שלמה ז״ל
9 Nissan 5777

He was a Rav and Marbitz Torah in Hamilton, Ontario and Syracuse, New York, and then settled in Toronto for the chinuch of his children.

He entered the world of commerce, but he lived in the world of Torah, chessed, and service to Klal Yisrael. His emunas chachamim was total; the counsel of gedolim was his guide.

When there was a young Jewish community without a local mikveh, he built a mikveh. Though he felt that his primary responsibility was to Torah life in Toronto, he supported institutions everywhere. And he helped individuals warmly, wisely, and generously. His personal guidepost was absolute emes. His word was like an ironclad contract.

He lived with Emunah and taught by example. We pray that we can live up to his aspirations.

Mrs. Osnas Alon
and children

מכתב הסכמה מהרב הגאון ר' מתתיהו סולומן, שליט"א משגיח דישיבת לאקווד

בס"ד

אלול תשע"ו

הנה רצוני לכתוב שורה להגיד כמה נהניתי בראותי הקונטרס שערך בתו של ידידי, אהובי הר"ר מנדל קויפמאן זצ"ל מגייטסהעד בעניני אמונה, ביטחון והודאה לה'.

מאד ניכר מבין השורות החינוך על מבועי התורה והיראה והאמונה הטהורה.

יהי רצון שיהא זה לזכות ולעלוי נשמתו של אביה ר' מנדל זצ"ל, שמידת האמונה והשמחה הקרינה על פניו, ופיו היה תמיד מלא בשבח והודאה לה' ושם שמים שגור על פיו.

וכאשר הספר "מילה אחת אמן" עושה רושם גדול עד היום על אלפי בני ישראל כן יתרחב ההשפעה בעניני אמונה לקרב לבבות אל אבינו שבשמים.

איני צריך להגיד גודל החשיבות של התחזקות באמונה בימינו, הלוא דברי חז"ל גלויים וידועים. ויה"ר שבכוח חיזוק זה נזכה במהרה לגאולה השלמה.

Rabbi E. Falk
146 Whitehall Road
Gateshead, NE8 1TP
England
TEL: 0044-191-4782342

פסח אליהו פאלק
מח"ס שו"ת מחזה אליהו
'זכור ושמור' על הלכות שבת
'עוז והדר לבושה' על צניעות דלבוש
מו"ץ בק"ק גייטסהעד יצ"ו

בס"ד

אור לכ"ג טבת תשע"ח לפ"ק פה גייטסהעד יצ"ו.

נשלח אלי מא"י ספר באנגלית הכתוב ע"י בתו החשובה של ידידי
וידיד כל בית ישראל הרבני הנגיד הצדיק מורה"ר ר' מנדל קופמאן
זצ"ל מגייטסהעד ורעייתו החשובה ע"ה. הספר מבוסס כל כולו על עניני
אמונה ובטחון וכח התפלה וכו' וכתוב בחום ואהבת ה' שודאי תמשוך לב
הקוראים בו להכיר בוראם בכל קורות חייהם. שם הספר הוא "מלה אחת
- אמונה" וכל כולו מעשה אומן כתוב ע"י מי שנתחנכה על ברכי אביה
ואמה וספגה בלבה כל היקר ליהודי הדבוק בה' ובתורתו. כותבת הספר
היא לא הראשונה לומר "מילה אחת - אמונה" דכבר אמר בדומה לכך
הבורא עולם "מה ה' אלוקיך שואל מעמך כי עם ליראה את ה' אלוקיך"
ובמלות קצרות אלו כרוכה כל המהות של יהודי חרדי לדבר ה'.

והנה אני נמנע מלתת הסכמות בכל האפשר מחמת גודל האחריות,
אולם כאן יצאתי מגדרי בראותי גודל הטירחא שטרחה הכותבת
להואיל לבני גילה, וגודל הס"ד שהיה לה לאסוף ולסדר הרבה דברים
יקרים ומעשים מופלאים מגדולי ישראל, וגודל התועלת שיכול לצאת
מהדפסת ופרסום ספר זה. ואני תפלה שנוצר תאנה יאכל פריה ותזכה
כותבת הספר שתחי' לראות פירות מעמלה לזכות את הרבים בעולם
שרעב כל כך לחיזוק באמונה. ובודאי ספר זה יהא לנחת רוח לנשמת
אביה ואמה החשובים זצ"ל שחיו באמונה והודאה תמידית להבורא
עולם, וגידלו בניהם בדרך התורה והיראה.

הכותב לכבוד החיזוק שיצא בעז"ה מספר זה.

פסח אליהו פאלק

Table of Contents

Acknowledgments

THE STORIES IN this book were written with great care to present true life examples of *emunah*, which should enhance the *divrei chizuk* presented alongside, to form light and easy-to-read words of encouragement so desperately needed today.

Much time was spent thoroughly clarifying the numerous details in each story, in most instances hearing them from the people involved, so that they could be written precisely the way they took place.

I am deeply grateful to all the people who agreed to share with me their personal challenges, divulging deep sentiments, whether under their real name or a fictitious one.

I sincerely appreciate Mrs. Tzirel Strassman's devotion as she accompanied me to various interviews and recorded them and other stories so beautifully with her talented flair and heartfelt words.

I thank R' Nachman Seltzer for using his fantastic gift of writing to bring vividly to life the true stories he wrote.

I thank Mrs. Rochel Gross for the stories she skillfully wrote or translated.

I thank Mrs. Chana Nestlebaum for taking my manuscript and turning it into the wonderfully polished, finished product.

I am grateful to the *chashuve* staff of ArtScroll, each one for his or her part in bringing this book to perfection. Especially to Mrs. Miriam Zakon for her expert advice and talented touch, given in such a caring and pleasant manner.

I thank my close family for the help, support, and enthusiasm they shared with me while writing this book.

מוֹדֶה אֲנִי לְפָנֶיךָ ה׳ אֱלֹהַי וֵאלֹהֵי אֲבוֹתַי, עַל כָּל הַחֶסֶד אֲשֶׁר עָשִׂיתָ עִמָּדִי, וַאֲשֶׁר אַתָּה עָתִיד לַעֲשׂוֹת עִמִּי וְעִם כָּל בְּנֵי בֵיתִי.

E. Stern

Shevat 5778 / January 2018

אור זרוע לצדיק ולישרי לב שמחה

לעילוי נשמת

ר׳ זכריה מנחם קויפמאן זצ״ל

בן ר׳ משה קויפמאן זצ״ל - גייטסהעד

דבק בה׳ ובצדיקים באהבה ובאמונה טהורה
חוט של חן וחסד היה זרוע על פניו
שהקרין אור כשמש וחימם כל סובביו
היה אוהב שלום ורודף צדקה וחסד
הקים בית של תורה וזכה לראות
בנים ובני בנים עוסקים בתורה ובמצוות

נלב״ע ז״ך טבת תשע״ו

Prologue

The Emergency Shabbos Flight

REB ELIMELECH'S* BOUTS of unexplained pain had been getting worse. Now he sat in an oncologist's office with his wife, watching as the doctor pored over the MRI scans he had brought along. The doctor at last looked up at his patient and cleared his throat.

"Mr. Gutman, I'm sorry to have to tell you that you're seriously ill. It doesn't look good."

He gave Elimelech several referrals, and appointments were set up immediately.

Soon the couple was making the rounds, but to their great relief and comfort, they were accompanied by Reb Shia,* a local medical referral expert who knew how to cut through the red tape and ask the right questions. The doctors were well acquainted with Reb Shia. They respected his professionalism and admired his *mesirus nefesh* for his fellow Jews.

Nevertheless, the news was grim. "We're sorry, but there's nothing we can do for you," the doctor told Elimelech. "There's nothing to be gained from beginning a round of treatment. The sickness has progressed to the point of no return."

They thanked the doctor and left the office. Reb Elimelech was silent, lost in thought. At this point, his wife chimed in.

"Could you please do us a favor?" she asked Reb Shia. "Please set up a meeting for us with Rabbi Elyashiv. Today if possible."

---

* Names marked with an asterisk have been changed.

"Today is Friday," Reb Shia said, "when he doesn't usually see visitors. But since this is a matter of life and death, I will see what I can do."

The meeting convened twenty minutes later around the simple dining-room table of the *gadol hador* in Yerushalayim. Reb Shia arrived equipped with the entire case history, and Rabbi Yosef Shalom Elyashiv listened to the facts with grave attention. When Reb Shia finished summarizing the situation, Rabbi Elyashiv spoke.

"There doesn't seem to be much of a question here. The doctors all concur that there isn't anything left to be done and no reason for treatment."

Reb Elimelech looked at the tablecloth, his downcast eyes brimming with tears. Rabbi Elyashiv, though clearly feeling for the patient, didn't suggest treatment, but gave him a *berachah* for a *refuah sheleimah*. The meeting had wound its way to an end.

His wife chose that moment to ask her question.

"Rebbe," she bravely began, "it seems inevitable from how the Rav has answered us that I will soon be a young widow and my children will be orphans without their father. Right now, our children are very young and have no idea about our current critical situation. But, *b'ezras Hashem*, they will grow up, and I know that they will wonder about the circumstances surrounding their father's passing. I am sure that one day they will want to know if I did every single thing possible to save his life. Will I be able to tell them that I did?"

Her pleading words hung in the silent room, in the air redolent with *sefarim* and holiness.

At that moment, something changed in Rabbi Elyashiv's demeanor. A look of urgency took over.

"Reb Shia," he said, "I want you and the patient to board a plane right now and fly to the United States for treatment."

Although it was almost Shabbos, the *gadol* insisted that they act immediately to save Elimelech's life. Two cabs arrived: one to take Mrs. Gutman home, and the other to transport Reb Shia and Elimelech to the airport.

It wasn't long before Elimelech was undergoing emergency surgery in a New York hospital. After hours of waiting,

Reb Shia finally saw the surgeon enter the waiting room. An exhausted but satisfied smile was on his face.

"It looks like your friend has a new lease on life," he said.

After several weeks of recovery, Reb Elimelech was once again flying, this time toward life: toward his wife and his children, who would now never have to wonder if their mother did her best to save their father's life.

The story, inspiring as it is, begs a question. What caused Rabbi Elyashiv to change his mind? After all, the *gadol* had seemingly accepted the doctor's prognosis and had made it seem pretty clear that he didn't have any hopes for a miracle. The moment Mrs. Gutman opened her mouth, everything changed. Why?

Reb Shia decided to ask Rabbi Chaim Kanievsky to explain his father-in-law's apparent change of heart. After relating the entire story to Reb Chaim, he received the following explanation:

"When you first presented the information to my father-in-law, it was clear that everyone had given up on Reb Elimelech's life. The doctors saw nothing to be done and you concurred. Even Reb Elimelech had given up hope for a miracle. According to *derech hateva*, the natural order of the world, there was no chance for things to change.

"Then Reb Elimelech's wife wanted to know if anything in the world could possibly be done to save her husband. She wasn't willing to give up all hope. She had *emunah* and *bitachon* that the doctors' prognosis could be wrong and that there could be other avenues to pursue. She didn't want to have to answer to her children that she hadn't tried her best to save their father's life.

"Once my father-in-law saw this, he realized that there was room for her *emunah* to save her husband's life. The change took place only once it was clear that this young wife still believed that nothing was over until the Ribono shel Olam decreed it so. At that point, my father-in-law recognized the urgency and *paskened* that they fly to America — even on Shabbos — because the *emunah* shown in this case was powerful enough to actually change nature."

(*Derech Sichah* 684)

Introduction

*L*IFE IS LIKE an ocean. Sometimes the waters are calm and the waves roll smoothly and peacefully. But frequently a storm erupts, and the waves become wild, rising higher and higher, roaring loudly, threatening to overpower anything that gets in their way. When that unexpected storm breaks out and the waves are already above our head, they will soon drown us unless we are thrown a rope that we can grab hold of. It must be an extremely sturdy rope that is anchored by a very strong force, powerful enough to pull us up, above the turbulent waves, to safety.

Rebbe Elimelech of Lizhensk once sat at *seudas shelishis* with his disciples crowded around his table, thirstily drinking in his holy words of wisdom. Suddenly he paused and asked them, "What is *chevlei Mashiach*?"

They responded with silence, waiting to hear what Reb Elimelech would answer. He said, "Before Mashiach comes, HaKadosh Baruch Hu will take a rope and hang it from one end of the world to the opposite end. Then He will shake the rope up and down with great force. Those who hold on very tight will survive. But those who loosen their grip will fall."

This rope is the *emunah* and *bitachon* that connect us directly to the Ribono shel Olam Himself, Who can pull us up and beyond the mightiest waves. This violently shaking rope, this *chevel*, is called "*chevlei Mashiach*." By grasping it with all our might, it will save us from the fearsome challenges that precede Mashiach's coming.

At those precise moments when all seems lost, we have the opportunity to grab hold of the rope and access this wondrous world of *emunah* and *bitachon*. We can ascend to great heights and accomplish far more than we ever did when everything ran smoothly. It is a beautiful, secure world where we have the full support of the

Strongest Force in the universe and enjoy the most intimate relationship with Hashem.

Many people have the mistaken belief that they're not in control of their thoughts and emotional reactions to events in their lives, and they allow their emotions to control their behavior and moods. This is a very mistaken attitude. With *emunah* and *bitachon*, a Yid can work to control his thoughts and emotions, building his trust and striving for the loftiest aspirations. He can develop new perspectives, reaching the highest levels of *Yiddishkeit* and achieving accomplishments way beyond the laws of nature.

Working on *emunah* might seem to be a task only for very righteous people, who are far above our *madreigah*. It might seem brazen to even dare write about such lofty concepts as *emunah* and *bitachon*. A wonderful *mashal* of the Chafetz Chaim from his introduction to *Sefer Shemiras HaLashon* eradicates any hesitation we may have about attempting to climb such a tall ladder, even though we realize we may still remain on the lower rungs:

Jewels on the Beach: A Mashal

A young man has a few hours to spend at the seashore before he will be picked up to return home. He walks along the beach and is astonished to see that the stones and pebbles are shining brilliantly, reflecting beautiful colors. Taking a closer look, he confirms that these are not ordinary shells but precious jewels.

He stares at the thousands of jewels and diamonds lying on the sand. Each one is worth a fortune. What should he do? He has only a short time, and he'll never manage to pick up so many thousands of them.

Should he shrug his shoulders and say, "What's the point of making an effort to pick them up? There are too many. I'll never be able to collect all of them." Should he just give up, then, before he even begins?

Of course not!

He'll bend down and grab as many as he can without thinking twice, not wasting a second, and he'll arrive home a very wealthy man.

The levels a person can reach with *bitachon* are infinitely high, but every small step we climb is a major accomplishment. For one thing, each and every thought of *emunah* that a person has is tremendously precious to the Ribono shel Olam. For another, it influences the quality of our life in this world and our portion in Olam HaBa and makes an impact on all the heavenly spheres. It enriches our life with so much *menuchas hanefesh* and *simchas hachaim*, tranquility and joy, even if we didn't reach the top. Although we cannot manage to amass it all, we can still become very wealthy.

May this book be a source of *chizuk* to everyone who reads it and enable them to enter the majestic world of true faith in Hashem, providing a strong rope to hold onto in the face of mighty waves. May it turn desperation into hope and depression into joy and tears of despair and self-pity into tears of *deveikus* to the Ribono shel Olam, so that everyone will merit a content and tranquil life and consequent salvation.

Part 1:
Practical Emunah

Chapter 1
Mastering the Skill

Emunah is knowing and believing. Bitachon is taking the knowledge and putting it into practice.
(Chazon Ish, Sefer Emunah U'Bitachon 2:2)

The Definition of Emunah

A LIFE LIVED WITH *emunah* is a peaceful, tranquil, and joyful life. No problems or worries, no pressure, no tension or fear of anyone or anything. It is a life filled with happiness, full of hopes for the future. No sadness, remorse, or bitter memories of the past. No jealousy. A truly calm and blissful life!

Does this sound like a fantasy?

Is there anyone who sails through life without experiencing any difficulty in *parnassah*, without any illness, pain, hardships, problems in family life, or *tza'ar gidul banim*? Life is not a picnic! When problems arise, they are real, big, threatening, and overpowering.

Does *emunah* really take away our problems?

Emunah solves all problems. Sometimes, in the course of time, the problems disappear altogether. And sometimes a problem remains in the form of a challenge, but the worry, fear, and anxiety disappear. In its place, a wonderful feeling of *kirvas Elokim*, of closeness to Hashem, fills us with warmth, joy, and serenity.

In the most hopeless situation, when a person has every reason to despair, his *emunah* can save him. Is it correct to display faith and trust even when naturally and logically there is no hope?

Yes. This is the very definition of *emunah. Emunah* begins where logic ends! That is, what seems logical from our limited perspective. Logically it may seem as if there is no hope, no way out of our situation — until salvation seems to appear out of nowhere, from a place we didn't expect it. The stronger our *emunah*, the faster the wheel of salvation will move. *Emunah* itself is the force that turns the wheel. It's actually quite natural.

Let's look at the differences between a person living with *emunah* and a person without *emunah*:

WITH EMUNAH	WITHOUT EMUNAH
Content	Often complaining
Never worries	Feels anxious
Calm, relaxed	Nervous, no *menuchas hanefesh*, fearful
Focused on tasks to be done	Distracted state of mind, lacks energy
In high spirits, happy, cheerful	Depressed, sad
Confident	Lacks confidence
Is helpful and friendly to everyone	Easily angered and insulted

If a person would examine one of his life's challenges and calculate how much of his suffering is the actual problem and how much is the accompanying worry, pain, anguish, and fear of the unknown, he would discover that often the problem itself is relatively small compared to the side effects that blow it up into a huge burden. With *emunah* there are no "side effects." There is only the net problem.

Emunah Training

SO HOW DOES one acquire *emunah*?

The answer lies in the very root of the word. *Emunah* (אמונה) has the same root as *imun* (אימון), "training." *Emunah* is an *umanus* (אומנות), a skill that can be only acquired with *imun*, with practice.

A recruit must go through intensive training before he can be considered a soldier. A medical student has to study for many years, but his knowledge alone won't qualify him as a doctor until he goes through practical training. A violinist must invest thousands of hours of practice to master the skill. Even the most famous violinist practices for hours each day to ensure that he will perform at his best.

Emunah is a skill like any other. It can't be acquired without training. It takes hard work to become professional. Life's trials and tribulations, some minor, some major, provide us with practical training. There is no other way to master the skill of *emunah*.

If you are presently facing a difficult situation, be aware that you have been chosen by your loving Father to join a professional course. You have won a scholarship! He has chosen to personally train and coach you because He sees great potential in you. He is accompanying you every step of the difficult trek, guiding you and waiting for you to pass the test with flying colors. He has full confidence in you. That's why He picked you for this challenge.

Let's imagine a child who is confined to a wheelchair due to an injury. The doctors promise him that with intensive physiotherapy he can overcome his disability. He will have to invest time, patience, strength, and willpower to perform daily exercises that might be extremely painful. It might take days, weeks, or months until he sees any improvement, but if he is persistent, he will be able to leave his wheelchair and walk.

Likewise, we attain *emunah* through practice and exercise. It requires hard work in painful situations, but if we persist, we can overcome major handicaps. Without it, we may remain stuck in a wheelchair forever.

Switching the Channel

*I*T HAD BEEN a strenuous day for Ahuva. It was 11 p.m. and every limb in her body ached and her eyelids felt heavy. She collapsed into bed, exhausted, when suddenly the telephone rang.

Ahuva didn't even have the strength to stretch out her hand and lift the receiver, never mind speak to anyone. But the caller seemed to be adamant that his call not be ignored. The ringing went on and on until Ahuva realized that if she didn't answer, all her children would wake up.

"Mazel tov!" her brother shouted excitedly as soon as she picked up. "Shoshi has just become a *kallah*. We're drinking the *l'chaim* now. Come over quickly."

"What!" Ahuva screamed. She sprang out of bed, dressed, and ran out of the house at full speed. Shoshi was her oldest niece. This was so exciting!

A few minutes earlier, Ahuva had collapsed into bed and didn't have the strength to lift a finger. Where did she suddenly get such a boost of energy?

Sometimes it's not our situation that makes us feel so weary. It's how we view it that makes the difference. Here's another example:

Yehoshua walked along the street, bent under the weight of his burdens. He was drowning in the debts incurred by marrying off five children, and he had another three who were of marriageable age. The food he ate would get stuck in his throat. He couldn't concentrate on a *blatt* Gemara or on any task, for that matter. He felt he could hardly smile anymore. He just wanted to run away and escape from all his problems.

A bus pulled up right in front of him. He boarded the bus and sat, sinking into his seat, until the bus arrived at the last stop. As he disembarked and trudged down the street, his face was clouded with worry. Then someone tapped him on his shoulder. He found himself face to face with a kind-looking stranger. For some reason, he took up the offer to rest on the nearby bench and pour out his heart. The stranger listened attentively, sympathetically.

Finally, he took out his wallet and asked Yehoshua, "How much money do you need so that you can get back on your feet again?"

Yehoshua said, "If I had $150,000 I could invest it and slowly, slowly begin to repay all my loans. It would also leave me with a small dowry for my next child in line."

The total stranger opened his checkbook and wrote out a check for $150,000 made out in the name of his new acquaintance. "My name is Reichmann," he explained. "In two years' time I will meet you here at this bench, and I hope you will be able to return the loan to me. By then you will be feeling better, and earning a good salary like you used to."

Yehoshua took the check in disbelief, feeling as if he had been rejuvenated. The heavy boulder had been removed from his shoulders.

He tucked away the check while he considered exactly what to do with the money. Meanwhile, with an extra spurt of energy, he was hired for a well-paying position. He became very successful and was soon earning a handsome sum. The check remained untouched in his drawer. *I would rather pay back all the loans with my earnings before I use it*, he decided.

Within two years the loans had all been paid back and Yehoshua had married off his next son. His financial status was stable. He even had a neat sum in a savings account. He had not touched the check. He set out on the appointed date to meet Mr. Reichmann, proud to be able to return the check and relate his success story.

He noticed Mr. Reichmann in the distance. As he watched him approaching, a passerby remarked, "There's that mentally disturbed man who hangs around the neighborhood giving out checks and claiming that he's Mr. Reichmann!"

Yehoshua's salvation had turned out to be based on nothing more than an illusion, but it was enough to restore his faith in his future, and that faith was all he needed to find solutions to his problems.

Truly, a different mind-set can transform a person who is exhausted, physically or emotionally, into a new person infused with strength. This is the power *emunah* has to enable a person going through the most trying and overwhelming circumstances to get back on his feet feeling refreshed and joyous, ready to stride through his challenge.

Such a transformation doesn't come in one day. It requires readjusting one's thoughts and reprogramming one's mind-set. With perseverance and willpower, there is no limit to the *madreigah* one can reach in *emunah*, and there is no limit to the supernatural powers and miracles *emunah* can engender.

Laying the Foundation: Acceptance

*B*EFORE WE EMBARK on our journey in search of *emunah*, there is one fundamental principle that must be learned and learned well.

In the present, a person may feel that he is a failure. His life hasn't turned out as he dreamed it would. As a result, he may feel annoyed and frustrated. He must stop a moment to think, *Who am I angry with? Who caused all my problems? Did I choose my plight? Did I pick my parents or children or determine who my spouse would be? Did I choose whether or not to be wealthy or healthy or whether to live in peace and comfort — or in pain?*

This person surely did not make those choices. Every individual's life situation is chosen for him down to the most minor detail, given to him by the only One Who is in charge: HaKadosh Baruch Hu. So we can calm down. We are not to blame, and neither is anyone else. There has been no mistake. This is our fate, designed specifically for us. We didn't choose it, but if we choose to accept it, we can learn to deal with it and rise from the challenge instead of becoming broken, downcast, and overwhelmed.

A Lesson at the Market

*Y*OSEF MEIR OF Machnovka was a grandchild of Reb Itzikel Skverer. One day, young
Yosef Meir took a stroll in the marketplace.
When he arrived home, Reb Itzikel greeted
him and asked him where he had been.

"I went to the cattle fair," Yosef Meir replied with a grin.
"I heard a rumor that Eliyahu HaNavi is around there, and I
thought I might meet him."

"*Nu*, did you meet him?" his grandfather probed.

"No, I didn't."

"So what did you see there?"

The sharp-witted boy knew he must provide a sufficiently
clever answer to satisfy his illustrious grandfather.

"I'll tell you what I observed," he answered spontaneously. "I saw many oxen tied up waiting to be sold. There were
some that resigned themselves to their fate, and they stood
in line patiently until they were fed and given to drink. There
were others that pulled and kicked wildly, angrily trying to
break free of the rope. They were beaten and bruised un-
necessarily."

He took a deep breath and continued. "Every person
has his own *pekel*. Some accept that it is from the Ribono
shel Olam and they are calm. Hashem accompanies them
throughout their challenge, and they manage to cope. Others try to fight. They're not prepared to accept their lot, and
they cause themselves superfluous pain and anguish."

Reb Itzikel kissed Yosef Meir on his cheek and he told
him with obvious delight, "If that's what you observed, then
maybe you didn't see Eliyahu HaNavi, but he certainly saw
you!"

The Ohr HaChaim writes (on *Bereishis* 36:27) that when a person accepts his *yissurim*, that is his best remedy.

When a person stops trying to get his way at all costs and blaming others for his failings, and he resigns himself to Hashem's will,
he is *zocheh* to *yeshuos*.

Know That Hashem Loves You

*H*OW DO WE reach this level of acceptance when we're struggling with pain or disappointment? The first and foremost significant step we can take is to internalize that *Hashem loves me!*

Our problems are real and threatening, and anxiety may fill our mind constantly. We can't instruct the mind to stop thinking, but we can dispose of all the troublesome negative thoughts by replacing them with positive ones.

The most inspiring, strength-infusing positive thought we can use to fill us up with happiness and energy is expressed in three words: "Hashem loves me."

This is the meaning of the verse "*Asaprah el chok Hashem amar eilai bni atah ani hayom yelideticha* — I am obliged to proclaim that Hashem said to me, 'You are My son; I bore you this day'" (*Tehillim* 2:7). This is a *chok* (חק), a decree — the first rule for withstanding any challenge — which should be *chakuk* (חקוק), engraved on our heart: We must reassure ourselves again and again that "*bni atah*" — we are Hashem's children and He loves each of us dearly like a father loves an only child.

Imagine the great love a father has for his only precious child. Hashem's love for us is so much more than that. It's more than the love we have for ourselves. It's more than any love that ever existed in the world.

Every single Yid is deserving of this love, regardless of how low he has fallen or how much he has sinned. As long as one has a parent, he is always someone's child. Hashem is our Father, and He will always be there for us. We must engrave this in our hearts and tell ourselves again and again: Hashem loves us so very much. He doesn't hurt us and He doesn't punish us brutally. He does only what is absolutely best for us. He is looking after us every moment of the day.

As the *pasuk* says, "*Im esak Shamayim sham atah v'atziah she'ol hinecha* — If I ascend to heaven, You [Hashem] are there [with me], and if I make my bed in the lowest depths, behold You [Hashem] are there [to protect me]" (ibid. 139:8). We can't run away from Him. We can't hide anywhere. And He won't leave us either: never, ever. He is standing by our side watching us, caring for us, not diverting His attention from us for one split second, regardless of how far we have distanced ourselves from Him.

What can we do to allow ourselves to feel His love for us? In the midst of our anxiety, we should open our eyes wide and begin to notice every little act of *hashgachah pratis* — individual supervision — that Hashem shows us every day. We can take a few minutes at the end of each day to review how many times we felt His special *hashgachah pratis*. We can make a mental note of the kindnesses He performed for us in one day and say, "Thank You."

We can take note of the various coincidences of the day when it seemed that just "by chance" things worked out conveniently. Rearrange the letters of the word מקרה, "chance." They form רק מה', "[they were] only from Hashem." He is showing us His love each time, and we should allow this love to trickle into our heart. How lucky we are to be His dear children!

Moishy felt someone slap him hard on the back. He whirled around aggressively, ready to defend himself, only to see his closest friend grinning from ear to ear.

We must turn around and look over our shoulder to see who is slapping us. We will realize that no one is attacking us. It is only an affectionate slap from our closest Friend. Then the slap won't even hurt. We will no longer be angry.

Shloimy's parents accompanied him as he was wheeled through the hospital corridor to the operating room. He was going to have his right arm amputated.

He knew that this would prevent his illness from ravaging his entire body. He was aware that he was fortunate the illness had been discovered in time and he had a chance to save his life.

Shloimy woke up several hours later. Acute pain seized him. He wanted to scream. Tears began streaming down his face as he absorbed the terrible reality: he had only one arm.

He opened his eyes, and he met the gaze of his father standing right next to him. His father smiled at him lovingly, a smile full of compassion and understanding. He could detect his own pain reflected in his father's face.

Shloimy was undergoing a tremendous ordeal. His body writhed in pain. He was left handicapped, but his spirit was intact. He was thankful that his life would be saved. He relied on his father's decision to perform the operation, and the love and encouragement of his father and his sharing in his pain gave him the strength to survive.

The trying ordeals we go through may be excruciating. But our loving Father chose to give them to us for our benefit. He is there right next to us the entire time. Our pain hurts Him much more than it hurts us. This is what a person must think about while he is suffering.

The *Orchos Tzaddikim*, in the section entitled *Sha'arei Simchah*, explains that internalizing this knowledge and believing it and feeling it with one's whole heart is a positive mitzvah: "*Ki ka'asher yeyaser ish es bno Hashem Elokecha meyasreka* — Just as a man will chastise his son, so Hashem, your God, chastises you" (*Devarim* 8:5).

These precious words are Hashem's personal message to us: "I love you. You are My dear child, and if I cause you pain, it's only intended to help you, to save you. Your pain hurts Me, too."

Thinking about this will soothe our pain and calm us down. Every moment we think about it is a mitzvah from the Torah.

This moving story was heard from Rabbi Ezriel Tauber, whose close relative was present at the time:

The Convert's Response

The *beis din* in Flatbush was crowded with prestigious *rabbanim*. The *av beis din* addressed the convert standing nervously at her place awaiting the *psak din* that would determine her future. Would she be accepted into the Jewish congregation to become a full-fledged Jew?

"Do you realize that it's very hard to be a Jew?" he informed her sternly. "The mitzvos are difficult to observe, and the penalty for committing sins is very harsh."

"I'm aware," she replied confidently. "And I'm prepared nevertheless to accept all the consequences of this."

The *rabbanim* used every possible argument to dissuade the woman, but she stuck to her conviction.

Finally, the *av beis din* shouted, his voice booming, permeating the entire room, "If you become a Jew, it is possible you may not have Olam HaZeh, and it's possible you may not have Olam HaBa!"

There was a hush in the room. Everyone held his breath. Would these sharp words weaken her resolve?

The *giyores* candidate pierced the silence with a heart-rending cry: "I don't need Olam HaZeh, and I don't need Olam HaBa," she sobbed. "I just want to be a child of HaKadosh Baruch Hu!"

Not one eye remained dry. The *giyores*-to-be understood the essence of *Yiddishkeit*.

Ashreinu mah tov chelkeinu! How fortunate we are to be the beloved children of the Ribono shel Olam, Who has the power to do anything. As long as we know this, we are safe, secure, and cared for. Our *emunah* will be strong no matter what life brings us. We will not question His ways, and we will be confident that He will help us.

Bearing the Unbearable

SOMETIMES OUR CHALLENGES may be so overwhelming that our pain is unbearable. Too many problems come at us at once, and we feel justified in giving up. After all, how much strength are we expected to have? At times like these, we might feel as if Hashem is slapping us very harshly in the face. We begin to wonder, *Why? Why me? Has Hashem left me?* However, as the following story from the *sefer Meir Einei Yisrael* (Vol. 2, p. 266) shows us, even when we've lost everything, we can still save ourselves by holding even more tightly to the last thing we have, the one thing that can never be ripped away from us: our *emunah*.

Fire in Radin

In the era of the Chafetz Chaim, a fire broke out in Radin. The leaping flames mercilessly ravaged dozens of houses in the Jewish neighborhood, until they stopped right outside the house of the Chafetz Chaim.

Kind neighbors welcomed the homeless families of Radin into their homes and helped them with whatever they needed until their houses were in livable shape again.

Half a year later another fire broke out. This time it started with the Chafetz Chaim's house and continued in the other direction until it burned down the last house in Radin. With no fire engines, the people in town formed a bucket brigade to fight the raging fire.

Reb Chaim Tzvi Sinai was a *yeshivah bachur* in the Yeshivah of Radin at the time. Many years later, when living in Ramat HaSharon in Eretz Yisrael, he related to the rabbi of Ramat HaSharon, Rabbi Yaakov Edelstein, what he saw during the fire.

As one of those standing closest to the Chafetz Chaim's house, Reb Chaim Tzvi threw bucket after bucket of water onto the tzaddik's burning home. He knew that the Chafetz Chaim didn't own expensive belongings and fancy furniture, but surely he had precious manuscripts that were worth more to him than all the money in the world. Reb Chaim Tzvi imagined how desperate he must have felt as it all went up in flames.

Then Reb Chaim Tzvi caught sight of the Chafetz Chaim, who was mumbling something to himself as he watched his house burn down. The *bachur* had to know what he was saying in the midst of such devastation, so he handed his task to another boy and edged closer to where the Chafetz Chaim was standing. Here is what he heard:

"Dear Father in Heaven. You are so good and kind and merciful. You care for us, Your children, so much. You decreed a *gezeirah* that all the houses in Radin must burn down; surely this is for our benefit although we don't know why. But You didn't burn them all at once so that all the families would be homeless with no one to help them. You first burned down half the town so that there would be others to help them. Only when every one of those families had rebuilt their homes did You burn down the rest of the town, so that those who are now homeless have neighbors to turn to. How good You are to us! You look after us and never abandon us!"

This glimpse into the response of a true *ba'al emunah* in the midst of his misfortune is a powerful beacon, sufficient to illuminate the way out of even the darkest tunnel. It shows us that a person can have almost everything he holds dear taken from him: his money, his health, and even his children. But one thing can never be taken from him: his *emunah*. He is able to choose whether to drown in the engulfing waves or rise above them and see the kindness of the Ribono shel Olam. And in the merit of his *emunah*, he will see wondrous salvations, and he will earn the most coveted place in Gan Eden.

Hashem is constantly at our side, as David HaMelech says, "*Achazta b'yad yemini* — You grasped my right hand" (*Tehillim* 73:23). He is *always* holding our hand. But although we can't see it clearly, during the hard times He lifts us up and holds us in His arms: "*Al kapayim yisa'uncha* — On [their] palms they will carry you" (ibid. 91:12). It's only with effort that we are able to picture it and feel His love, which fills us with a sense of security and allows us to feel relaxed.

The most difficult times are a very special opportunity in life when we can enjoy the most elevated feeling a Yid can ever experience: closeness to Hashem. We can spend this time worrying and bemoaning our fate, angry that we have been abandoned. Or we can use it to soar higher and higher, connecting closely to our dearest Father, observing how He wondrously solves our problems.

When your life has turned stormy, you can say out loud:

> "Ribono shel Olam, You are my Father and I am Your dear child."

> "I know that now when things are rough, You are holding me in Your arms."

> "I know that this is from You and what You do is good for me, although it hurts me."

> "I won't despair. I trust You and I'm waiting to see You bring my salvation."

> "I know that You will help me. Please help me quickly."

> "Help me to correct my behavior. And help me to have *emunah* and *bitachon* because I know that this is what You want from me now."

Real Life Emunah
There Are No Rotten Tomatoes:
The Story of a Daughter at Risk

Mrs. Rose* of Yerushalayim suffered a traumatic life challenge. She underwent terrible anxiety until she managed to save herself from drowning under turbulent waves.

She and her daughter share their experience in the following interview. Baruch Hashem, they are able to talk about it freely today as a positive experience.

My daughter Ita* was not your regular, run-of-the-mill child. She was smart and had a quick tongue, but she didn't like to study or be involved in extracurricular activities. She was an introverted child who liked to do her own thing.

I tried to push Ita to be more outgoing, to care more about her schoolwork, but to no avail. She was a free spirit, an independent soul.

As she got older, Ita started flouting the strict dress code in our chassidic home. My husband and I grew more and more alarmed as Ita's sleeves crept above her elbows, her hair fell far below her shoulders, and her hemlines did not cover the knee.

But nothing prepared us for that terrible day.

Ita had been moody and preoccupied for days, but that was nothing new. For months I'd been treading on eggshells around her, not wanting to provoke her, never sure whether to say something or keep quiet about her mode of dress, unacceptable speech, and neglect of her studies.

I was brushing my teeth when she stood by the bathroom door and dropped the bombshell.

"Ima," she said, "I'm getting married."

"You're what?"

I could hardly speak through the toothpaste. I could hardly speak anyway.

"I'm getting married."

I could tell she was perfectly serious. "To whom?" I was near hysterical.

"To Roni Afulai."* Her voice was flat, expressionless.

"Ita! Stop it! Who is he? Where did you meet him? Who is he?"

"Roni's a bus driver. I see him every day on my way to school. We've been going out for the past few weeks, and we've decided to get married. Roni's not religious, and from now on, neither am I."

Ita moved out of our house and married Roni. It was a high-profile wedding, abuzz with journalists and photographers representing all of Israel's media outlets. A *frum*, sheltered chassidic seventeen-year-old girl, the daughter of a respected *rav*, Torah lecturer, and writer, had defied her parents and was marrying a nonreligious Kurdish bus driver. Sadly, these days it might not have caused such a stir, but back in those days, the unthinkable had happened. We were literally the talk of the country.

Six hundred guests attended the wedding. All six hundred of them had come for the *chasan*. Ita did not have her mother or her father or a single friend or relative at her wedding. From that day on, we cut off all contact with her and instructed our family members to do the same.

"She'll miss you so much, she'll come back to you on your terms," a psychologist advised us. "A seventeen-year-old can't cope on her own."

But Ita didn't contact us.

And thus began my journey. A journey of self-recrimination and self-analysis. I thought of everything I had done wrong. Everything I should have done right. I should have shown Ita more love. I should have admired her hair when she brushed it instead of shaming her for it. I should have accepted Ita's quiet, reserved nature instead of pushing her to be something she wasn't. I should have given her the approval she craved so that she wouldn't have had to look for it elsewhere.

No mother should ever have to go through what I went through. Day after day, I would wake up thinking of Ita and go to sleep thinking of Ita and think of her all the time in between. As much as I tried to put her out of my mind, I couldn't. Neither did "well-meaning" people allow me to forget what had happened. The heart-piercing comments about causing such a *chillul Hashem* and the accusing letters that arrived through the mail...

After a year of no contact with my daughter, I was convinced that the psychologist had erred by encouraging me to cut off all ties. I had heard through the grapevine that Ita had had a baby. I had to reach out to her! I was desperate to know if she was happy, if everything was okay. I broke the icy stone wall and called up Ita to say hello.

When we next met, she was holding the most adorable nine-month-old baby — my grandson. My first grandchild. She was happy but lonely, she told me. She wanted to come visit; she wanted to see her siblings. But I knew that as long as Ita didn't dress like a Jewish daughter, my husband would not allow her to come home. He wouldn't speak to her and wouldn't allow our other children to speak to her either. She didn't attend their bar mitzvahs, graduations, or weddings.

I tried to strengthen my *emunah* during this trying time. Actually, a year after she married, I began to suffer serious panic attacks. It seems that the feelings of heartache, guilt, and degradation had begun to take their toll. My vision would blur, I couldn't catch my breath... It took five years of intensive therapy and exercises to recover. (Today, I am studying psychology and, drawing upon my personal experience, I am able to help people overcome anxiety without the use of medication.)

I kept telling myself that whatever I would have done,

nothing could have changed Ita's destiny. When people are complimented for a good child, they say, "It's all from Hashem." Why don't we say the same about a challenging child? Why all the self-blame? Ita's path had been paved by Hashem, and in any case, her choices – good and bad – were her own.

Rabbi Yisrael Lugassi's *sefer, Ner L'Ragli,* helped me a lot. It brought home to me that I wasn't responsible for this tragedy. Yes, I had to learn from my mistakes, and, yes, I had to try to do better with my other children, but that didn't change the facts.

Another crucial thing I learned was to let go of my ego. Many times, as I agonized over the turn Ita's life had taken, I honestly questioned myself: How much of this pain is because it hurts you that Hashem's daughter has rejected His Torah, and how much of it is because it's your daughter? Once I got my ego out of the picture — "What will people say about you? Where did you go wrong? How could this happen to the daughter of a *talmid chacham* like your husband?" — it became much easier to bear.

And I didn't stop praying for a miracle.

One Purim, eleven long years after Ita had left home, she asked to speak to my husband.

"He's not going to speak to you, Ita," I told her. "You know that." We had gone through this before.

"Please give him the phone," she begged.

I handed my husband the cordless and left the room. "Phone for you" was all I said and walked into the kitchen to put the finishing touches on my *mishlo'ach manos.*

A few minutes later, he walked into the kitchen. I released my breath.

"Ita's coming," he said.

"What did she say?" I asked, wondering what magic spell she had cast on him.

"'Tatty,' she told me, 'doesn't it say about Purim, *"Kol haposheit yado litol nosnim lo —* All who put out a hand, give to them"? Please let me come home!'"

And Ita came home. She came without her husband — just the kids — and she dressed appropriately only for the occasion, but she came home.

Not long afterward, Ita's husband also came, putting on a *kippah* for the meeting. I'll never forget the day my husband set eyes on him for the very first time.

"*Baruch haba!*" he said, and warmly hugged his son-in-law as if they'd known each other for years.

We all cried as we watched. There was still a long, arduous journey ahead of them. They had no intention at that time to make any commitments, but in the end, they miraculously arrived at their destination!

Looking back, I now see that there was a master plan to all this. Ita was destined to marry her wonderful husband this way and give birth to her precious children and bring them all back to Torah. Her lifestyle is very different from ours. She wears a beautiful wrapped head covering while I wear a *sheitel*, and she lives in a neighborhood very different from our own. But this path in life is her calling, and this was how Hashem led her there.

Today she works for Arachim and has a remarkable impact on girls who have slipped in their religious observance. She turned off the road we lived on to get back onto another street, the right address for her.

Ita and I are co-speakers at events, where we tell the audience our story. We participate in Shabbatons sponsored by Arachim for the purpose of encouraging mothers and siblings going through what we did. We tell them what to do (mostly what not to do) and what to tell themselves when going through this *nisayon*.

Once children show no interest in Torah, there is nothing one can do except to show them love, help them feel they still belong, and *daven*. Speeches, arguments, and impassioned pleas are mostly useless. But every single *tefillah* helps! Nothing goes to waste! If not now, then at some point down the line. Don't give up! For sixteen long years, I *dav-*

ened and cried, and never gave up hope. *Baruch Hashem*, Ita is now back home.

May Hashem bring all lost Jewish souls back home.

Ita's Story: An Interview

What was it like for you to say goodbye, possibly forever, to your family and friends at the age of seventeen?

I felt I had nothing to lose. By the age of twelve or thirteen, I had the sense that I wasn't fully accepted. My parents didn't accept me because as the oldest, I didn't fit the mold of the model child they'd expected me to be. My friends didn't accept me because I wasn't exactly like them. And my teachers didn't accept me because I wasn't *frum* enough for them, meaning I wasn't the exact same carbon copy as the hundreds of students the school was turning out each year.

Was it hard for you, not having any contact with your family for so many years?

It was extremely, *incredibly* difficult. Very, very difficult. Don't let anyone fool you when they tell you they're happy making it on their own. A child is tied to his parents' home with invisible ropes of steel.

I remember once being banished to my room on Shabbos because I wouldn't conform to the rules. I lay burrowed under my blankets, angry and bitter. My mother came into my room and tried to talk to me, but I ignored her. Then she brought me a plate bearing warm, sesame shnitzel and left it on my bedside table. That shnitzel spoke more than she could ever have said. It spoke of love, hope, and promise.

Later, as much I tried to convince myself that I didn't need my family, that I didn't want to live like them, deep down I yearned for connection — and for my mother's sesame shnitzel.

What eventually brought you back to Torah?

There was no defining moment. It was a very gradual process. Perhaps it began after the birth of my fourth child. His feet were deformed when he was born, and he had to wear a cast for the first few weeks of his life. The night before the bris, which had been delayed, I removed the cast. He screamed as I removed it, he screamed while I bathed him, he screamed while I fed him, and he screamed most of that night. As the early hours of the morning passed, with me trying in vain to soothe him, it suddenly dawned on me, *The baby wants his cast. He misses the security.* And I started wondering, as I cried along with the baby, *Maybe I miss my cast, too?*

Then and there, I decided that I wanted a proper bris for him. I wanted a rabbi to attend this baby's bris, to speak and bring a different atmosphere to the ceremony.

I phoned up Arachim and asked them to send me a rabbi. I described exactly just what type of rabbi I needed under the circumstances. The time of the bris drew near, and the guests started filing in, one of them uninvited and unwanted by everyone but me. My husband shot me daggerlike glances that demanded, "What's this?" But he wasn't about to make a scene.

The rabbi was exactly what I had ordered. After he had delivered his winning speech and left, my husband asked me, "Tell me, are all rabbis like this?"

We asked the rabbi to deliver a weekly lecture at our home and invited a few couples, friends of ours, to attend. We were entertained, if not fully persuaded, by his keen insights and masterful delivery.

Another turning point was when my third child, Noa,* was in the second grade. By then she was visiting my parents and playing with her cousins, and she wanted to be more like them. "Please, Mommy," she begged, "I want to attend a *dati* school."

It took a long time for my husband to agree ("Learning

is only fun when it's coed," he maintained), but eventually, he gave in.

When my oldest son was fifteen, after learning for some time with an *avreich* from Lev L'Achim, he insisted on enrolling in a full-time yeshivah. I think that's what finally did it. My husband saw he was losing this tug-of-war, and he joined us on our journey to a complete, *frum* lifestyle.

What can parents and teachers do to prevent their children from going off the derech?

Kids who go off the *derech* are usually sensitive and intuitive. There is also far too much focus on the external, on actions rather than on meaning and depth. For instance, *tznius* is often presented as a forbidding set of cold, hard rules instead of as an expression of our essence as daughters of the King.

I sometimes wonder why it takes a child showing signs of defecting from Torah life for mentors to sit up and pay attention and use all their powers of persuasion to bring the child back home. If all those powers of love and concern had been harnessed earlier, perhaps so much heartache on either side could have been avoided.

Too often, I was yelled at and put down and threatened when I acted out. I was labeled bad, a rotten tomato, a wicked influence, and a host of other unflattering epithets.

That doesn't endear a person to Torah.

There's a *pasuk* (*Tehillim* 102:18) that is close to my heart: "*Panah el tefillas ha'arar v'lo vazah es tefillasam* — He will have turned to the prayer of each devastated one and not have despised their prayer." The word *arar*, "devastated one," has the same letters as the word *ra*, "bad." Hashem desires the *tefillos* of the "bad" ones, those who are being told all day how they are "rotten tomatoes." They must know that Hashem loves them. He doesn't reject them.

The first time I felt connected to Hashem was during the time that I wasn't living a Torah lifestyle; I was grappling with doubts and yearning for a foothold somewhere.

I remember one specific day as if it were yesterday. My children were already attending religious schools, and the secretary at my daughter's school had called to tell me that the principal wanted to set up an appointment to meet with me. I knew exactly what she wanted to speak to me about. I had felt it coming. They knew we had a TV at home, and they wanted me to throw it out or they would kick out my children.

I hesitantly brought the matter to my husband, and he responded with a resounding "No! No one's going to tell me how to lead my life!"

He left the house, and I cried bitter tears. I felt so confused. I myself didn't know what I wanted, where I stood, who I was. I verbally cried out to Hashem, "Please, Hashem, help me!" I raised my arm, and I could feel, literally feel, a cloud of warmth on it.

Soon after, my husband came home and said, "You know what, Ita? I've decided to get rid of the television."

Never before had I felt Hashem's presence in my life as I did then.

I had to take such a long, convoluted journey to find Hashem! I consider it my mission to use my life experience to help youth who are struggling with their identity, to help them find Hashem before they do things they may regret forever.

Mrs. Rose and her daughter can be contacted via the author.

Understanding the Mitzvah

*I*S THE MITZVAH of *emunah* mentioned in the Torah? The Rambam (*Sefer HaMitzvos*, beginning of section 2) explains that the mitzvah of *emunah* is the first mitzvah in the Ten Commandments: "*Anochi Hashem Elokecha asher hotzeisicha me'eretz Mitzrayim... — I* am Hashem, your G-d, Who took you out of the land of Egypt..." (*Shemos* 20:2).

The Ramban disagrees. He claims that *emunah* is the foundation of the entire Torah and mitzvos. Our whole *Yiddishkeit* is based on *emunah*. Without faith a person is not a Yid! It's the root of every mitzvah, not a commandment on its own.

The *Nesivos Shalom* (part 1, *Yesodei HaTorah, ma'amar* 1, *osos* 2, 3) reconciles the opinions of the Rambam and the Ramban. He explains clearly and beautifully as follows:

Emunah is present in the heart of every Jew. It's the air a Jew breathes. It's the foundation on which his life as a Jew is based.

But working on having *emunah*, training oneself to think with *emunah*, reading about *emunah*, talking with *emunah* — that is the mitzvah of "*Anochi Hashem.*" Therefore, even if a Jew doesn't achieve complete faith, as long as he's *working* on having *emunah*, he is fulfilling the mitzvah perfectly and he can merit salvation, as it says, "Walk about in the streets of Yerushalayim and look... If you will find a man...who seeks faith, then I will forgive her" (*Yirmiyah* 5:1).

Hashem promises that as long as a person strives to be a *ba'al emunah*, even if he hasn't yet reached high levels, He will forgive him and help him. It's sufficient that he is sincerely trying and working on it. He receives reward for every bit of effort he makes to strengthen his faith.

The *Nesivos Shalom* goes on to explain that the mitzvah of *emunah* is divided into two parts. The two parts together form the basis of our *emunah*, and they are found in the mitzvah of "*Anochi Hashem.*"

It says, "*Anochi Hashem Elokecha asher hotzeisicha me'eretz Mitzrayim* — I am Hashem, your G-d, Who took you out of the land of Egypt." Why does Hashem introduce Himself as the One Who took us out of Egypt? He doesn't mention a word about creating the world. We would have expected Him to say, "*Anochi Hashem Elokecha asher barasi es hashamayim v'es ha'aretz* — I am Hashem, your G-d, Who created the heavens and the earth." Isn't the creation of the world more monumental than the Exodus from Egypt?

The *Nesivos Shalom* clarifies that "*Anochi Hashem*" means "I am Hashem Who created the world." This is the first part of the mitzvah of *emunah* — to believe that "I, Hashem, created the entire world and all living beings and I control everything that happens in the world, all the time."

But then there is another fundamental part of *emunah*, and that is "*asher hotzeisicha me'eretz Mitzrayim.*" At the liberation from Egypt, Hashem saved a whole nation — men, women, and children — freeing them from slave labor, persecution, and torture after 210 years. Hashem performed open miracles for them until they reached the Yam Suf, where He completely changed the laws of nature: the sea split, allowing the Yidden to pass, and then the waters came together again, onto the Egyptians who had pursued them.

At this time, the nation wasn't worthy of Hashem's kindness. In fact, they had no merits to deserve being helped. They had fallen to the lowest spiritual level, the forty-ninth level of *tumah*. As they walked through dry land in the middle of the Reed Sea and Hashem began to drown the Egyptians, the prosecuting angels argued, "Why are You saving the Jews? They worship idols; they're sinners just as much as the Egyptians!"

That is when Hashem showed everyone that the Jewish people are His children. It doesn't matter if they are deserving or if they are sinners. As long as they rely on Me, I will look after them. Even without any merits, as long as Jews believe that their Father will save them, He will.

Yetzias Mitzrayim was the greatest miracle that Hashem ever performed for *Am Yisrael* at a time when they were sinking deep into impurity. This is the foundation of our *emunah*. We have a special mitzvah requiring us to talk about *yetzias Mitzrayim* every day, to mention it in Shema and in Kiddush. This is because internalizing that Hashem does miracles for us regardless of whether we deserve it or not is the very basis of our *emunah*. And this applies to every individual, always.

This second part of *emunah* is just as significant as the first part. Knowing that Hashem is in control and that no one can do anything without His consent and that He can perform miracles is not enough. We must assure ourselves that even if we are not deserving, He will help us out because He loves each one of us like a father loves his firstborn child — as Hashem had lovingly referred to us "*bni bechori Yisrael* — My firstborn son is Yisrael" *(Shemos 4:22)*.

As long as we turn to Hashem for help and we sincerely believe that He will help us, He *will* help us, regardless of our level in *Yiddishkeit*. This is *bitachon*: we can stop worrying because He will be there for us always.

When we work on believing this, we are also fulfilling the mitzvah of "*Tamim tiheyeh im Hashem Elokecha* — You shall be wholehearted with Hashem, your G-d" *(Devarim 18:13)*. As Rashi explains, we should not worry about what might transpire.

Just being a Yid is the greatest reason to jump for joy. We need only rely on our Father, and He will help us regardless of whether one is a tzaddik or the greatest sinner! He is the kindest Father Who looks deep into our heart and reads our thoughts. The sincere *emunah* He finds there outweighs any amount of sin.

Say It Out Loud

Yidden in need of a salvation would pour out their hearts to Reb Mordche of Lechowitz and beg him to promise them a *yeshuah*. He had a very special *segulah* that he used before he could assure them that things would take a turn for the better.

He would tell them, "According to the laws of nature, there's nothing to do. I can't help you either. But if you will have *emunah*, you will enter a world beyond nature. There, there's hope. There, things can change. Anything can happen."

He pointed out the example of the Jews trapped between the Reed Sea and the Egyptians. Though they lacked merit, Hashem instructed Moshe to urge them to march forward. The faith in Hashem that they exhibited by entering the sea would save them, even if, according to strict justice, they were undeserving.

Reb Mordche then took hold of the destitute person's hand and instructed him to repeat, "*Ani ma'amin b'emunah sheleimah shehaborei yisbarach shemo hu borei u'manhig l'chol haberu'im...* — I believe with perfect faith that the Creator, may His Name be blessed, created and supervises all of creation [and He alone made, makes, and will make all things]."

Then they repeated together, over and over again, various verses of *bitachon* from *Tehillim* until Reb Mordche felt that the Yid's hope was rising and he trusted in his Father's ability to help him. After that, Reb Mordche would tell him to go home and carry on the "therapy" until his *yeshuah* arrived.

Reb Mordche's therapy called upon the person to verbalize his faith. It wasn't enough to just listen, think, and feel. He learned this from the words of Yirmiyahu, when he rebuked the Jewish people for their lack of faith. He said, "*Emunah* is lost; it is detached from their speech" (*Yirmiyah* 7:28). In order to "feel" *emunah* and truly have *bitachon*, we need to speak it aloud; it must fill our mouth. This will cause the faith to actually sink into our heart.

We can use any words we like, whether in English or in Hebrew, to verbalize our *emunah* and instill it within us:

"Ribono shel Olam, I know this is from You."

"I know You are doing what is best for me."

"I am relying on You, and I'm waiting for You to help me."

When things don't work out the way we hoped, say, "Ribono shel Olam, I know this is Your will. *Gam zu l'tovah!* This, too, is for the good."

Or quote verses such as "*Rabim machovim larasha v'habotei'ach baHashem chesed yesovevenu* — Many are the agonies of the wicked, but as for the one who trusts in Hashem, kindness surrounds him" (*Tehillim* 32:10). The Midrash explains regarding this *pasuk* that a person can be steeped in sin. He may be a *rasha*. But as soon as he trusts in Hashem his woes will disappear. He will be "surrounded by kindness" (*Midrash Tehillim; Yalkut Shimoni*).

Or recite the verse "*Rabos ra'os tzaddik u'mikulam yatzilenu Hashem* — Many are the mishaps of the righteous, but from them all Hashem rescues him" (*Tehillim* 34:20). A tzaddik is someone who shall live through his *emunah* — "*tzaddik b'emunaso yichyeh*" (*Chabakkuk* 2:4). As soon as a person has *emunah*, Hashem will solve *all* his problems.

It also says, "*Hashleich al Hashem yehavcha v'hu yechalkelecha* — Cast your burdens on Hashem and He will sustain you" (*Tehillim* 55:23). When we say this *pasuk*, we are telling the Ribono shel Olam, "I'm throwing up my *pekel* to You. Catch it. Look after me. The burden is too heavy for me to carry."

We will feel immediate relief. Our shoulders will feel lighter. Our heartache will disappear. We will feel calm.

This *segulah* and advice is an age-old remedy. David HaMelech said, "*He'emanti ki adaber* — I believed because I spoke" (ibid. 116:10). "I achieved *emunah* only because I spoke about *emunah* aloud, repeating it over and over again."

When we feel particularly sad and depressed, we can say the following verse: "*Mah tishtochachi nafshi u'mah tehemi alai hochili l'Elokim ki od odenu yeshuos panai v'Elokai.*" The meaning of this verse (ibid. 43:5) is beautiful and comforting: "Why are you downcast, my soul, and why are you disturbed on my account? Hope to Hashem [because the day will come when] I shall yet thank Him for the salvations of my countenance and because He is my G-d."

We can say it again and again. David HaMelech quotes this verse in Chapters 42 and 43 of *Tehillim* three times! We should repeat it until we are convinced that in the near future we will be thanking Hashem for bringing our salvation.

We can choose any words or any verse and repeat it each time we feel down, until our effort bears fruit. The words will sink in and we will be calmed.

When a person strengthens his resolve with *emunah* at a difficult moment, he fulfills the *pasuk* "*Kaveh el Hashem chazak v'ya'ametz libecha v'kaveh el Hashem* — Hope to Hashem; strengthen yourself and He will give you courage, and hope to Hashem" (ibid. 27:14). His effort is so precious in the eyes of Hashem. Reb Yitzchak Eizik Safrin of Kamarna writes in his *sefer Nesiv Mitzvosecha* (*Nesiv Emunah*, p. 3, *os* 4) that the purification of the soul that a person achieves when he accepts aggravation with *emunah* is equivalent to fasting thousands of times!

Ask Without Limitations

*H*OW MUCH MAY a person hope for the best and trust in Hashem?

Through an incredible insight on the following *pasuk* in *Tehillim*, the Vilna Gaon provides an answer.

The *pasuk* says, "*Im lo shivisi v'domamti nafshi k'gamul alei imo kagamul alai nafshi* — I swear that I calmed and silenced my soul like a suckling child at his mother's side, like the suckling child is my soul" (*Tehillim* 131:2).

David HaMelech says, "I imagine that I am a newborn baby nursing from his mother. Like this child depends on his mother, my soul depends on Hashem."

The baby only has to suck, and he receives all the nutrients and nourishment he requires. But what happens if he doesn't suck? His mother's milk supply will dwindle until it dries up altogether. If he sucks more frequently, the milk supply will increase abundantly. If a mother nurses twins, there will be sufficient milk for both of them. It's the sucking that produces the supply.

This is a precise analogy to the *ba'al bitachon*, explains the Vilna Gaon. *Emunah* and *bitachon* — relying on Hashem — produces the abundance! The more we believe in Him, and the more we earnestly rely on Him to provide for us, the more He will give us. The bounty the Ribono shel Olam can give us is endless.

But just as a baby who gets his milk from another source — for instance, a bottle of formula — can no longer rely on his mother's milk, we also cut off our supply when we turn elsewhere for our needs. Along these lines, the *Chovos HaLevavos* writes, in the introduction to *Sha'ar HaBitachon*, some very sharp and frightening words:

> A person who doesn't trust in Hashem and trusts in someone or something else (such as his boss or any other influential person, the *shadchan*, his wealth, or his wisdom or strength), HaKadosh Baruch Hu withdraws His personal supervision and leaves him.

This point should come as no surprise, as the Torah carries Hashem's warning to us in *Parashas Bechukosai*: "*V'halachtem imi keri, v'halachti af ani imachem b'keri* — If you go with Me with happenstance [i.e., if you forget about Me and you see everything as happenstance], then I, too, will behave toward you with happenstance" (*Vayikra* 26:23–24).

Rabbi Ephraim Wachsman of Monsey explains that as soon as a person's *emunah* and *bitachon* in Hashem wavers, he automatically places his trust in someone or something else. That is dangerous because it means that he has stopped "sucking." If he stops sucking, then his milk supply dries up.

This is not a punishment for lacking *emunah*. It's the natural consequence. When you stop drawing from the unending heavenly supply, the system collapses. Where there's no demand, there's no supply.

A person fixes his own destiny by the measure of *bitachon* he has. If he sincerely believes in the innermost depths of his heart that Hashem will provide for him, Hashem will provide for him!

"*Anochi Hashem Elokecha... Harchev picha v'amaleihu* — I am Hashem, your G-d... Open your mouth wide and I will fill it" (*Tehillim* 81:11). "Open wide your mouth" means asking Hashem for all our heart's desires without restriction and believing with certainty and confidence that He will give it to us. Then, says Hashem, "I will fill it." When we make ourselves into a receptive vessel, Hashem fills up that vessel. We receive all that we believe He will give us — even when it seems impossible.

Be Solely Dependent on Hashem

*T*HE *NESIVOS SHALOM* brings a beautiful *mashal* from the *Midrash Shocher Tov* on the verse "*Elokai becha batachti al eivoshah* — My G-d in You I have trusted; let me not be shamed" (*Tehillim* 25:2):

Depending on the King: A Mashal

A wanderer once came to the city of his king and lodged outside the palace gates. The king's guards found him and began to beat him. He told them, "Don't hit me. I belong to the king's household." They looked at him in disbelief, but they decided to wait until the morning so they could speak to the king.

They led him to the king and told him that the man claimed to be a member of the royal family. The king asked him, "Do you know me personally?"

He answered honestly, "No."

"So how can you belong to my family?"

The man answered, "I am not part of your household, but I'm one of your loyal subjects in your kingdom and I rely on your kindness."

The king turned to the guards. "This man depends on me. Leave him alone!"

That is what David said to Hashem: "My G-d, I am relying on You — don't let me be shamed!"

It's clear from this *midrash* that the commoner had no reason to count on the king's favor. But the king was impressed when he saw the earnest respect and sense of reliance his subject had for him, and for this alone he was prepared to help him.

The *Nesivos Shalom* explains that when a person sincerely believes that Hashem will certainly help him because he is relying solely on Him, then he "forces" Hashem to help him. He transforms himself into a dependent son of Hashem.

With such *bitachon*, there are no inspections; the palace gates are immediately opened wide. All the locked and bolted *sha'arei Shamayim* are accessible, and we are brought with priority treatment straight to the King.

We need only say, "*Al eivosh ki chasisi vach* — [Father,] let me not be ashamed, for I take refuge in You!" (*Tehillim* 25:20) and automatically Hashem assumes responsibility.

Rabbi Elimelech Biderman uses a wonderful *mashal* to illustrate how relying on Hashem guarantees our salvation:

Two people stand in close proximity on the sidewalk of a busy street. One is a young businessman who is waiting to meet his partner, and the other, an elderly gentleman, is waiting for a lift. The old man, seeing no bench in sight, leans on the young man for support. Several minutes pass and the young man sees his partner waving to him. Will he rush away and let the old man topple over? He would have to be pretty ruthless to do so!

If we lean on Hashem for support, He has no choice; He must help us because He surely won't let us topple over.

Pray for Success

*T*HERE IS ONE blessing in *Shemoneh Esrei* in which we *daven* to merit the privileged treatment due to *ba'alei bitachon*.

In the blessing of *Al HaTzaddikim*, we say, "*V'sein sachar tov l'chol habotchim b'shimcha be'emes v'sim chelkeinu imahem...* — Give a good reward to all who sincerely believe in Your Name, and put our lot with them..." We ask Hashem to help us have true *bitachon* and to be counted among those tzaddikim who are *ba'alei bitachon*.

"*U'l'olam lo neivosh ki vecha batachnu* — And we should never be ashamed when we sincerely rely on You." We beg Hashem to always justify our total reliance on Him and to never let us down.

"*Baruch atah Hashem mishan u'mivtach latzaddikim*—Blessed are You, Hashem, Who is a pillar of support and a secure haven for tzaddikim." Who are the tzaddikim? — "*Tzaddik b'emunaso yichyeh* – The righteous person lives through his faith" (*Chabakkuk* 2:4) — anyone who has genuine faith in Him.

This *berachah* is recited by Jews all over the world three times a day. It's a special prayer asking Hashem to reward the *ba'alei bitachon*, including us, for their devotion to Him by allowing them to realize their hopes and aspirations and fulfill their dreams without disappointment. Rabbi Ephraim Wachsman says it's worth being a *ba'al bitachon* just so that all of *Klal Yisrael* will be praying for us three times a day!

Mastering the Skill

*W*E HAVE NOW learned the steps in mastering *emunah*:

- Recognize Hashem's love and kindness and that everything He does is for the best.
- Verbalize our faith in Hashem when we feel that stress and panic may overcome us.
- Accept and make peace with challenges.
- Ask for anything and everything we desire with total dependence and sincerely believe that Hashem will provide it.
- Pray for success.

The more we practice these steps, the more "professional" we will become in our goal of mastering the skills of *emunah*. At last, we will be able to say to Hashem, "I am relying on You — don't let me be ashamed!"

And He won't!

Chapter 2
Gratitude

*O*NE WHO HONORS Me by offering thanks and makes this his way of life, I will show him the salvation of G-d.

(Tehillim 50:23)

You may have come this far and still not found your way to true *emunah*, perhaps because the steps you learned in Chapter 1 are not steps you feel you can take. It might seem a little naïve to you. "Just relax and give my burdens to Hashem? How can I relax when disaster is right around the corner? I'm not a starry-eyed kind of person. I'm a realist. I'm a thinker, not a dreamer."

But you don't have to shut down your thinking brain to train yourself in *emunah*. In fact, your deep-thinking nature is an asset that you can use in a remarkably positive way. It's a matter of changing course. The more you think about Hashem and become aware of His constant involvement in your life, the sooner your worries will be replaced by gratitude and the priceless benefits that it brings.

Gratitude Makes Us Aware of Our Countless Gifts

A PERSON'S MIND WORKS nonstop. It's impossible to switch off the mind and say, "Stop. That's enough, no more thinking." But we can load our mind to the brim with positive thoughts that literally don't allow negative ones to enter.

Here is the best method to do this:

Devote a few minutes a day, when you are alone, to recollect on some of the *chasadim* that Hashem has done for you and say, "Thank You." You can thank Him for *chasadim* He has done for you in the past: for your health, for *parnassah*, for the loving parents and family He gave you. You can reminisce about all the small and big gifts He continuously gives you. You can thank Him for each and every one of your organs that are intact.

Imagine a person who has a malfunctioning kidney. He has been on dialysis for a few years, suffering greatly. Only a kidney transplant can save his life and transform him into a new healthy being. It's impossible to describe the overwhelming gratitude he will feel toward the compassionate person who donates a kidney to him. So how can we ever express enough gratitude to our Father Who gave us not only two healthy kidneys for free, but also two ears, a nose, healthy lungs, a heart, liver, and stomach...? The list is endless. Every minute of the day, He is supervising the healthy functioning of our body.

> The exercise class was finished, but before the students left, the teacher told them, "Here's one more exercise to do before you go home. Everyone put one hand on your heart."
>
> The students obeyed.
>
> "Now feel it beating. It's strong, it's regular, it doesn't miss a beat. Take a moment right now and be thankful. That's your life force, right there where you can feel it, giving you strength and health to get through your day."

The word *ashir* (עשיר), "wealthy," is an acronym for *einayim, shinayim, yadayim, raglayim* (עיניים, שיניים, ידיים, רגליים) — eyes, teeth, hands, feet. There is no wealthier person than one who can see, who can eat delicious foods with his own teeth, who has two healthy hands to serve him and two healthy feet that enable him to walk. If a person would tie his hands behind his back for one hour, he would realize how helpless he is without the use of his hands.

We can thank Hashem for caring for us in so many different ways. We can thank him for opportunities He sends us to perform mitzvos. These precious moments of thankfulness will help us forget all our troubles and focus instead on the endless *chasadim* He has given us and gives us every day.

If we do this exercise properly, we will certainly feel tears rolling down our cheeks. These tears are magic, healing waters that rinse and soothe all wounds. We will feel happier. So much tension will disappear. If we do this day after day, then slowly, gradually, we will feel a transformation. Stressful emotions won't plague us anymore. We will find ourselves expressing appreciation to Hashem throughout the day, beyond those moments we devote to this purpose.

It's interesting to note that even university researchers and wellness coaches have concluded that gratitude is good for our physical well-being. Joni Emmerling, a life coach in Greenville, North Carolina, is one of many who recommends keeping a gratitude journal. "Being grateful for your blessings cancels out negative thoughts and worries," she says. She advises people to take note of accomplishments of which they're proud and small things for which they are grateful.

There's something else we will definitely notice after a short while. It will suddenly strike us that several major problems have somehow sorted themselves out. Hashem will offer proof that the love we are displaying is mutual! This is tried and tested.

What Hashem Really Wants

*H*ASHEM GAVE US prayer and offerings as ways to serve Him, but it's our acknowledgment of Him and our gratitude that He desires most of all:

All the wild beasts in the forest are mine... If I were hungry, I would not tell you, for the whole world belongs to Me. Do you think that I need to eat the meat or drink the blood of your sacrifices?... *All I need is that you thank Me, and when you will call Me for help, I will save you...*

(*Tehillim* 50:10–15)

In the first verse of the Shema, Hashem describes to us the all-encompassing love He desires: "*V'ahavta eis Hashem Elokecha b'chol levavecha u'v'chol nafshecha u'v'chol me'odecha* — You shall love Hashem, your G-d, with all your heart, with all your soul, and with all your possessions."

What does *b'chol me'odecha* refer to? The Gemara explains, "Thank Him for every measure that He metes out for you, whether good or harsh" (*Berachos* 54a). (The words *me'odecha* and *middah*, "measure," share the same root.) When we are in the midst of a difficult situation and we turn to Hashem wholeheartedly, like a child crying on his father's shoulder, soaking in his father's love, comfort, and assurance, we experience the most profound and precious moment of connection in our lives.

A person can live a fruitful life full of accomplishments — he may have kept all the mitzvos with the greatest stringency — but he may have missed out on the essence of his life as a Jew if he has not learned how to feel and express gratitude.

Gratitude Empowers Our Prayers

GRATITUDE NOT ONLY helps us put life in the right perspective, but it also paves the way to having our prayers answered. This story, heard from Rabbi Simcha HaKohen Kook, the rabbi of Rechovot, illustrates the powerful role gratitude plays:

The Gift of Eyesight

Mr. Hirsch* of Rechovot was stricken with an eye affliction. After many failed treatments, it became clear that the only person who might be able to help him was an ophthalmologist in the United States. The cost of an initial consultation and follow-up treatment was exorbitant, but what won't a man do to save his sight?

He traveled to America filled with hope, apprehension, and prayer. After a comprehensive examination, the doctor told him, "I'm sorry to break this to you, but one eye is damaged beyond repair and the other might very well follow suit. There is nothing I can do for you."

Utterly crushed, Mr. Hirsch walked out of the hospital and found the nearest shul. He walked inside, put his head against the *aron kodesh*, and began to pour out his heart to his Creator.

Suddenly, a *Rabbeinu Bachya* that he had recently heard in a *derashah* in Rechovot came to mind:

Yaakov Avinu was about to confront his brother Esav, who hated him passionately and was approaching with four hundred men, intending to murder him. Yaakov desperately beseeched Hashem for mercy, beginning with the words "*Katonti mikol hachasadim...* — I am undeserving of the kindnesses [You have done for me until now]" (*Bereishis* 32:11).

Rabbeinu Bachya advises that this is the correct way for anyone to pray when he needs a big *yeshuah*, as David HaMelech says, "*Tovasi bal alecha* — I have no claim to Your benefit" (*Tehillim* 16:2). Hashem is the Master of the world Who does kindness like a master bestows favor on his servants, under no obligation but purely out of *chesed*. Only after a person contemplates the kindnesses Hashem does for him and has done for him in the past, even though he is totally undeserving, can he then pray for his needs and his prayers will be answered.

With this in mind, Mr. Hirsch broke down in uncontrollable sobs.

"Ribono shel Olam," he cried again and again, "I beg forgiveness for the fifty years in which I enjoyed the wonderful gift of eyesight without adequately thanking You for it."

The man then proceeded to enumerate the countless gifts Hashem gave him, expressing his heartfelt appreciation for each of them.

After three hours of intense thanksgiving, the man tearfully uttered one more statement before leaving the *beis midrash*: "Ribono shel Olam, I so much want to thank You for many more years of healthy eyesight."

The next day he requested that the doctor do one more thorough examination before his return to Eretz Yisrael. The specialist consented, although he told his patient that he didn't think there would be any gain. When the results came back, the doctor referred to his notes and previous test results again and pored over them deep in thought until he finally exclaimed, "I've changed my mind. I would like to perform the operation, after all. I think it will be successful."

The patient didn't dare ask any questions about the sudden change. The operation took place without delay, and a few days later he flew back home with two healthy eyes!

This is not the end of Rabbi Kook's narrative. Rabbi Kook told this story in one of his *shiurim*, and among the listeners was a father of two unmarried girls who had already reached the ages of twenty-nine and thirty.

How many tears had they already shed praying for their *zivug hagun*! Which *segulah* had they not yet tried?

Now their father came home and introduced a new idea. He explained to them the power of gratitude to the Ribono shel Olam. The girls and their parents each took upon themselves to spend several minutes daily contemplating and thanking Hashem for the great *chasadim* He performed for them each and every moment, past and present. They started to feel grateful, and a happy atmosphere began to replace the thick black cloud that had darkened their home.

Within a short period, both girls were married.

"People realize that with prayer our requests will be fulfilled, but they don't realize that learning to thank HaKadosh Baruch Hu for the numerous kindnesses we take for granted brings us so much more blessing," says Rabbi Asher Druk, quoting his uncle, renowned Kabbalist Rabbi Yaakov Meir Shechter. "The more a person thanks Hashem, the greater the abundance of blessing he receives."

A *pasuk* (*Tehillim* 50:23) states this clearly: "*Zovei'ach todah yechabdani v'sam derech ar'enu b'yeisha Elokim* — One who offers thanks honors Me and one who orders [his] way, I will show him the salvation of G-d." If we devote time every day to thanking Hashem for His abundant gifts to us, we will soon automatically find ourselves feeling very lucky. Our perspective will change from one of sorrow, anxiety, complaints, anger, bitterness, and worry to one in which we are constantly perceiving Hashem's kindness and special acts of *hashgachah pratis* that He performs for us all the time.

This is the most efficient way to attain *deveikus* to Hashem, *ahavas Hashem, yiras Shamayim*, and *emunah* and *bitachon*.

It heals our emotional wounds and opens for us all the gates of salvation.

The Gratitude Notebook: A Means That Changes Everything

*S*OMETIMES IT SEEMS that only a miracle from Heaven can solve our difficulties. We may be challenged by massive debt, serious health issues, problems with *shalom bayis*, or the *chinuch* of our children, and there appears to be no way out.

Here is a special secret heard from Rabbi Shlomo Zalman Auerbach that will work wonders and actually change your life in an instant.

Reb Shlomo Zalman's Eitzah

One day a distinguished man came to Reb Shlomo Zalman to seek his advice. He was a *rosh kollel* who had been supporting *avreichim* for many years. Recently, he'd fallen on hard times and simply couldn't put the money together each month. The distressed *rosh kollel* related that the terrible pressure he felt each month trying desperately to obtain the needed funds was affecting his health. It reached a point where he literally became ill. He couldn't sleep at night and suffered from panic attacks during the day.

After consulting with a psychologist, he was advised to close the *kollel*. This was the only way he would preserve his health and sanity, the professional warned him. Before taking such a step, he approached Rabbi Yitzchak Lorincz, son-in-law of Rabbi Trager from Antwerp and the head of Binas HaLev (an organization that helps people deal with emotional problems), and asked him to accompany him to Rabbi Auerbach, who was Rabbi Lorincz's grandfather.

"How long have you had the *kollel*?" Reb Shlomo Zalman asked him.

"Twenty-five years," the *rosh kollel* replied.

"Surely this is not the first time you are experiencing difficulties?" Reb Shlomo Zalman asked. "You must have had other times when you saw tremendous *siyatta d'Shmaya* and you managed to put the money together."

"True," the man confirmed. "But now it has become a tremendous pressure, and I just can't cope anymore."

"I have a wonderful medicine for you," Reb Shlomo Zalman offered. "Start keeping a gratitude notebook. Every time you feel the slightest *hashgachah pratis* or any *chesed* from Hashem, write it down in the notebook. Before each *tefillah*, take out the notebook and read its contents, and remember to thank Hashem in your *tefillos*, especially during *Modim*, for all His *chasadim*. I have no doubt that doing so will help you feel less stressed and bring about a *yeshuah*."

The *rosh kollel* followed the instructions faithfully. He recorded even small things, like the fresh milk arriving at the grocery early in the morning just as he reached the store, his son bringing home a positive note from his teacher, or small donations he received for the *kollel*.

Shortly he began to feel much happier and more relaxed, and, to his wonder, he raised money in all sorts of unexpected ways, easily allowing him to pay the *yungeleit*. In fact, until this very day, he is still supporting the *kollel*.

(*Chochmas HaNefesh HaYehudis*)

This was Rabbi Shlomo Zalman Auerbach's recommended *eitzah*. It works for anyone who wishes to try it!

Singing Hashem's Praises

*A*NOTHER *SEGULAH* THAT has brought many *yeshuos* — especially in the area of *shidduchim* — is to recite *Mizmor L'Sodah* (*Tehillim* 100), which is literally a "Song of Thanks." The account below comes from a young woman named Leah* who was unmarried, nearly twenty-four, and feeling disheartened.

Leah's Song

Leah read about the power of thanking Hashem for all His kindness and decided to give it a try. She took upon herself the *segulah* of reciting *Mizmor L'Sodah* thirteen times a day for thirteen days. She sang the chapter out loud each morning, paying attention to the words and letting her heart flow. Then she added her own words of thanks for the gifts Hashem had given her.

She even thanked Him profusely for delaying her *shidduch* until now, for surely the time had not been ripe. She thanked Him for enabling her to experience real heartfelt *tefillos* and to take on many different *chesed* projects and other mitzvah commitments.

At the end of the thirteen days, Leah had no desire to give up her new routine. Those moments of gratitude each morning had uplifted her entire life. She began another round of thirteen days, and on day 13, the *shidduch* suggestion arrived that turned her into a *kallah* a short while later. But she didn't stop there; she took on a new round of thirteen days to thank Hashem for her *yeshuah*.

What is the miraculous code in *Mizmor L'Sodah*?

The chazzan who often leads the prayer of Shacharis in the Shesilei Zeisim shul in Bnei Brak relates an amazing story:

The Power of the Mizmor

One day the chazzan came across the ruling in the *Shulchan Aruch* (OC 51:9): "The paragraph of *Mizmor L'Sodah* (in Shacharis, after *Baruch She'Amar*) should be recited in song, since all the songs will in the future be nullified except for the song of *Mizmor L'Sodah*."

He decided to adopt this practice from then on when he led the prayers at his minyan in the morning. Several months later a member of his family was diagnosed with a life-threatening illness. The chazzan traveled immediately to Tzefas and headed to the *kever* of Rabbi Yosef Karo, the Beis Yosef. He begged, "May the tzaddik be my *meilitz yosher* in the merit of keeping his *psak halachah* in the *Shulchan Aruch* to sing *Mizmor L'Sodah* aloud and renewing a practice that the majority are not aware of."

Two weeks later, a new round of tests were performed on his relative. There was no evidence of any disease. It had simply disappeared.

As we declare in *Mizmor L'Sodah* itself, "*Ivdu es Hashem b'simchah bo'u lefanav birnanah* — Serve Hashem with joy; come before Him in song!" This is a secret potion for happiness.

David HaMelech teaches us that no material pleasure can make a person truly happy. The only way to attain serenity is by training oneself to feel grateful for what one has at present, which evokes songs of praise and gratitude to Hashem.

This is a clear promise written in the Torah. There is one verse in the Torah that talks about failing to serve Hashem with joy. The Torah lists terrible curses that will take place, not just because we failed to keep the mitzvos, but "*tachas asher lo avadeta es Hashem Elokecha b'simchah u'v'tuv levav merov kol* — because you did not serve Hashem, your G-d, amid gladness and goodness of heart when everything was abundant" (*Devarim* 28:47).

But how exactly do we fulfill this requirement of a cheerful heart? The Gemara explains, "With songs of thanks and praise" (*Arachin* 11a).

As the Ramban says, the whole purpose of a Jew's life is to recognize his Creator and thank Him. If he keeps mitzvos but is angry, sour, and full of complaints, then he has failed in his purpose and he forfeits Hashem's blessings.

We know that "*middah tovah merubah*"; Rashi states (on *Shemos* 34:7) that our reward for fulfilling Hashem's will is *five hundred times greater* than our punishment for sins. When we imagine all the terrifying curses described in *Parashas Ki Savo* for those who serve Hashem resentfully and transform them into wonderful blessings — five hundred times over — we can understand why so many people have seen *yeshuos* from making an effort to thank Hashem and sing His praises.

Gratitude Brings More Good

*T*HE MORE WE thank, the more Hashem says, "You're grateful? Then I want to give you much more *chasadim*." What a wonderful way to feel happy and allow Hashem to shower us with more and more kindnesses.

In *Parashas Vayishlach*, Yaakov Avinu *davened* before he went to meet Esav. He declared, "*V'atah amarta heiteiv eitiv imach* — You said, 'I will certainly deal kindly with you'" (*Bereishis* 32:13). The Divrei Yisrael, Rabbi Yisrael of Modzhitz, writes that if you accustom yourself to saying, "*Heiteiv*," to notice and to thank Hashem for all the good things He gives you, then Hashem says, "*Eitiv imach* — I will make things even better for you!"

No Sighs

The holy Rebbe of Ruzhin once heard his daughter sighing. "My dear daughter," he told her, "please don't groan and sigh. You should know that one sigh leads to another sigh, but one thank-you leads to another thank-you."

He then told her a story that illustrated his point:

A wealthy man constantly grumbled about his lot, provoking Heaven to withdraw more and more blessing from his life. Only when he was reduced to the lowest possible situation — a pauper who was sick with leprosy and thus unable to even beg — did he stop complaining.

Suddenly, he realized that as bad as things were, they could always be worse. *As it says,* he told himself, "*What does a living man have to complain about? It's enough that he's alive*" (*Eichah Rabbasi* 3:39; *Midrash Rabbah* ad loc.). With that first awakening of gratitude, Heaven began to reverse his fortune until he became wealthier than ever. But this time, his wealth filled him with gratitude and happiness.

"It's best not to complain," the Rebbe warned his daughter. "Accept everything with happiness and gratitude. This will lead to such an abundance of blessing that you will always have what to be grateful for."

We human beings know that we don't enjoy giving to a person who is never satisfied with what we give. Yet it's a pleasure to give to someone who is grateful and appreciates any favor we do for him. The Ribono shel Olam doesn't have human feelings. He doesn't need our appreciation for it to be more enjoyable for Him to give to us. However, when we express discontent, we're declaring that things are unfair. We're demonstrating that we would run the world differently. This is a blatant expression of lack of faith, and it invokes harsh judgment.

But when we thank Hashem for every small kindness and even for the things that are hard for us, this gives Him *nachas* and arouses His heavenly mercy. He says, "You trust Me blindly, and you are full of gratitude although you have it hard. I will give you much to be thankful for." Thanking Hashem despite adversity arouses great mercy and kindness and leads to open miracles.

Real Life Emunah
Forty Days of Gratitude

Leah,* a reader of the monthly inspirational newsletter Kol Todah, is among the many who can testify to the impact of gratitude on a person's life:

It had been seven years since our *chuppah*, and we still hadn't been blessed with children. Just when I thought my life couldn't get any worse, Mrs. Braun,* the headmistress of the school in which I taught, summoned me into her office. After praising my teaching abilities, she dropped the bombshell. My frequent absences due to medical appointments and procedures were having a negative effect on my students' learning. While the seminary understood my plight, the students came first. As of September, a new teacher would be replacing me.

Now I truly felt as if I had nothing: no job, no money, no child. As I made my way home in a fog, I whispered, *Please, Hashem, I've suffered so much already. Please give me a baby. Please make my life easier to bear. I can't hold out much longer.*

My thoughts traveled back to my childhood. My father had died when I was only two years old. It wasn't easy to grow up as an orphan, with everything that entailed. When finally I married the perfect boy, I hoped to put my past behind me and build a family of my own. But it was not to be.

I felt totally crushed. As I was waiting for the bus, feeling very sorry for myself, I noticed a flyer on the bus stop bench, apparently left behind by a passenger. "*Kol Todah*" was the title, and then the subtitle, "Gateways to Gratitude: Giving Thanks to Hashem." There was a *devar Torah* about the importance of thanking Hashem and a phone number one could dial to hear inspirational *shiurim* and more personal stories.

I'm certainly not feeling very grateful right now, I thought, *and if there's one thing I need, it's chizuk. I'm going to call this number.*

I listened in fascination to the *shiurim*. I signed up for the newsletter and read each issue with great interest. There I learned that when a person complains and feels dejected, he brings down on himself more to complain about. But when he looks out for things to thank Hashem for, he brings down yet more blessings for which to be grateful.

At first, I felt very challenged by the idea. Was I not allowed to complain? But after thinking about it, I began to wonder if maybe by feeling so sorry for myself, I had overlooked the bounty of blessings that I do have. Maybe I wasn't such a pathetic individual after all.

"Thank Hashem for one full minute every day," one speaker on the hotline advised. "And for the first forty days, find something new to thank for every day. You'll see — it's not that hard!"

Intrigued, I took up the challenge the very next day. Before I began, I had to drive away the thoughts that came so naturally to me: my litany of complaints about my hard life. And then I began to search for things to thank for.

I looked around my small rental apartment. "Thank You, Hashem," I began, "for this apartment. For the fridge and the freezer, the table and chairs, the beds and the closet, the couch and the phone."

I was looking around for more things to thank for until I noted with relief that my minute was up.

The next day I did it again. "Thank You, Hashem, for the food in the fridge, the clothes in the closet, the books on the bookshelf. Thank You for the plates and the cups, the forks and the knives. Thank You for the running water — the, um — Oh, *baruch Hashem*, my minute's up!"

As the days went on, I noticed more and more to be thankful for: My senses and all the pleasure they gave me.

A walk in the fresh air and legs that can carry me. Even the lavender scent of my fabric softener!

By the time the forty days were up, my mind-set had undergone a complete transformation. Instead of merely being part of a one-minute, forty-day regimen, thanking Hashem had become a natural part of my thought process. Instead of being plunged into depression after another unsuccessful round of treatment, I would thank Hashem for everything that did go right in my life: the loan I'd been granted, the freelance job, the doctor's referral. I felt showered with blessings. Hashem owed me nothing. Everything He gave me was a special gift, and whatever He chose not to give me — well, a daughter can always ask.

On one of my doctor's visits, he suggested that I try an innovative treatment. "It has only a 20 percent success rate," he warned me, "so don't get your hopes up too high."

I thanked Hashem for this opportunity, that there was yet hope for me. And wonder of wonders, it worked! Eight years after my wedding, I was blessed with the greatest gift of all — a precious baby girl. Three and a half years later, I was blessed with another baby daughter. I have so much to thank for. The day isn't long enough!

Although we will never know *cheshbonos Shamayim*, I can unequivocally say that my quality of life has immeasurably improved thanks to my new awareness of the power of gratitude. And for that, I am immensely grateful.

Gratitude Opens the Way to Yeshuos

*T*HE THINGS WE lack can indeed be very significant. But if we work on feeling grateful, we grasp that what we do have is *much* more significant.

Naturally, our problems fill our mind and are blown out of proportion, but this is the very challenge of *emunah!* The more we focus on our blessings, the more we will feel happy and relaxed, and the more *nachas* Hashem will have from us. Slowly the problems will disappear.

Rabbi Nachman Seltzer relates a touching story about a boy who went off the *derech,* which pained his parents terribly. One day the parents suddenly realized that perhaps they should concentrate more on thanking Hashem for their other six children who were giving them so much *nachas.* They hoped that this would ease their pain and allow them to feel happier and truly grateful. They and their children worked on feeling gratitude to the Ribono shel Olam, and then, the unbelievable happened. Their son decided to join them for the Seder night; the happy atmosphere at home drew him in.

Gratitude is at the heart of a lifelong cycle that brings more and more goodness into our lives.

Real Life Emunah
Miracle after Thirty-Two Years

Shevat 5739/1979. Reb Shimon,* the son of a renowned *talmid chacham*, walks to his *chuppah* arm in arm with his prestigious father and father-in-law. Hundreds participate in the joyous wedding celebration and shower the new couple with blessings to build a *bayis ne'eman b'Yisrael*.

Shevat 5749/1989. A decade has passed but unfortunately, the couple does not yet have children. Their names are on everyone's *Tehillim* lists as Yidden beseech Heaven to grant a child to this special couple.

Shevat 5759/1999. Twenty long, difficult years of waiting have passed since their wedding, but they still haven't merited cradling a baby in their arms. Many people have lost hope and try to offer them words of comfort.

Shevat 5769/2009. Three decades from the wedding. Reb Shimon is a beloved and respected leader. Hundreds come to glean *chizuk* from his refined soul, which radiates *emunah* and *bitachon*, despite his personal hardship. At this point, most people find it hard to believe he will ever have children. The only ones who never stop hoping and *davening* are Reb Shimon and his *rebbetzin*.

And then —

Adar Beis 5771/2011. Yerushalayim awakes to the glorious news that Reb Shimon and his *rebbetzin* have become parents to healthy twin girls! It is just over thirty-two years since their wedding!

Reb Shimon is a very modest person who disdains honor and fame. He agreed to be interviewed only on condition of anonymity. He hopes that by telling his story he will strengthen and encourage others not to give up, no matter what.

"It's impossible to describe the heartache and pain we suffered. So many people discouraged us along the way. They all despaired for me, yet look at me today — I'm a father!

"I remember once going to a big *mekubal*. I begged him to promise me that we'd have children, but he promised me we wouldn't! Another time I went to a great tzaddik, one of the leading *gedolei hador*, who also wanted to convince me that it wasn't *bashert* for us to have children. He tried to comfort me that I could leave a *zecher* in this world through teaching my *talmidim*. Can you imagine how despondent I became that even great tzaddikim predicted that we had no chance?

"But I refused to give up. We kept telling ourselves that Hashem can do anything. We have to stay strong. Rebbe Nachman of Breslov says there is no *ye'ush* in the world. We must never lose hope.

"For two whole years, we went every single weekday early in the morning to the *kever* of Rachel Imeinu, who was also barren for a long time until Yosef HaTzaddik was born, to recite the entire *Sefer Tehillim*. Every time, I was certain that it would be my final *tefillah* there, for surely Hashem would help us already. I will never forget the day I woke up in the morning after completing a whole year of *tefillos* at Kever Rachel. The *yetzer hara* came to me and filled my mind with despairing thoughts: *What's the point? You tried so hard, you didn't miss a single weekday of davening this year at this holy site, yet still, you have not been helped. Just give up already!*

"With supernatural *kochos*, I strengthened myself and fought my inner voices of gloom and hopelessness. *I will not give up*, I told myself. *I am going back to Kever Rachel for a second year of Tehillim!* And, *baruch Hashem*, at the end of the second year, we finally merited a *yeshuah*. At that time, my wife and I took on a very special commitment, and although we can't presume to know *cheshbonos Shamayim*," Reb Shimon concludes, "we both strongly feel that we were helped in the merit of this mitzvah."

The *rebbetzin* explains:

"When we had already been married for over thirty-one years, I was talking to a friend who told me about a very special *sefer* that she had just finished reading called *The Garden of Gratitude*, by Rabbi Shalom Arush. In his *sefer*, Rabbi Arush, backed by many sources, urges people to constantly thank Hashem for everything they experience in their lives: for all the good they have, of course, but also for all the minor, bothersome little events that occur throughout the day, and even for all the major *nisyonos* and *tzaros* they go through.

"He relates stories of people who were having tremendous challenges, yet they stayed upbeat and thanked Hashem throughout, and they ended up having wondrous salvations. My friend suggested that my husband and I try the same. We should thank Hashem for our *nisayon*, and maybe in that *zechus* we'd finally merit a child.

"To be honest, I found the suggestion preposterous. How could I thank Hashem for thirty-one miserable years filled with so much pain and suffering? What good was there in decades of disappointments, failed treatments, tears, and heartache? But after talking about it with my friend, we came up with some ideas. It had obviously been *bashert* for me to suffer, so maybe if I'd have had a child earlier, the child would have been sick. Who knows what we might have had to endure? In that case, it was a blessing that this didn't happen. In addition, all those years of *tefillos* and yearning had brought me so much closer to Hashem. Wasn't that something to thank Him for?

"I discussed it with my husband and we came up with many more reasons to be grateful to Hashem. We both took our new commitment very seriously. From that day on, we began to thank Hashem all the time, for everything. We really, truly, and honestly thanked Hashem, even for the tremendous *nisayon* of being childless for over thirty years.

"And you know what happened to me in the process? I became a different person! I felt that I had been born anew. I'd been so consumed with my burning desire to have children that this was the only thing that had occupied my mind. But once I began to thank Hashem for His great *chesed* to me, I felt as though I'd shed a huge burden. I felt so much lighter and happier. I began to notice things I hadn't paid attention to in a long, long time — like how beautiful trees and flowers are and what a stunning world Hashem created for us to enjoy. The words of *Tehillim* that I recited and the *tefillos* I *davened* suddenly had so much more meaning beyond the one thing I craved.

"Because my husband and I felt so grateful to Hashem, and we saw the good even in our *nisyonos*, we felt truly happy. And then, after two weeks of keeping to this commitment, the breakthrough came. We discovered we were on our way to becoming parents! It's hard to describe our emotions.

"We continued thanking Hashem in the months that followed. Our refrigerator broke down, and we said, "Thank You." Then our washing machine broke, and we thanked Him for that, too. A while later, a large closet fell apart. We began to laugh at that point because it seemed as though everything that could break was suddenly breaking down. Apparently, our home was being rejuvenated in honor of the new arrival!

"When our beautiful daughters were born on that glorious winter day, we knew that every *tefillah* said, every *berachah* received, and all the good deeds done throughout the years had surely brought the *yeshuah* closer. But it's hard not to make the connection to our commitment to constantly thank Hashem, especially as we were helped only two weeks after we undertook this.

"My father, a *chashuve rav*, explained that the *sefarim* write that sometimes the gates of *tefillah* are locked for reasons beyond our comprehension. However, when a person brings a gift to the King, he is always allowed through and no angels can obstruct his way. Expressing gratitude to Hashem is like offering Him a present, so the doors are opened wide to allow us to stand before Hashem. Once we are there, He takes a look at our needs and provides us with what we are lacking."

"*Bo'u she'arav b'sodah* — Come and enter His gates with thankfulness!" (*Tehillim* 100:4).

Indeed Chazal say, "From the day the Beis HaMikdash was destroyed, the gates of prayer are locked" (*Berachos* 32b). The Sfas Emes (*VaEschanan* 5638) comments that the gates of prayer may be locked, but the gates of praise and gratitude to Hashem are always wide open.

There's Great Opportunity in Small Troubles

*T*HE POWER OF gratitude in the face of great challenges is truly wondrous. But one doesn't need to wait to suffer major *nisyonos* to experience this power. Suffering, according to the definition of the Gemara, includes even the small irritations that beset us each day.

This definition comes up because the Gemara informs us that someone who has not endured any suffering for forty days is not a *ben Olam HaBa*. He is devouring his reward in this world. Therefore, someone for whom life has been going fairly smoothly might come to believe that he falls into this category. The Gemara reassures us that suffering can come in the form of minor annoyances like being poured cold water instead of hot water, reaching into one's pocket for a coin and pulling out the wrong one, or putting on a garment inside out, or having a garment sewn only to find that it still does not fit (*Arachin* 16b).

Everything that doesn't go exactly according to plan, or anything that causes us even minor aggravation, is considered *yissurim*. This gives us an unbelievable opportunity to acquire the benefits of acceptance and gratitude at the low cost of a flat tire, a lukewarm coffee, or a misplaced credit card!

Rabbeinu Yonah in *Sha'arei Teshuvah* (Ch. 4) guarantees that when we accept aggravation cheerfully, understanding that it's Heaven-sent and it is beneficial for us, we are at that moment tearing up evil decrees and saving ourselves from far worse troubles that were supposed to befall us. He quotes two verses that support this concept:

1. "*Ki chamas adam todeka she'eiris cheimos tachgor* — When a person thanks You for his troubles, You hold back the remnants of Your anger" (*Tehillim* 76:11).

2. "*Odecha Hashem ki anafta bi yashov apcha u'senachameini* — I thank You, Hashem, for You were angry with me and in the merit that I thank You for Your judgment, may You retract Your anger" (*Yeshayah* 12:1).

The *yissurim* mentioned in the verses above refer to *all* suffering, major and minor. When various people or events irritate us, we should feel elated that Hashem sent us this aggravation, offering us a special chance to accept it happily and cancel far more serious suffering. We should grab the opportunity.

It is said in the name of the holy Chozeh of Lublin that if a person knew how much mazel it brings him when a dish breaks in his home, he would take all of his dishes out of the cupboards and break them all! We're accustomed to saying mazel tov when a dish breaks, but for every small annoyance, we should also be saying mazel tov, since it's a chance to cancel a harsher judgment and bring good fortune.

If we simply say, "*Baruch Hashem*," we not only save ourselves from suffering, we enhance our lives tremendously. We will always be calm, and nothing will get us angry or frustrated. We will create for ourselves the most delightful life.

Gratitude Even for Troubles

ABBI ELIYAHU ELIEZER Dessler explains why thanking Hashem despite suffering has the power to evoke heavenly mercy:

Hashem runs the world *middah k'negged middah* (measure for measure). Our behavior determines how He will behave with us. When we accept the attribute of judgment — the pain and suffering — with love and thank Hashem for it, believing that it is good for us, then according to the law of *middah k'negged middah*, Hashem's attribute of judgment must turn into mercy.

(*Michtav MeEliyahu*, Ch. 5)

Rabbi Dessler's words are astounding! If we receive our troubles in the spirit of judgment and punishment, that is what they will be for us. However, we have the power to turn it all around — to receive our troubles in the spirit of kindness in which they are given to us, to trust that they reflect Hashem's mercy and love. And then, that's what they will become. In the true account below, we see how a grateful heart can truly snatch a person from the jaws of disaster:

Terror Attack at Gesher HaMeitarim

Recently I read several inspiring stories that stirred me to thank Hashem for all the good in my life. It was the last day of Chanukah 5776/2015 and, feeling a tremendous awakening, I took my siddur in my hand and recited Hallel with intense concentration. When I had finished Hallel, I recited *Nishmas*, slowly saying each word, and concentrating on the wealth of meaning behind it.

It wasn't as if my life was all peaches and cream. I was twenty-three years old and still hadn't found my *bashert*. I also had two older siblings who were single. Each of us was longing to set up a home of our own. Yet, as I *davened*, all I thought about was Hashem's tremendous *chesed* to me. Feeling uplifted, I decided to go to the Kosel and express my thanks to Hashem in that holiest of places.

On the way home, I took the light rail train to the Gesher HaMeitarim at the entrance to Yerushalayim and then crossed over to the 59 bus stop to catch a bus home. I was engrossed in a book and wasn't paying attention to what was happening around me when I suddenly felt an enormous tremor, heard a loud crash, and then found myself on the ground! I heard screams of fear and bewilderment. I saw shards of splintered glass on the asphalt, splatters of blood, and fierce jets of water streaming down the road.

Terrified, I realized there had been a terror attack. I got up and started running, instinctively shouting in panic, "*Hatzilu!*" As I ran, I noticed blood streaming down my knee and realized I'd been injured, but I knew that I had to keep running, running — along with the many hysterical people who were scattering in every direction.

Amid the confusion, I found myself being led to the nearby emergency medical center, where I was treated for minor cuts on my knee. It was there that I learned that a terrorist had rammed his car into the bus stop, targeting the very bench where I had been waiting. He'd crashed into a fire hydrant, which took the brunt of the collision, thus saving my life. Fourteen people were injured, some were hospitalized for many months, but, *b'chasdei Hashem*, none were murdered. I was unscathed aside for a few cuts in my leg and some glass that I carefully removed from my hair.

I was astonished when I realized what a miracle I'd experienced. So it didn't just happen to people in the magazine articles I had read. I, too, had experienced firsthand how Hashem performs miracles for those who recognize the good He does for them.

And have I mentioned my name yet? Believe it or not, it's Yudit — Yehudis — which means thanks.

You Can Live a Better Life

THERE ARE MANY dramatic accounts of people who have seen salvation from long-standing, difficult troubles, all by shifting their focus from what they're lacking to the myriad gifts they are being given each and every moment of the day.

But even if a person's life is basically on track — he has a good family, a decent livelihood, no major health problems — gratitude can bring him into completely new territory, both spiritually and in his everyday life.

This story was heard from an *avreich* living in Eretz Yisrael who discovered on his own the tremendous influences that gratitude activates:

Opening New Pipelines

"Don't ask what happened," I said to my wife at suppertime.

On cue, she asked, "What happened?"

"You know that payment plan I worked out with the optometrist to pay for my eyeglasses? Well, this month, when I tallied our budget, I didn't reckon in those postdated checks, and as luck would have it, our account was in deficit and the check bounced. What a headache! It's not just the expense. It's all the phone calls and explanations. It had to happen just this month!"

My wife made all the appropriate clucking noises and expressions of sympathy. Then we went on to talk about all the other semicalamities of daily life: the letter from school that one of the children needs dental treatment, the stifling weather.

The next day, on my way home from work, mulling over the day's occurrences and preparing to share them with my wife, it suddenly occurred to me that my dinner discussions each day were basically a list of complaints! How had this happened? I had so much to be grateful for! Why was I always focusing on the negative?

Something has to change, I thought to myself. *From this very evening, I'm going to try to focus only on the good and to thank Hashem for everything.*

"So how was your day?" my wife asked.

"Great!" I beamed. "*Baruch Hashem* for my *chavrusa*, who challenges my learning in the most profound way. And thank heavens for the air-conditioning; when I stepped outside into the heat, I truly knew to appreciate it!"

The look of surprise on my wife's face was priceless. "Why, that's wonderful!" she said, sounding really pleased. And then she told me of the note Shimmy's rebbi had sent home about his attentiveness in class and the shoes she'd found on sale. There was no mention of looming dentist appointments and rising electricity bills. It seemed my resolution had caught on fast.

Ever since, my life has undergone a complete turnabout. It's mind-boggling how, by recognizing Hashem's goodness in my life, I opened new pipelines for more and more blessings to come pouring down from Above.

Just after my resolution to be thankful, my *chavrusa*, a building contractor, mentioned to me that he was currently involved in building a new housing project on the outskirts of the *chareidi* city where we lived. We were renting a small apartment at the time. When we were newly married, it was adequate, but now that our family had grown, we longed to buy a spacious home of our own. When I told my *chavrusa* of our dream, he offered to sell an apartment to me for two-thirds of its market value. The offer was too good to refuse.

I went home that evening and together with my wife drew up all kinds of calculations on paper. Could we do it?

"We are so extremely lucky!" I exclaimed. "Hashem has helped us this far. He'll surely help us further!"

That year we moved into a brand-new apartment. And as I continued to thank, our blessings grew — including some new family members. Once again, we felt we had to move to bigger quarters. But how? "Hashem has given us so much until now," I assured my wife in what had now become a familiar refrain. "He'll surely help us further."

And He did. The neighbor who lived above us had to make a quick sale of his apartment, which had one more room than ours and room to expand further. Miraculously, we found a buyer for our apartment who was willing to pay us the same price our neighbor was asking for his. And so we moved to a more spacious apartment without having to shell out more money and without having to acclimate to a new neighborhood — or even hire a moving van.

As the years went by, I developed a fierce desire to live in Yerushalayim. My wife shared that passion, but we knew it wasn't something we could swing financially. Without going into the details, I will tell you that we were able to make the move, turn some of our property into rentals, and come out financially ahead of where we had been. Once again, we declared in wonder, "*Hodu laShem ki tov!*" Which *kollel avreich* can afford to buy himself an apartment in Yerushalayim? Hashem had arranged the impossible for us.

Apart from the good fortune we are blessed with, the atmosphere in our home has undergone a complete transformation. I can honestly divide my life into two: before my wonderful commitment and after. We feel Hashem is always looking out for us, and whatever happens, even the irritating, frustrating events that comprise daily life are for the good. By osmosis, my children, too, have adopted our attitude and the phrases "*Chasdei Hashem*," "What *hashgachah*!" and "*Gam zu l'tovah*" have become catchwords in our home.

Hodu laShem ki tov!

Nothing is too big or illogical for Hashem to provide us, and when we thank and trust Him, we have access to a special account of unlimited credit!

There is one common thread running through the stories above. Each of the narrators began to feel truly fortunate, and they began to experience a close connection to the Ribono shel Olam. One person even said, "Ever since my commitment to devote a few minutes every day to thanking Hashem, my relationship with *mein tayere Tatte* changed so dramatically that I literally feel like a *ba'al teshuvah*!"

Another admitted, "Married life was often full of challenges. Since I began my thanking exercises, instead of becoming irritated by my spouse's shortcomings, I thanked Hashem for the opportunity to work on my *middos* to be accepting and understanding. I thanked Him for all my spouse's virtues and flaws as well. Our *shalom bayis* improved tremendously."

How to Grab Each Opportunity

*W*E'VE NOW DISCOVERED through many *pesukim* and incredible true stories of *yeshuah* just how much goodness gratitude brings into our lives. There is no person who doesn't have the occasion and reason to thank Hashem, and yet we often forget. Either we're so accustomed to certain gifts that we stop noticing them, or we're so overwhelmed with our *nisyonos* that we have trouble focusing on the good.

Awareness in the following three situations is the key to seeing *hashgachah pratis*, feeling Hashem's *chesed*, and remembering to thank Him:

1. Thank Hashem for all the kindness He does for us all the time, for all the things we take for granted. Appreciate the *hash-*

gachah pratis and *chesed* we experience on a regular basis. Be aware of it and say, "Thank You."

2. Thank Hashem for all the things that could annoy us: the stifling hot weather, the bus that was full and the long ensuing wait for the next one, the broken dish, the lost item, the flu, the missed appointment, the ruined garment, the child who cried all night, the traffic jam. Become accustomed to dismissing these irritations by smiling and saying, "*Baruch Hashem!*"

3. Thank Hashem for the difficult challenges He custom-designed for us to enable us to grow. Realize that these situations are the very best for us, even if we can't understand why.

As soon as a person begins to notice and use these opportunities for gratitude, he feels like a changed person. Chazal say, "*Meshaneh makom meshaneh mazel*" (*Rosh Hashanah* 16b). Changing your place changes your mazel. When we become a changed person, we have changed our place — our *madreigah* — and our mazel completely changes.

Rabbi Avraham Chersky of Stamford Hill, London, has a magnet that he distributes as a reminder to say "thank you" in every situation:

There is another important point to remember while we accustom ourselves to thanking Hashem. It may sound odd, but a person should even thank Hashem for his own careless mistakes. Nachum Ish Gam Zu exemplifies this trait. He had been entrusted with a chest containing the last remaining gems and gold of the Jewish nation. His mission was to bring it to the caesar to appease him and get him to stop his relentless persecution of the Jews (*Ta'anis* 21a).

While Nachum Ish Gam Zu slept in an inn on the way, thieves entered his room, stole the treasure, and replaced it with dirt. In the morning, Nachum realized what had happened. However, he didn't blame himself or bemoan what certainly seemed to be a national disaster. He went forward with his mission, waiting to see what Hashem would have in store.

At the end of the story, he witnessed a miracle in which the dirt turned into lethal weapons that the Romans were able to use to defeat a stubborn enemy. The caesar gratefully sent Nachum back

THE 4 PILLS FOR A HAPPIER LIFE
You can transform pain and worries into happiness and mitzvos!

Many people suffering from aches and pains have said or had in mind the 4 Baruch Hashem's (Thank You God) with feeling and saw them miraculously vanish. When you are faced with a challenge, take these pills by saying the 4 Baruch Hashem's with feeling and you will receive heavenly aid to weaken them or even overcome them.

BARUCH HASHEM:
That I have not experienced this difficulty till now

BARUCH HASHEM:
That this pain/problem is not any worse

BARUCH HASHEM:
That all other areas of my body/life are all right

BARUCH HASHEM:
This too is for the good - Gam Zu Letovah

Rabbeinu Yonah says: 'A happy heart heals a person from his illness.' (משלי יז כב)
Sfas Emess says: 'One who thanks Hashem for his pain will see it disappear because one does not deserve to suffer when thanking Hashem. (שפת אמת מכתבים ח) ועי' דברים רבה ד א)
Rav A. Chersky, 25 Egerton Road, London N16 6UE. Author of Booklet of Joy &Trust.

לעילוי נשמת האשה לאה בת יחיאל ע"ה, נפטרה יום א' בשבועות, ו' סיון תשע"ד.

to Judea with his chest filled with Roman treasure. The Romans needed a secret weapon far more than they needed more gems and gold. The thief had done the Jewish people a favor.

Nachum Ish Gamzu was right once again. Everything is for the good — even our own mistakes.

Does Gratitude Disable Our Bakashos?

*W*HILE WE ARE certainly allowed to *daven* to Hashem and beg Him to help us through our challenges, we need not worry that by switching gears and focusing on gratitude, our difficulties will go unaddressed. The fact that we are thanking Hashem rather than complaining to Him in no way detracts from His desire to help us, because He is even more concerned about our welfare than we are.

David HaMelech expresses this precisely in the *pasuk* "*Agilah v'esmechah b'chasdecha asher ra'isa es anyi yadata b'tzaros nafshi* — I will exult and rejoice in Your kindness, that You have seen my affliction; You are known of the trouble of my soul" (*Tehillim* 31:8).

Just as fleece keeps sheep warm and insulated even in the freezing cold weather, the feelings of gratitude to Hashem form a warm, insulating cushion around the heart that doesn't allow troubles to pierce it and cause us pain. Moreover, when we approach Hashem with gratitude rather than demands, the *yeshuos* we are granted do not consume our merits. The reason is quite simple. We know that everything in the world belongs to Hashem.

The Gemara explains that before we make a *berachah*, our food and drink belong to Hashem (*Berachos* 35a). But once we make a *berachah* and praise Hashem, the food is ours to enjoy. Therefore, saying a *berachah* is like paying for the food. In the same way, explains Rabbi Aharon Yosef Luria (*Avodas Panim*, letter 11), when we constantly thank Hashem for every kindness He does for us, then we rightfully deserve the gifts without forfeiting any of our merits.

Moments Meant for Thanking

THERE ARE MANY moments built into our daily routine that are meant for contemplating Hashem's *chasadim*. We can infuse ourselves with gratitude by using those moments fully, paying attention to what we are saying and letting our thoughts and words stir our emotions. Here are some of the many opportunities that arise every day, and they are packed with potential that shouldn't be wasted:

1. *Saying Asher Yatzar.* When we say this *berachah*, we are thanking Hashem for the miraculous functioning of our body, with all its limbs and organs.

2. *Reciting Birchos HaShachar.* Each blessing offers an opportunity to focus on yet another gift that Hashem gives us upon

waking up each morning. Anyone who has been disabled by a broken arm or arthritic hands can understand the joy we should feel saying *Matir Assurim*. The fact that we can stand upright, walk with balance, shed our fatigue, and take on a new day are all gifts we can mindfully acknowledge as we say the morning blessings. If we think about what we're saying, we will feel more and more fortunate and cared for with each *berachah* we say.

3. *During Shemoneh Esrei.* When we say *Atah Chonein*, that is the moment to focus on the gift of speech, hearing, and understanding. A man who specifically wanted to thank Hashem for these gifts once asked Rabbi Chaim Kanievsky how to do so, and he recommended this *berachah*. *Modim* in the *Shemoneh Esrei* is a prayer for all the miracles and wonders Hashem performs for us every moment of the day. It ends with the words "Your mercy is never ending, and Your kindness never, ever finishes — because we always hope in You." Just saying these words reminds us how much we have to be grateful for.

4. *Reciting Birkas HaMazon. Bentching* after a meal gives us the right words for thanking Hashem, not only for the food we've eaten, but for the *parnassah* and abundance He generously provides for us.

5. *When things go right.* When we need a miracle and receive it, we're naturally overwhelmed with gratitude. But when things go according to our plans, according to norms and expectations, there's so much more to be grateful for. We didn't have to endure hardship; Hashem gave us what we wanted readily, with an open hand.

The following wonderful stories highlight the importance of thanking Hashem when we receive His goodness.

Orit's* Story

I was thirty-five years old, happily married, and a mother of five healthy, adorable children, living in Gan Yavneh, Israel. Life was good.

One evening, I experienced severe abdominal pain. I felt I

was going to pass out, the pain was so severe. Doubled over in agony, I was rushed to the emergency room, where tests and ultrasounds revealed that my gallbladder was seriously inflamed. I was informed that the gallbladder would have to be surgically removed. But first, the doctor instructed, I must be put on a zero-fat diet for six weeks, to alleviate the inflammation.

From the very next day, I abstained from eating anything that had the slightest fat in it. I cooked without oil and grilled instead of frying. *Baruch Hashem* I felt instant relief and did not experience any other attacks. I was so grateful to feel well again, and I began to view all the blessings in my life with new appreciation. How lucky I was to have my family, my home, and no pain!

But the threat of the operation loomed in my mind. I was very afraid. The doctors had explained to me that the gallbladder was responsible for dealing with all the body's fat. If the gallbladder would be removed, then the fats pass on to the pancreas, which can also get inflamed, and then there is no simple cure.

At that time in my life, I had read the book *Just One Word: Amen* and was inspired to say the *berachah* of *Asher Yatzar* with special *kavannah*, reflecting on each word. A thought crept into my mind: *Asher Yatzar is such a powerful prayer of thanks to Hashem, where we can express our gratitude for every single organ that functions correctly. Gedolim have promised that saying this blessing with devotion can prevent illness. I'm now making a commitment to say this blessing with kavannah. May G-d help me that I recuperate without the need for the operation!*

"You have created the human being with wisdom… If one sealed body part opens or one open cavity is sealed, it is impossible to exist for even one hour…" Every word of the *berachah* was so meaningful. I felt so grateful for every minute that my body was functioning, realizing how much can go wrong and how blessed I was that it didn't. My heart, my liver, my brain, my pancreas, my blood vessels — a whole biology book of organs, muscles, capillaries were in perfect working order. How lucky can I be?! Several times daily, I recited the *berachah* with deep concentration, feeling increased gratitude each time for the marvelous blessing of life.

After four months, I had lost close to twenty pounds and was feeling more fit than ever. I thanked Hashem continuously for my good fortune in being alive, healthy, and well, while begging him to save me from the surgeon's knife.

My surgery had been scheduled for Lag BaOmer, but was postponed for two months due to a doctors' strike. After leaving a hospital medical meeting where a new date for surgery was assigned to me, it occurred to me that the doctors' decision to operate was based on the discharge forms the doctor on duty at the ER had given me over half a year earlier. *How can they schedule surgery without referring me for new tests?* I wondered. *This is medical negligence!*

It was too late to reassemble the doctors to a meeting, so I went home and asked my medical practitioner for a referral for an ultrasound. He saw the logic in that and complied.

It was a Friday morning and the operation was scheduled for Sunday — two days later. That very day, as the ultrasound technician in the private clinic in Ashdod printed out the results, he blurted out to me, "I'm not supposed to tell you this — you're officially meant to hear it from your doctor — but I simply must inform you that there is no reason at all to perform surgery. The inflammation has certainly improved."

Enormously relieved, I hurried out to tell my husband the good news. I managed to arrange an urgent consultation with our private doctor and the unbelievable was confirmed. Surgery would not be necessary after all!

All that was left for me to do was to call the hospital to inform them that I was canceling the operation. What a series of *hashgachah pratis*: the doctors' strike had resulted in the operation being postponed for another two months, which had made me decide on the spur of the moment, two days before the operation, to schedule additional tests. If not for the strike, the operation would have been on Lag BaOmer as planned.

I thanked Hashem from the bottom of my heart for this

wonderful miracle, and for His incredible *hashgachah pratis* — and for Him listening to my heartfelt thanks and prayers every time I said *Asher Yatzar*.

Until today I must maintain the fat-free diet. Simultaneously, my children and I say the blessing of *Asher Yatzar* from a written text. I also encourage them to keep a gratitude journal, where they jot down *hashgachah pratis* occurrences and Hashem's *chasadim*. I certainly feel healthier — physically, and spiritually too.

What to Be Grateful For

A young man went to Rabbi Shach and asked him if it was necessary to make a *kiddush* for his firstborn child, a daughter. Rabbi Shach asked the man if he had been married for ten years. The man replied that he had been married for less than a year.

"If you had been married for ten years and this was your first child, would you make a *kiddush*?" Rabbi Shach asked.

The man answered that, of course, he would make a huge *kiddush* to share his joy and gratitude with everyone.

"If so, then you should now be making an even bigger *kiddush* to thank Hashem that you didn't have to endure ten years of waiting for a child!"

When we sincerely thank Hashem for all the blessings He's bestowed upon us, He doesn't have to get our attention in other, less pleasant ways. Here's a great story to teach us that vital lesson:

Dollar Bills From Heaven: A Mashal

Gedalia left his office in a high-rise building with bundles of hundred-dollar bills tucked away in his bag. He was on his way to his attorney to close a business deal, and he was feeling on top of the world. Acting on his energized mood, he decided to ride the elevator to the rooftop of the building and take in the magnificent cityscape below.

As he stepped out onto the roof, a gust of wind slammed shut the heavy metal door right behind him. To his dismay, the handle was broken, and he realized he was locked out. He walked toward the fence overlooking the busy street below. People were swarming around like busy ants. He tried to scream, but he gave up quickly. There was no way anyone would hear him.

He returned to the door and began to bang with all his might. The top floors were unoccupied, and not a soul was in hearing range. He began to panic. Would he die here of cold and hunger?

Suddenly he had a brainstorm. He would throw down several hundred dollar bills, and surely people would look up to see where the notes were dropping from. Then they would notice him waving for help.

He allowed a handful of bills to flutter down to the street. The passersby gladly picked them up, and without a glance upward, they went on their way. How disappointing! Didn't it interest them to know who had thrown the bills down?

With each passing minute, he grew more frantic. His wealth and success would mean nothing if he were to die there with his bag full of money. He began to toss bundles onto the street. A commotion erupted as people gathered around excitedly to pick them up. Then they moved on, rushing to their destinations without a glance upward.

Gedalia began to cry. "How could people be so stupid? Do they think that Mr. Wind has sent them a gift?"

Then he realized something. He was just like the people down there. Had he ever looked upward to thank the One Who had sent him his wealth and health and family?

As he pondered this, his gaze fell on a pile of stones. He began to throw them down to the street, one after another. Frightened and outraged, people were soon peering upward, searching for the source of the danger. As soon as they spotted Gedalia, they called the police to arrest the troublemaker. In a matter of minutes, the police arrived, and Gedalia greeted them with stark relief as he told his story.

We often overlook the "hundred-dollar bills" Hashem sends into our lives. We take what He gives us and move on without a thought. How much better would our lives be if we turned our gazes upward at those moments, rather than waiting for the sharp sting of a pebble to attract our attention!

Saying "thank you" leads to *bitachon* and to every *middah tovah*. When we thank, we feel

- appreciative and not demanding,
- optimistic and not pessimistic,
- content and not grumpy,
- satisfied and not deprived,
- hopeful and not hopeless,
- elated and not depressed,
- complacent and not anxious,
- accepting and not angry.

Gratitude is the best therapy and the best remedy. It's a worthwhile investment.

The Essence of a Jew: To Thank

THE WORD *YEHUDI*, "Jew," literally means "to thank." The exact same word also means "to admit," since thanking is in essence admitting that we owe someone a debt of gratitude. Hashem doesn't owe us anything. Everything we have is a gift, and our only purpose in this world is to acknowledge Him.

The Ramban states this in his famous commentary at the end of *Parashas Bo*:

The underlying reason for all the mitzvos is to recognize and thank the Ribono shel Olam. The sole purpose for mankind to exist is so that a person will thank his Creator. A Jew does not have a portion in the Torah of Moshe if he does not thank Hashem for open miracles and routine *chasadim* alike.

If gratitude is the essence of a Jew, then it makes sense that the greater the Jew, the more he is aware of how little he deserves and how much Hashem does for him. We can catch a glimpse of this crystal-clear awareness through the ways of our *gedolim*:

- The Chafetz Chaim thanked Hashem aloud every day for all the kindness He showed him. Eyewitness accounts of this come down to us from people who overheard him through his closed door as he stood alone in his room verbalizing out loud his words of thanks.
- The Yesod V'Shoresh HaAvodah, Rabbi Alexander Ziskind, writes in his famous will: "I thank Hashem for the pleasant home and furniture He bestowed upon me, for the letters my sons wrote to keep me informed of their welfare that I enjoyed reading, for the respectful garments I was able to purchase and was pleased to wear, for having enough money to buy daily necessities, for the fragrant scent of the tobacco in my snuffbox, for the dish that fell yet did not break..."
- Rabbi Yisrael Salanter was known to thank Hashem for every small kindness. He once related a story that had inspired him to do this: He was traveling with several students on a cold winter evening when they stopped at an inn for coffee. The innkeeper named a high price and the students protested that it was too high. Indignantly, he told them that they weren't just paying for the coffee, but also for the mugs and the chairs and the roaring fire. Reb Yisrael took a lesson from this: that every blessing we say contains within it dozens of other reasons to be thankful. The *shehakol* on our water includes gratitude for the ability to hold the cup, swallow the water, and so forth.

Thanks in Advance

*H*ERE IS ANOTHER powerful idea.

Chazal (*Midrash Rabbah, Vayikra* 27:2) explain a *pasuk* in the most incredible way. The *pasuk* says, "Who has preceded Me that I have to pay, since the entire universe is Mine?" (*Iyov* 41:3).

In this verse, Hashem is asking, "Who can pay Me in advance so that I must pay him back?"

Chazal explain that we can't expect payment for anything we do for Hashem, because we can't do anything unless He gives us the resources to do it. Even when we perform a mitzvah such as affixing a mezuzah on the door of our home, Hashem has preceded us by giving us the home to live in.

There is only one mitzvah a person can do in advance that will cause Hashem to say, "I owe him." That mitzvah is thanking Hashem in advance.

If a person is filled with faith that Hashem will give him salvation, and he sincerely thanks Hashem in advance, Hashem will be obliged to give him the salvation!

In the time of Yehoshafat, Ammon and Moav marched into Eretz Yisrael to conquer the land (*II Divrei HaYamim* 20). Although the Jews were vastly outnumbered, the prophet Yehoshafat strengthened their *emunah* with the promise that Hashem would perform miracles for them. With tremendous *bitachon*, they went out onto the battlefield, thanking and praising Hashem for the miraculous victory He would certainly perform for them.

When they stepped onto the battlefield, Hashem helped them ambush the enemy, and their adversaries began killing each other in confusion. Ultimately, all the enemy soldiers were killed. It was an outright manifestation of G-d's *hashgachah*! And all the Jews had done was praise Hashem.

When we pay for something in advance, the seller is obligated to give it to us. Praising and thanking Hashem before the salvation occurs is the one way available to us to "pay" for Hashem's gifts in advance. When we do this with a full, sincere heart, Hashem is obliged to give us what we are seeking.

Conclusion: We Are Hashem's Delight

*I*N *AKDAMUS*, SAID on Shavuos, we recite:

If all the trees in the universe were paper, and all the oceans and rivers in the world were ink, and every single person that exists on this planet was the most eloquent writer, they could still not even begin to compose even a minute portion of Hashem's praises.

Does Hashem need us to praise Him? The *Akdamus* goes on to describe the magnificent empire of trillions of angels that praise Hashem every second. Every day Hashem creates more and more angels who sing *shirah* and rush to fulfill His every command. We would seem to be less than nothing by comparison.

Yet Hashem covets the praise of simple Yidden who wish to express gratitude. He delightedly places their praises on His head, so to speak, to form the royal crown that adorns the King of kings. *Ashreinu!*

Chapter 3
The Power of Prayer

Hashem is close to all those who call upon Him, to all who call upon Him sincerely.
(Tehillim 145:18)

Now that we are brimming with gratitude, we can fully utilize the power of prayer. When our prayers come from a heart filled with appreciation, when they are not bitter and full of complaints, they are taken straight to the heavenly throne.

No Prayer Too Small

ALL WE NEED to do is ask for Hashem's help and believe that He can give us both the trivial and major things we desire. Nothing we *daven* for is too petty. The following parable, related by Rabbi Yosef Zalman Bloch, the son of the late Telz *rosh yeshivah*, illustrates this point:

There was once a gracious couple who took in a teenage orphan. They paid for expensive medical treatments that he needed and cared for him as if he were their own child. They married him off and set him up in a home near their own.

One day, he came to dine with them. At the end of the meal, his father realized that there were no drinks on the table. He asked his son, "Aren't you thirsty? Why didn't you ask for a glass of water?"

The young man replied, "I really was thirsty, but you already gave me so much. I didn't want to ask you for another favor."

His father was deeply offended. After all he had done for this young man, did he really think something so small posed a challenge? The only possibility was that, after receiving so much, the young man wished to avoid feeling further indebted.

When we refrain from asking Hashem for everything we need, we appear oblivious to the fact that it is He Who already provides us with everything. It's as if we are saying, "This I can take care of myself. I don't need to bother Hashem about it."

Constantly asking for help from Hashem proves that we're aware that all our success comes from Him. He's so pleased that we have asked for His help that He wishes to grant our requests. The more we recognize His *hashgachah* by praying to Him, the more we will merit *siyatta d'Shmaya*.

In addition, when we ask Hashem for the small things, we are able to perceive how our prayers are answered. For example, a man is driving around and around the block looking for a parking space. Finally, he turns to Hashem and says, "Please, Hashem, help me get to work on time. Please let a space open up for me!" In moments, he notices a car pulling out of a parking space, right in front of his office building. Immediately, he feels Hashem's loving care and His listening ear. Had he not prayed for the space, he would have been happy to get it, but the experience would not have drawn him closer to his Father in Heaven and strengthened his trust in Him.

A person who regularly prays for the small things — "May I find a good suit at a good price," "May my challah come out fluffy," "May my children behave on the bus," "May I get my project finished," "May I get a good grade on my test," and so forth — constantly sees answers to his prayers. The more we ask for Hashem's assistance for trivial necessities and notice how He answers our prayers, the more we gain a tremendous *chizuk* in the power of prayer. We feel that we are living in a world of small but constant miracles, as the story below illustrates:

For the first Shabbos after Pesach, Mrs. N. decided to bake bread with a certain type of flour for a family member who was sensitive to wheat flour. She searched the stores for the flour but couldn't find any that had been produced after Pesach. So she *davened*, "Please, Hashem, allow me to bake this challah for Shabbos!"

To her amazement, on Friday morning someone knocked on her door and delivered a parcel containing this very flour with a note attached: "I really wanted to send you a cake for Shabbos, but since I can see I just won't manage, I am sending you the flour."

Her friend had meant this as a joke, but Hashem had sent a messenger right to her door to bring her what she had sincerely asked for!

When we witness how Hashem can easily send us the small things we require, we come to truly believe in the power of *tefillah* to obtain much bigger requirements.

Insurance on Our Emunah

*N*OT ONLY DOES this type of *tefillah* build our emunah, but it insures it for the long run. It instills *emunah* deep in the recesses of our hearts and keeps on nourishing it, prayer by prayer, so that we maintain a vibrant connection to Hashem throughout our lives.

In a conversation with the Chazon Ish, recorded by Rabbi Elazar Tzadok Turchin, the coauthor of *Shoneh Halachos* in conjunction with Rabbi Chaim Kanievsky, we learn the importance of constant prayer even for those immersed in learning. (This was recorded in *Be'er HaParashah* by Rabbi Elimelech Biderman.) The Chazon Ish once advised Rabbi Turchin, "When a person sees that his shoes are torn and he wishes to go and buy a new pair, should he just take money and go off to the store? No. He should pause before he leaves his home and ask the Ribono shel Olam, 'Please help me find the right store and the most comfortable shoes for a reasonable price.' Then he can go shopping, and he will see *siyatta d'Shmaya*."

Then the *gadol* posed a question to Rabbi Turchin: "Where do some of those diligent *yeshivah bachurim* who excel in learning and are considered the top boys disappear to after they marry and leave yeshivah? Why does their *hasmadah* and *yiras Shamayim* dwindle and ruin the promising future predicted for them while they were in yeshivah?"

The *gadol* observed that because people believe *emunah* comes naturally, even some of the most brilliant *talmidim* have trouble maintaining their level of *emunah* once they leave yeshivah.

"The truth is," he said, "that those boys were already missing something while they sat in yeshivah. They didn't work daily on acquiring *emunah*, and this is what caused their downfall as soon as they left the sheltered walls of the *beis midrash*."

This remarkable anecdote implies clearly that *davening* for mundane requests is not only the right thing to do, but it is imperative for the acquisition of lasting *emunah* and *yiras Shamayim*.

Answered Prayers Are "Natural"

*W*E MIGHT HESITATE to *daven* persistently for something because we're afraid that it requires a miracle, and this will deduct from our merits. The truth is just the contrary. We might not deserve a certain gift, but once we pray for it, we will rightfully deserve it. The Maharsha explains why this is so in his commentary on the following episode related in the Gemara:

Rav Acha once went to learn in Abaye's *beis midrash*. During that period, a destructive demon had been roaming the *beis midrash* and harassing those who learned there. When Abaye heard that Rav Acha had come to town, he instructed everyone to refrain from offering him accommodations so that he would be forced to sleep in the *beis midrash*. He trusted that Rav Acha, because of his lofty piety, would be able to defeat the demon.

The demon indeed tried to harm Rav Acha, but he prayed to Hashem seven times, and with each prayer, the demon lost one of its seven heads. The next day, Rav Acha questioned Abaye for putting him in harm's way and forcing him to depend on a miracle to save himself.

(*Kiddushin* 29b)

The Maharsha asks: Was it correct of Abaye to rely on a miracle at Rav Acha's expense? Even if he was so certain that a miracle would occur, was it fair to force Rav Acha to use up some of his merit in the process?

The Maharsha answers that when a person *davens* and his *tefillos* are answered, this is the most natural way to obtain what he needs. No merits are deducted from his account, even if it entails a miracle. An answered prayer, even in the form of a miracle, is simply nature at work. Hashem created a world that runs on the power of *tefillah*.

We Have to Ask

WHAT ACTIVATES THIS natural flow of salvation from Heaven is the act of praying to Hashem; we must ask in order to bring His bounty into our lives. In fact, there may be a gift that Hashem has already prepared but has not given us yet because He's waiting for us to ask for it. If we don't ask, we may never receive it. What a missed opportunity!

But this is the way Hashem runs the world. When we ask, we get what was destined for us, and when we don't ask, we might lose it.

The greatest example of how this system works occurred during the Creation. On the third day, Hashem created grass, trees, plants, and vegetation, but they never sprouted (*Rashi, Bereishis* 2:5). Not until the sixth day, when Adam HaRishon was created and prayed for rain, did the world's exquisite trees and vegetation sprout forth above the ground. Likewise, there are many gifts Hashem has prepared for us, but He gives them only after we pray for them.

These prayers don't have to wait for a fixed time. We can ask Hashem for help from the moment we wake up in the morning until we fall asleep at night: "*Ki eilecha ekra kol hayom* — For I call on You all day long" (*Tehillim* 86:3). Hashem never gets sick and tired of us.

We can confide in Him and ask Him to solve our problems: "*Eshpoch lefanav sichi tzarasi lefanav aggid* — I pour out my troubles to Him; I declare my distress before Him" (ibid. 142:3). He is the ideal life coach, psychologist, therapist, doctor, professor, adviser, mentor, *rav*, and Rebbe. He is always available to us without an appointment, any time we want, for however long we want. He listens, He understands, and He can help us more than anyone else: "*Al tivtechu vinedivim...she'ein lo seshuah* — Do not trust in nobles ...for he holds no salvation" (ibid. 146:3).

This idea of speaking to Hashem doesn't apply only to times when we need something — even something simple. It's a way of life that has a powerful impact on every aspect of our lives. The commentators explain that this was the secret of Yosef's success. How could a young boy of seventeen, betrayed in the most cruel way by his brothers and sold as a slave to Egypt where he was completely alone and exposed to the worst form of *tumah*, remain unscathed?

The *Midrash Tanchuma* (*Vayeishev* 8) says that all day his lips moved in prayer, in gratitude to Hashem and in requests for help. He was so busy mumbling the entire day that Potifar asked him, "What are you whispering all the time?" He answered, "I am praying to G-d that He help me." He didn't stop calling to Hashem for help and he conversed with Him throughout the whole day. This is how he survived.

Believe That Tefillah Works

WHEN WE *DAVEN*, we must believe in the power of our *tefillah*. Then, there is no limit to what we can accomplish. However, we often underestimate this power. It is written, "*Kerum zulus livnei adam* — When baseness is exalted among the sons of man" (*Tehillim* 12:9). Regarding this verse, the Gemara says, "This refers to what belongs to the uppermost spheres that control the universe, yet people belittle it." Rashi there explains, "For example, prayers" (*Berachos* 6b).

If we only knew what a powerful instrument we have in our hands, we would take advantage of it and use it to get all we wish for. The amazing story below shows us the power of praying with a heart full of conviction:

The Promise

Reb Yankel, a Vizhnitzer chassid living in Bnei Brak and father to fourteen children, had a daughter in *shidduchim*. No suggestion seemed to go anywhere. One day he met a Yid who often asked him for a donation. This time, too, he asked for money, and Reb Yankel told him, "I will give you as much as I can at the moment, but please don't ask me again next week because I really can't afford more."

The Yid didn't bother him again for some time, but one Sunday evening a few weeks later, he again begged for financial assistance. Reb Yankel felt he just could not help him on a regular basis. He told him, "Listen, I have a daughter, and we are desperately looking for a *shidduch* for her. If she gets engaged by the end of this week, I will give you a thousand dollars!"

He gave the Yid his daughter's name to *daven* for her and they parted. This *ehrliche Yid* desperately needed the money. He took this opportunity very seriously, *davening* heartfelt *tefillos* and fasting.

The next morning a *shadchan* called. He suggested a *shidduch*, but Reb Yankel wasn't impressed with the suggestion. Instead, he asked the *shadchan* about a boy who had been suggested earlier and rejected by the other side. "I'll try calling them again," the *shadchan* promised.

Later that evening, the *shadchan* was back on the line. "Yes. They are prepared to go ahead."

From there, things began to move quickly. Reb Yankel went to meet the boy, and the mother met his daughter. Another few meetings between the *bachur* and the girl — and on Thursday evening they were drinking *l'chaim!*

Friday morning Reb Yankel handed over the sum of one thousand dollars to this *ehrliche Yid*.

Reb Yankel then decided to share his good fortune. He had a friend whose daughter had been in *shidduchim* for six years and was still not engaged. He made a deal between his friend and the *ehrliche Yid* that the Yid would *daven* for the girl, and the father would pay him $1,500 if the girl got engaged within one month.

Again the Yid took to *davening* very seriously. On day thirty the girl got engaged, and the man earned his much-needed sum of money.

The needy man's prayer was what David HaMelech calls "*tefillah l'ani ki ya'atof* — the prayer of the afflicted man when he swoons" (*Tehillim* 102:1). This Yid begged with all his heart that this be his opportunity to earn the money he needed so urgently, and Hashem answered him in such an open manner.

Pure Kavannah

*A*TEFILLAH FROM THE depths of the heart is always answered. It can even overturn a Divine decree.

In the generation of *Yetzias Mitzrayim*, Hashem decreed that 600,000 Yidden would die in the Wilderness after the spies spoke *lashon hara* about Eretz Yisrael. All those Yidden who cried and complained for no reason, incited by the spies, would have to wander around in the Wilderness for another forty years and would die before entering Eretz Yisrael.

The Midrash explains that these deaths would occur every year on Tishah B'Av (*Eichah Pesichta* 33). On *erev Tishah B'Av*, the people would beg and pray to Hashem that they should wake up alive the next day, but the decree stood, and every year, another 15,000 Jews perished. Finally, in the fortieth year, when there was only one group of 15,000 remaining of that generation, they knew there was no chance that any of them would live through another Tishah B'Av. Their *davening* took on a new urgency: either Hashem would hear their pleas, or they would perish. They lay down that night trembling, crying and pleading with Hashem to annul the decree.

When the sun rose on Tishah B'Av in that final year in the Wilderness, not one of them had died. This is the power of a real, sincere plea. This time no thought crept into their minds that maybe it would happen to someone else. They knew that entreating and beseeching Hashem in prayer was their only hope. These prayers were all answered without exception.

"*Karov Hashem l'chol korav l'chol asher yikra'uhu v'emes* — Hashem is close to all who call to Him, to all who call to Him sincerely" (*Tehillim* 145:18). When a person offers a real, sincere plea from the depths of his heart, Hashem will have mercy on him and answer him even if he is a thief in the midst of performing a burglary and he begs to be saved from the police (*Ein Yaakov* on *Berachos* 63). A sincere *tefillah* is always answered whether the person is a tzaddik or a *rasha*.

When a person calls out for help from Hashem in a time of distress, he is expressing the purest form of *tefillah*, and he fulfills a positive commandment from the Torah. It's his intention — his *kavannah* — that transforms his words into a power that can change reality, as the following story, told by Rabbi Yitzchok Zilberstein, author of *Aleinu L'Shabei'ach*, illustrates:

What Are You Building?

Reb Meir Binet was a contractor in Tifrach, a southern town in Eretz Yisrael. One of the projects assigned to him was to build a *mo'adon* — a youth center — for secular youth. He was not at all enthusiastic about this assignment. He decided to consult with the Shomrei Emunim Rebbe, who spent much time during the week in the quiet, southern town of Ofakim engrossed in Torah and *avodah*. The Rebbe's reply was astonishing.

"Build the *mo'adon*, but your intentions all along should be to build a yeshivah!"

This is exactly what he did. Years later, this very location hosted the yeshivah of Tifrach, which today is one of the most prestigious yeshivos in Eretz Yisrael where hundreds of top *bachurim* are learning.

Another contractor might have built the exact same building, and it would have remained a youth center. What transformed reality was Reb Meir Binet's *kavannah*. Likewise two people can *daven* three times daily, and one can be building *olamos* while the other can be building daydreams. The *Kuzari* says that *tefillah* without *kavannah* is like a body without a soul. However, with *kavannah*, *tefillah* is so powerful that it can break all boundaries.

Why Keep Asking?

NOT ONLY DO our sincere prayers have the power to accomplish everything, but also, there is no limit to how often and how much we may use this power. If we ask a human being to do us a favor and he refuses, we may try asking again. But if we ask a third time, he might retort, "I told you no. Leave me in peace." We wouldn't dare ask again. But we may ask Hashem again and again, and He listens each time. If He still hasn't answered us, we may continue pestering Him as many times as we want.

We might wonder, though, if we should perhaps just accept no for an answer. After all, we know that Hashem wants what's best for us, and if He hasn't granted our request, perhaps we should conclude that it isn't beneficial for us.

This is the wrong way of thinking. Every prayer brings us closer to Hashem. What might not have been good for us before can become advantageous after we have purified ourselves with so many *tefillos*.

Our forefathers were childless because "Hashem desires the prayers of the righteous" (*Yevamos* 64a). Hashem knew that they would continue *davening* from the depths of their hearts, reaching ever-greater levels of elevation and closeness with Him. Therefore, He craved their *tefillos*.

They set an example for every Jew for all time. Our unanswered prayers are never a sign that we should pull away from Hashem, close up our hearts, and accept defeat. Rather, they are an invitation from our Father to come closer, to dig deeper into our hearts, and reach new levels of *emunah*. From there, anything can happen!

Tehillim: Ours Eternally

*W*E COULDN'T POSSIBLY discuss the power of prayer without mentioning the greatest tool we possess to communicate with our Father: none other than *Sefer Tehillim*. We can turn to our *Tehillim* whether we feel like dancing and singing praises to Hashem or we feel like crying bitter tears and pouring out our heart in sorrow.

David HaMelech suffered persecution all his life, initially from his own brothers and then his father-in-law, Shaul HaMelech. Even his loyal adviser Achitofel betrayed him. He suffered terrible *tza'ar gidul banim* when his son, Avshalom, revolted against him. For many years, David was on the run.

Even before he was anointed king at the age of twenty-seven, he spent all his days out in the fields as a shepherd, having been expelled from his own home due to false presumptions. Yet he composed verses of song and praise in the midst of all his worries and was forever thanking his Creator.

These are such powerful words that even if we recite them without total comprehension, it's as if they are being uttered by David HaMelech himself with all his holy *kavannos* (as we recite in the prayer before saying *Tehillim*). These psalms are soaked with David's tears of pain and joy. They are filled with *deveikus* to Hashem, *emunah*, and pure trust.

All of this *kedushah* is absorbed into our bones as we recite each word, and we naturally acquire David HaMelech's peace of mind and serenity. One can't imagine the power of each and every word to bring us close to our Creator and to bring any salvation we might need. Indeed these words were composed with *our* problems in mind.

Anyone who turns to *Sefer Tehillim* in a time of need or a time of thankfulness is amazed at the way these ancient words seem perfectly suited to each occasion, even thousands of years after they were written. That is how it was meant to be. As the Midrash teaches, "R' Yudan says in the name of R' Yehudah that these psalms were not intended only for David himself. They suit any situation any Jew will find himself in, for all generations to come" (*Midrash Tehillim* 18).

This idea is confirmed by the *Ma'or VaShemesh* (*Mishpatim*), which cites the Radak: "David HaMelech prayed for all matters that *Klal Yisrael* will require until the coming of Mashiach. He prayed for remedies for all the sick and for the healthy to remain in good health, for abundant *parnassah* for all Jews, and for the annulment of all evil decrees."

Furthermore, reciting *Tehillim* is a *zechus* on par with Torah learning. One who recites *Tehillim* will not be accused of wasting time that could have been spent learning. He will receive reward as if he were learning the complicated *masechtos* of *Nega'im* and *Ohalos* (*Midrash Tehillim* 1:8; *Yalkut Shimoni*, *Tehillim* 613).

What gives *Tehillim* such power to bring *yeshuos*? The *Noam Elimelech* reveals the mystical secret. He explains that there is one upper sphere called the *Olam HaTehillah*, the World of Praise, which is a world full of compassion where no accusing angels have any influence. Through saying *Tehillim*, a person connects himself to this upper sphere where the Satan has no control and evil decrees just melt away.

Any Jew who has opened *Sefer Tehillim* and prayed earnestly will attest that the *tefillos* helped him. The words of *Tehillim* have a remarkably soothing and comforting effect that result in instant relief. This is due to David's unique characteristic that no other tzaddik preceding him possessed: not only did David HaMelech give us the precise words with which to beseech Hashem, but it's also in his merit that our *tefillos* are answered.

Better Than Silence

*T*HE TIFERES SHLOMO writes that when Aharon's two sons died, Aharon was praised for remaining silent: "*Vayidom Aharon* — And Aharon was silent" (*Vayikra* 10:3). He didn't question Hashem's ways. But there is a greater level than that. After all the pain and calamities that befell David, he said, "*L'ma'an yezamercha chavod v'lo yidom* — So that my soul might sing to You and not be silent" (*Tehillim* 30:13).

He didn't remain silent. He continued to thank Hashem, even for the pain and the suffering. This is an outstanding trait that makes the words of psalms very sweet. It is why David was aptly named *"Ne'im Zemiros Yisrael"* — the Sweet Singer of Yisrael.

That ability to distill *emunah* out of suffering is the source of *Tehillim's* beauty and power. But the Gemara tells us that there was another talented poet whose works exceeded David HaMelech's in beauty, and that was Nevuchadnetzar, the Babylonian king (*Sanhedrin* 92b; *Rashi* ad loc.). When he opened his mouth to sing praises to Hashem, however, an angel slapped his mouth closed.

Reb Menachem Mendel of Kotzk explains that Nevuchadnetzar had it all: the wealth and power of the world's greatest empire of that era. How difficult could it have been for him to perceive Hashem's kindness? But once the angel slapped him, he was no longer interested in singing praises. His beautiful words thereby lost their value.

David, in contrast, had the power to sing praise to Hashem with remarkable *bitachon* even when he was suffering immeasurable pain. This power penetrates our *neshamah* when we recite the holy words (*Kol Todah*, Sivan 2016).

Furthermore, the words we recite evoke sweet memories of Hashem's most devoted servant, filling Him with compassion for us, too. David incorporated within the psalms every emotion that any person will ever feel, and thus the words have a mystical calming and elevating effect on every person.

The following famous story demonstrates the power of *Tehillim*:

The Chernobler Rebbe's Advice

Reb Chaim Eliezer Hershtik was a young chazzan living in Bnei Brak when he was offered the coveted position of chazzan in the Great Synagogue of Johannesburg. Before he left for South Africa, Reb Chaim sought a blessing from the Chernobler Rebbe, Rabbi Meshulam Zusha Twersky. The Rebbe blessed him and, just before Reb Chaim left the room, offered this advice:

"You should know that saying *Tehillim* has tremendous power. If you are ever in a difficult situation, or you meet somebody who's in a difficult situation, recite the entire *Sefer Tehillim*. If that doesn't help, recite it again, and again, until your *tefillos* are answered! The miracle of my salvation from Communist Russia came about only because of the power of *Tehillim*."

Then the Rebbe proceeded to tell him his story:

"I was a young boy living in the Soviet Union when the Communist regime became increasingly antagonistic to religion, and it became very hard to keep the Torah and mitzvos. It was also almost impossible to leave the country and get to the other side of the Iron Curtain.

"But I was determined to leave. My uncle, the illustrious Rachmastrivka Rebbe, had already moved to Eretz Yisrael, and I felt I had to join him there. I yearned to sit and learn Torah, but instead I was busy trying to elude the long arms of the K.G.B., always on the run from one yeshivah to the next.

"I applied for a visa to Eretz Yisrael and finally received an appointment at the visa office. Before I went, I recited the entire *Sefer Tehillim*.

"I entered the building with great trepidation. I told the officer the story written on my falsified documents, that I was in very poor health and upon doctors' recommendations had to move to a country with a warmer climate, that my family had already moved to Eretz Yisrael, and that in my frail situation I wasn't capable of taking adequate care of myself.

"The gruff officer dismissed me without a word. I knew that only a small percentage of applications actually reached the application committee, and, of those, an even smaller percentage of applications were issued visas. I also knew that by the mere act of applying for a visa, I had declared myself an enemy of the state and was now subject to the mercies of the notorious K.G.B.. In short, I was in grave danger.

"Every Wednesday, which was the day the committee convened, I recited the entire *Sefer Tehillim*. For a few weeks I did this, until I was finally told the incredible good news: my application had been accepted! I held the visa in my hand, my precious passport to freedom.

"I traveled to the port in Odessa from which my ship was due to leave, but to my dismay, I discovered that the ship was scheduled to embark on Shabbos. How could I travel on Shabbos?

"I pleaded with the captain to postpone the departure by a day, but he refused. I had no choice but to stay behind. Fellow *frum* passengers urged me to board the ship, explaining that it was *pikuach nefesh* and I would forever be doomed to remain in this giant prison called the Soviet Union, branded as an enemy of the state. But I felt I couldn't travel on Shabbos.

"I left the ship and made my way to one of Odessa's shuls. There I sat down and once again recited the entire *Tehillim*. Over Shabbos I recited it several times, and as soon as Shabbos was over, I made my way back to the port to check out my options. To my surprise, there stood the ship, as if waiting for me. I raced up the gangplank just in time to hear the ship's horn blast its departure!

"So remember, Reb Chaim," the Rebbe concluded. "Reciting *Tehillim* has enormous power!"

Soon after this conversation, Reb Chaim went to Johannesburg to serve as a cantor. One day, the leader of the community asked Reb Chaim a favor. A congregant was very ill, and the doctors said he didn't have much time left. The rabbi had been called away to be somewhere else. Could the chazzan step in for the rabbi and recite the final prayers with this dying man?

Reb Chaim agreed and went to the hospital, where the man lay, very sick, surrounded by his family. However, with the Rebbe's words in mind, instead of saying *Vidui*, Reb Chaim called together the family members and recited *Tehillim* with them, verse after verse, chapter after chapter.

After six hours, the entire *sefer* had been recited. The man's children entered their father's room and were met with a conscious father and a team of doctors astounded by his miraculous recovery.

Had the Rebbe foreseen this particular incident? That question will remain unanswered, but undoubtedly the holy words of *Tehillim* had worked wonders, as the Rebbe had guaranteed.

(*Bnei Emunim, Naso*)

Sefer Tehillim is our unwavering ally through thick and thin. When we use it to reach out to Hashem, we immediately feel His loving care surrounding us. Our *emunah* becomes stronger than ever, not because, like Nevuchadnetzar, we have it all, but because, like David HaMelech, we seek out Hashem even in our pain. We declare, "*V'lo yidom* — I will not be silent!"

Chapter 4
Defeat Despair!

Even if a sharp sword is poised over a person's throat, he should not refrain from praying for Hashem's mercy.

(Berachos 10a)

*I*T IS HIGHLY probably that as soon as you take impressive strides in strengthening your *emunah* and *bitachon* and your attitude becomes more positive, you will experience a serious setback. Beware! Your *yetzer hara* is becoming very irritated. The relationship between you and your Father is strengthening, your aspirations are too high, and you are growing too powerful.

He has a way to break you. He'll say, "Listen here, it's true that Hashem can help you, but *you* don't deserve it. You have so many *aveiros.* Hashem is angry with you at the moment. You have a bad mazel. There are people who have grievances against you. There's an *ayin hara* on you..."

Does this sound familiar?

Every person who is working on *bitachon* will go through these extremely dispiriting thoughts. These are natural thought patterns, but they can be completely overcome. You just have to take hold of the *yetzer hara* and throw him completely off balance.

Hashem Helps — Whether or Not We Deserve It

T HE *CHOVOS HALEVAVOS* in *Sha'ar HaBitachon* clarifies this troubling issue very clearly:

> The decisive factor that determines *bitachon* in a person's heart, and without which *bitachon* is not a reality, is as follows: He must be certain that the One He trusts will keep His word and will fulfill what He promised, and that He will even do him favors that He did not promise or undertake to do but will do them out of benevolence and kindness.

These words are the essence of our *emunah*. If a person begins to doubt whether or not he is worthy of Hashem's kindness, he is not a *ba'al bitachon*. *Bitachon* is being sure that not only will Hashem give what He promised to give, but He will also give generously and charitably that which He is not obliged to give.

The *Pischei Lev* explains:

> If a person doesn't rely on Hashem to deal kindly with him even if he is undeserving, he will always be wary that perhaps he is unworthy of the goodness Hashem gives only to those who do His will. This will put an end to his *bitachon*. But if he believes that Hashem will always help him out, even if he doesn't deserve it, he will always be able to rely on Hashem.

It is obvious that a person can never be sure if he is worthy or not. *Bitachon* is being confident that Hashem will help us as long as we truly trust in Him — regardless of whether we deserve it.

The Ramban (*Emunah U'Bitachon* 1) explains the *pasuk* "*Betach baShem va'aseh tov* — Trust in Hashem and do good" (*Tehillim* 37:3):

> Even though you know you are a *rasha* and you have no good deeds, nevertheless trust in Hashem since He is All-merciful, and He will have mercy on you, as it says, "*V'rachamav al kol ma'asav* — And His mercies are on all His works" (ibid. 145:9).

The Ramban also explains (*Emunah U'Bitachon* 3) that even if a person really doesn't deserve to be helped, Hashem will help him as a reward for his trust; he has no need to fear that he isn't worthy.

Bitachon takes us into the private chambers of the King, regardless of who we are. No prosecuting angels can get in the way. There, right next to the Throne of Glory, *ayin hara* and mazel don't exist. There we are secure under the protection of His wings.

Rabbi Avraham Dov of Avritch, author of *Bas Ayin*, would say that if a person doesn't believe that even when he is sinking and wallowing deep in mud Hashem is still there with him, he doesn't have *bitachon*. "*V'atziah she'ol hineka* — in the lowest depths, behold You are there" (*Tehillim* 139:8).

This trust is our heritage. We are descended from the 20 percent of the Jews who trusted in Hashem and followed Him out of Egypt into the Wilderness (*Midrash Tanchuma, Beshalach* 1). They were redeemed even though they had sunk to the lowest level of impurity.

These ancestors saw all the miracles at the Exodus from Egypt, the splitting of the Reed Sea, and the giving of the Torah. Every Jew alive today is descended from those who left Egypt — those who absorbed into their DNA that Hashem will work miracles for us, no matter how low we've fallen. It's an everlasting contract, a nonbreakable commitment. Our dear Father will always help us.

So when our evil inclination tries to destroy us with depressing thoughts, we must learn how to deal with them:

"Hashem is angry at me."
> *No, He isn't angry at you. He is slow to anger.*

"He doesn't love me anymore."
> *He always loves you no matter how you behave.*

"He is punishing me."
> *No, He always does what is very best for you.*

"He's not answering my *tefillos*."
> *He listens to every tefillah. Each one is precious to Him. Every tear you shed in beseeching for mercy He uses to wipe away gezeiros for you, your family, and for Klal Yisrael.*

"There's no hope."
> *There is no such thing as no hope: "Even if a sharp sword is poised over a person's throat, he should not refrain from praying for Hashem's mercy" (Berachos 10a).*

"I have a bad mazel."

> *Chazal say, "Change your place, change your mazel"*
> *(Rosh Hashanah 16b). As soon as your bitachon brings*
> *you closer to Hashem, you have changed your place*
> *and your mazel changes!*

"The gates of Heaven seem to have closed for me."

> *With tefillos and bitachon you can overcome the highest*
> *barriers, and all the gates of Heaven will open for you.*

"I don't deserve it."

> *You're right! You don't deserve it. And so what? Hashem*
> *will still help you if you rely on Him. You're His child.*
> *He is the most kind, compassionate, and loving Father.*

None of this means that we should become complacent about our flaws and errors. When things aren't running smoothly, and a person is desperate for a salvation, he should certainly make a *cheshbon hanefesh* and make every effort to improve his ways and increase his good deeds. But he shouldn't see these as payment for a *yeshuah*; they are only a means of arousing mercy. He can't possibly accumulate enough merit to outweigh what he owes Hashem.

A Father's Gifts

*S*O WHAT CAN we request from Hashem? We can't claim to deserve His *chasadim*. Neither can we allow ourselves to fall into the hopelessness that the *yetzer hara* tries to force into our hearts. How should we respond?

A person should approach the Ribono shel Olam and beg Him to shower him with *matnos chinam*, free gifts. We don't deserve it. We are in great debt to Him, but He is our Father and we are His beloved children. That's enough: "*Hashem amar eilai bni atah... She'al mimeni v'etnah* — Hashem told me, 'You are My son... Ask anything of Me, and I will grant it'" (*Tehillim* 2:7–8).

If the son of a billionaire needs hundreds of thousands of dollars for an operation, would anyone be surprised when the father readily gives every penny? It's natural for him to share his wealth with his beloved son. He doesn't assess his son's worthiness first.

He loves his son, wants to help him, and has essentially unlimited resources to do so.

Likewise, Hashem is our dear Father. He loves each of us like an only child. When we turn to Him and say, "Tatte, Your heavenly treasury is so vast. Please give me *matnos chinam* because I am Your child and I need help and I have no one else to turn to," He will answer us. A father gives gifts to his children for no reason.

It's interesting to note that it's just when we are so desperately in need of help that we begin doubting our worthiness to ask for it. As long as Hashem was keeping the problem away from us, we never stopped to wonder if we deserved His help. A healthy person doesn't think, *Do I deserve my good health?* Only when illness strikes does he wonder if he is deserving of an answered prayer.

Both are free gifts, both undeserved, both given by Hashem with grace, goodwill, and mercy. When we depend on that alone, we open up Heaven's vast storehouse of *matnos chinam*.

The Midrash tells us that Hashem showed Moshe many treasures set aside as reward for tzaddikim (*Tanchuma, Ki Sissa* 27).

Moshe asked in wonder, "Who will be worthy of receiving these treasures?"

Hashem told him, "These are for those who perform charitable acts."

Then Hashem showed Moshe another huge treasure-house. "And who will receive these treasures?" Moshe asked in amazement.

Hashem answered him, "These treasures are for those who study Torah."

Hashem showed him yet another treasure-house and explained that this was for those who honor *talmidei chachamim*, and so on. And then Hashem took him to see a massive treasury, so incredibly filled with treasures that Moshe couldn't see the end of it.

"And who merits to receive gifts from this massive treasure-house?"

Hashem explained to him, "To those who have mitzvos and good deeds, I give their reward, but to those who don't, I give free gifts from this treasure-house."

This treasury of *matnos chinam* is accessible to anyone who is aware that he is undeserving yet places full trust in the mercy of his Father and His ability to provide for him for free.

Thoughts That Materialize

*N*OW WE'RE READY to "switch on the engine" and zoom forward with our dreams and aspirations so that our wheel of salvation will begin to turn at top speed. Are our thoughts and feelings so powerful that they can control our destiny?

Yes.

The opposite is also true. A person who feels despondent, is full of self-pity, and imagines the worst is literally rejecting his salvation and weakening chances that his situation will improve.

Why?

The *Chovos HaLevavos* explains that this is a promise, as the *pesukim* say, "*V'habotei'ach baShem chesed yesovevenu* — One who trusts in Hashem kindness surrounds him" (*Tehillim* 32:10), and "*Baruch hagever asher yivtach baHashem v'hayah Hashem mivtacho* — Blessed is the man who trusts in Hashem, then Hashem will be his security" (*Yirmiyah* 17:7).

The *Chovos HaLevavos* also cites a verse regarding the opposite attitude: "*Arur hagever asher yivtach ba'adam* — Accursed is the man who trusts in people" (ibid. 17:5).

How can the reflections that go through a person's mind be so forceful?

The Maharsha explains that "in the way a person wishes to go he is led" (*Makkos* 10b). Who leads him? Angels lead him. Which angels? The Maharsha answers, "The angels that he created with his thoughts, with his own willpower and ambitions."

This *Maharsha* is an eye-opener. How many thoughts go through our head in one minute, in one hour, in one day? Every single thought creates an angel. If the thought is one of *emunah* and *bitachon* and a positive desire to persevere, we create holy angels who are ready to take us in that direction. Every time we imagine how Hashem will surely help us, we are anticipating our salvation, fulfilling the mitzvah of believing in G-d, and creating more and more angels. In one day we can become surrounded by hundreds of *malachim* who lead us to our goal: "*Ki malachav yetzaveh lach lishmarcha b'chol derachecha al kapayim yisa'uncha...* — For He will command His angels on your behalf to

protect you on all your paths. On their palms they will carry you..."
(*Tehillim* 91:11-12). Imagine the power of constantly trusting in
Hashem!

With that kind of protection, we will surely reach our destination!

But if the thoughts are of hopelessness, anger, and frustration,
of imagining how bad things are and will be, then the angels created are not holy angels. They don't lead a person to salvation.
They are angels that lead a person in the disastrous direction of his
thoughts. He is indeed cursed.

The *pasuk* says, "I was not secure ... I was not at rest; and
torment has come" (*Iyov* 3:25). When a person dwells on melancholy, on pessimistic thoughts, these thoughts, too, have a power
to materialize.

You Are Where You Think

THE BA'AL SHEM Tov explains that a person takes
up spiritual residence in the location toward which
he directs his thoughts. If he is preoccupied with
worries that he is being punished with *middas
hadin*, then he attaches himself to *middas hadin*. If, however, he
is certain that Hashem will do kindness with him, he is attaching
himself to *middas hachesed* and he draws *chesed* upon himself.

The *pasuk* (*Tehillim* 109:17) says, "*Vaye'ehav kelalah
vatavo'eihu v'lo chafeitz bivrachah* — He loved the curse so it
came upon him; and he desired not blessing." Which human being
loves a curse? A person doesn't actually long for tragedies, but he
might allow himself to daydream about them, dwelling on them
constantly and making no effort to get rid of them. Ultimately, his
habitual thoughts cause his fears to materialize.

But is every thought really in our control? To what extent is a
person responsible for his thoughts?

There is a difference between *machshavos* and *hirhurim*.

Machshavos are fleeting thoughts that cross your mind. For
these a person is not responsible. "*Machshavah tovah mitztarefes
l'ma'aseh* — When one has good intentions, Hashem adds it [the
reward] onto the [reward of] fulfilling [the mitzvah]" (*Kiddushin*

40a). However, if a person intends to commit a transgression yet refrains from carrying it out, he is not punished for the intention. It is our duty to dispose of undesired thoughts as soon as they enter our minds and, of course, not act on them.

Hirhurim, on the other hand, are thoughts that one dwells on and pictures taking place. Chazal say that if a person imagines himself committing a sin, it can be worse than the sin itself (*Yoma* 29a). Dwelling on melancholy thoughts and believing that the "worst will come" is a lack of *emunah*. This *is* in our control: we are obligated to refute such reflections.

A person can't fully focus on two things at the same time. If a person wishes to stop thinking about something, he can always switch channels. By repeatedly substituting his undesirable thoughts with positive ones, he will find that the negative thoughts gradually fade until they finally cease altogether.

The tried and tested way to "switch channels" is by taking time every day to think and thank: think about all the gifts Hashem gives us and thank Him for them. When we think positively, then all will be well in the end. As the Yiddish expression goes: *"Tracht gut, vet zain gut."*

For forty years, *mahn* rained down from Heaven every day, and the Jewish people in the Wilderness had delicious meals to eat without having to work. This was actually a test in *bitachon*. It was challenging to have to go to bed every night with not a morsel of food, relying on Hashem to send more the next morning.

But after one year, two years, and even twenty years, what was so challenging? They could see that day after day, Hashem never failed to send them this miraculous, tasty food.

Perhaps we should be asking the same question today! What are we so anxious about? Can't we see that Hashem has never abandoned us? Don't we see the miracles every day?

That is precisely the test! Will we concentrate on all the miracles and free gifts Hashem has given us and trust that He will continue to help us, or will we worry and fret about all our problems?

It's our choice where to direct our thoughts: in the positive or the negative way. Either way, thoughts are extremely powerful and can bring about dramatic results.

Envision Your Bright Future

A SURVIVOR OF YEARS in Auschwitz described how he was able to endure the horrendous, torturous conditions without losing his mind and the will to live. He related that he kept picturing the excitement he would feel at his liberation. He pictured the joy of reuniting with his family and building a life with a wife and children of his own. By keeping this vision constantly in mind, he found the strength to live day after day.

Rashi lets us in on a powerful tool for salvation that this Holocaust survivor understood. He cites a verse (*Tehillim* 18:4): "*Mehullal ekra Hashem u'min oyvai ivashei'a* — With praises I call unto Hashem, and I am saved from my enemies.*"

Rashi explains that David HaMelech is saying, "Even before the salvation I praise Him, since I am certain that I will be helped." These precious words teach us that even when a person is in deep trouble, he should be so confident in Hashem and His salvation that he is able to praise Him as though he can already see the salvation.

A Song Written in Prison

The Skulener Rebbe, Rabbi Eliezer Zusha Portugal, risked his life in Communist Russia to teach Torah and bring faith and encouragement to the souls of the Yidden trapped behind the Iron Curtain.

Many times he was arrested for his actions. Amid the suffering and the interrogations he endured, he would concentrate on picturing his salvation and praising the Ribono shel Olam.

At the thanksgiving celebration he held each year in America, on the day after Yom Kippur, he would sing a joyous song to the words "*Hodu laShem ki tov ki l'olam chasdo* — Give thanks to Hashem, for He is good; for His kindness endures forever" (*Tehillim* 118:1). He told the assembled that as a redeemed prisoner, he was among one of the four categories of people who are obligated to praise Hashem by reciting *birchas hagomel*, and for that reason, he composed this song.

The chassidim were surprised to learn that the song was not composed after his release, but, rather, while he was imprisoned! How was it possible to be inspired with such an upbeat song in prison?

The Rebbe explained, "I had to prepare a song then with which to thank Hashem when I would be released."

We see in this story the living expression of David HaMelech's words. Fixating on the *yeshuah* that we are confident will come keeps us from capitulating to despair. The *yetzer hara's* dire predictions fall on deaf ears. In this way, our positive thoughts create the momentum in *Shamayim* to carry us through to the salvation.

Tapping Into Joy

*T*HE MOST POTENT antidote to despair is its opposite: joy. But where do we find it in the midst of a very trying situation? There are circumstances where a person feels that there is just nothing at all for which to be joyful. But that's when the *yetzer hara* can gloat over his success. His ultimate victory is to squeeze every ounce of hope and joy out of a person so that he will be depressed. Then the *yetzer hara* has him firmly in his clutches.

For example, if a person has a child who has deteriorated spiritually, he might feel that he is to blame, or his spouse, or the influential friend or neighbor or harsh teacher. But no matter how and why it happened, he is still required to be joyful. How can he feel happy when he is carrying such a tragic *pekel*? The following story below about Rebbe Zusha of Anipoli, renowned as an exemplar of serving Hashem with joy, offers the answer:

Even in Jail...

The two holy brothers, the Rebbes Reb Zusha and, Reb Elimelech, once went on a journey together. They were arrested by malicious anti-Semites and thrown into a prison cell. They weren't allowed out of their cell even to take care of their bodily needs. Minchah time arrived and they wanted to *daven*, but the bucket of waste standing close by made the cell unfit according to halachah. They couldn't bear to think of missing a Minchah, and they begged the attendant to take the bucket away. He hurled a series of curses at them in response.

Reb Elimelech felt downcast. They couldn't even engage in a Torah discussion! He turned to his brother sorrowfully and asked him, "*Nu*, how is it possible to be joyful now?"

Reb Zusha pondered his brother's question. Suddenly he jumped for joy.

"I'll tell you how! If we are presently in this prison and we can't *daven* or learn, then this is Hashem's will. He placed us in this very circumstance. Let us be joyful that we can accept His will!"

With true elation, they began to dance together. The officer was puzzled at their behavior, and, assuming that their joy was somehow related to the bucket, he spitefully removed it.

If a person would realize how joy and confidence in Hashem's salvation literally bring his *yeshuah*, he wouldn't allow any despondent thoughts or feelings to overtake him. He would say what Reb Zusha said, "If this has happened to me, then this is Hashem's will. I can rejoice that I am able to accept Hashem's will even in this circumstance."

As soon as he feels this way, the *yetzer hara* is defeated. His "prey" has managed to reach the lofty level of accepting Hashem's will with joy in such a painful circumstance. The *yetzer hara* will then loosen his grip and flee, and from that moment the person will be able to breathe again!

Once we feel happy, we become capable of finding our way out of the most sticky predicaments: "*Ki v'simchah seitzei'u* — For with gladness shall you go out" (*Yeshayah* 55:12).

Conclusion: Our Thoughts Open the Door to Yeshuos

E'VE NOW LEARNED how to build our *emunah* and pave the way for a *yeshuah*, even when we can't see help on the horizon:

- We must never despair that we are undeserving of Hashem's help. Rather, we should acknowledge that no one can truly deserve the constant abundance Hashem gives him.
- Everything is a gift, given graciously by the Father Who never stops loving us, no matter how we fail.
- Whatever salvation we are waiting for, we can close our eyes and imagine the joy we will have when our salvation arrives. We can picture it vividly and begin to thank and praise Hashem, feeling full confidence in Him.
- We can guide our thoughts toward accepting our situation with joy, knowing that we are where Hashem wants us to be and doing His will even in difficult circumstances. With these thoughts, we drive out despair, defeat the *yetzer hara*, and set the stage for Hashem's unlimited goodness to flow into our lives.

Chapter 5
Why, Why, Why?

"I would have to unravel the whole creation of the world to prove to you the truth of My ways. I must go back to the creation of the world and lay out before you every event and every act that ever transpired so that you will see all the threads and then you'll understand. Every episode is woven together with the one before it and the one after it, and you can't possibly grasp it."

(Rabbi Shlomo Kluger on a Midrash)

*W*ITH *EMUNAH* THERE are no questions. Without it, there are no answers!

Why do some people enjoy a prosperous life of luxury without any worries about their livelihood, while others are bent under the heavy burden of earning a living, paying debts, and struggling for basic necessities?

Why do some have to wait many years, their hope turning into shame and desperation, until they find their *zivug*, while others stand under the *chuppah* at a young age without enduring any difficulties?

Why do some rejoice with a healthy child soon after their marriage and others go through years of heartache and medical treatments, shedding many tears until they embrace their very own child?

Why do some have ten, twelve, or more children and others have one, two, or none at all?

Why do some reap *nachas* from their fine and intelligent children and others suffer so much *tza'ar gidul banim*?

Why do some people live a peaceful, long life and others pass away at a young age, leaving widows, widowers, and orphans?

If Hashem really loves us and is able to give each one of us all we desire and need, why do pain, illness, and hardship exist?

And then there's the most common question of all: "Why *me*? Am I less worthy than...?"

The Question of the Ages

THESE SAME QUESTIONS were asked by many tzaddikim before us. Moshe Rabbeinu implored Hashem, "*Hodi'eini na es derachecha* — Please make Your way known to Me" (*Shemos*: 33:13). With these words, Moshe was asking Hashem to show him the plan by which He runs the world. Why are there tzaddikim who lead a life of suffering, and why are there *resha'im* whose lives are tranquil?

The Midrash offers a glimpse of the answer to this unknowable mystery:

Hashem bade him [Moshe] to go up to the mountaintop. Moshe saw a man in the valley below. He was stooping over a well to take a drink of water. As he did so, his money pouch fell out of his pocket and he left the well, unaware that he had lost it.

A while later Moshe observed another man approach the well. When he noticed the pouch on the floor, he took it and left.

Soon afterward, the owner returned to look for his missing pouch. Noticing a different stranger who had come to the well to drink, he suspected him of being the thief and shouted, "Return my money to me!"

The stranger, who was being falsely accused, responded truthfully, "I don't know what you're talking about."

The owner thought he was being deceived and drew a knife in a fit of passionate anger and murdered the man.

Moshe, from his observation point on top of the hill, exclaimed, "Explain Your ways to me, Hashem! How can You allow an innocent man to be killed?"

"I will reveal My heavenly plan to you," Hashem answered. "In truth, the carrier of the money pouch had stolen it from someone else. When he left it behind at the well, the true owner found it and retrieved his property. The third person who came to the well was a murderer. He had killed the father of the man who was looking for the purse [which he had stolen]. I brought the two together at the well so the son might avenge his murdered father's blood."

(Cited in The Midrash Says)

The thief, of course, had no halachic right to kill the murderer. He had the freedom of choice to abstain from the crime and allow the murderer to be punished by Hashem. However, due to Hashem's special foreknowledge that he would commit murder, Hashem brought him together with a victim who was deserving of capital punishment.

Hashem allowed Moshe a glimpse into the justice of His ways, but told him, "*Lo suchal liros es panai ki lo yirani ha'adam vachai* — You will not be able to see My face, for no human can see Me and live" (*Shemos* 33:20). Even Moshe Rabbeinu, who spoke to Hashem as a person speaks to a friend, couldn't fathom Hashem's ways, because they are simply beyond the realm of human understanding.

David HaMelech was also extremely disturbed by the misperceived injustice of Hashem's ways. He suffered persecution and *tza'ar gidul banim* all his life; he passed through one misfortune only to be confronted by the next. In *Tehillim*, his masterwork, He relates his pain and confusion, which plagued his mind and assaulted his *emunah*. "*Kimat natayu raglai*," he says. "My feet were almost turned astray" (*Tehillim* 73:2). He nearly abandoned the path of faith in Hashem because of the seeming absence of Divine justice.

He further describes his confusion and despair: "*Kineisi vaholelim shelom reshaim er'eh...ad avo el mikdeshei Keil* — I envied the merrymakers when I saw the tranquility of the wicked...until I came to sanctuaries of Hashem" (ibid. 73:3, 17). David HaMelech relates that he was greatly vexed and frustrated by his questions until his thoughts turned to "Hashem's sanctuaries," the eternal World to Come, where only the righteous receive reward and the fleeting pleasures and comforts of this world are like a vivid dream that vanishes upon awakening (*Radak*).

He also discovered that despite a person's *tzaros*, he can enter the Mikdash of Hashem, G-d's Sanctuary, and feel, while still in this world, the bliss that he will feel after 120 years. How? The last line of the chapter explains it: "*Va'ani kirvas Elokim li tov shati baShem Elokim machsi...* — But as for me Hashem's nearness is my good; I have placed my trust in the Lord Hashem/ Elokim ..."

David came to the realization that by enjoying a close relationship with Hashem, which usually comes about through the difficult circumstances themselves, a person is filled with a sublime joy that far surpasses the empty thrill of sensual indulgence.

The sage R' Yehoshua ben Levi was another great tzaddik who was troubled by the suffering of good people and the seeming blessings accorded to evildoers. The Midrash recounts that he fasted and prayed to be allowed to understand the reason:

One day, he met an old man hobbling on his walking stick. The old man greeted him and introduced himself as Eliyahu HaNavi. R' Yehoshua realized his prayers had been answered, and he begged to be allowed to accompany Eliyahu on his daily missions so he could get a glimpse of Hashem's ways. Eliyahu told him that he could come along, but only as long as he asked no questions, no matter what he witnessed.

R' Yehoshua agreed. They began their travels together and soon arrived at a ramshackle hut. A cow was contentedly grazing in the adjacent field. The owners, an impoverished couple, noticed them approaching and rushed out to greet them and invite them in for a meal. The man and his wife served them bread, fresh milk, and cheese. Then they offered them their own beds while the couple slept on the floor.

The next morning R' Yehoshua heard Eliyahu HaNavi praying that the couple's cow should die. Even before they left, they heard shrieks of horror as the woman found her only cow, her sole possession of value and her solitary source of food, lying dead on the grass. R' Yehoshua was alarmed at the terrible injustice Eliyahu had executed. But he kept his mouth sealed as he had promised.

They traveled on, and at nightfall, weary and hungry, they stopped at a glorious mansion. They tried knocking on the door, but no one answered. They looked through the window and saw the table laid with the most exquisite delicacies. The wealthy owner saw them and shouted, "Go away, you good-for-nothing beggars!"

They pleaded to be allowed in to spend the night. After much persuasion, the owner allowed them to rest on some rocks in the yard without even bringing them a morsel of food or a cup of water. He was too busy ranting about the failure of his workers to repair a wall in his home that had collapsed.

As soon as dawn broke, R' Yehoshua told Eliyahu, "Let's get away from this place as quickly as possible."

Then he saw Eliyahu praying that a miracle should occur and the wall should stand again erect. He was absolutely puzzled. *This wicked man surely doesn't deserve any miracles!* he thought.

Finally, after several more peculiar events, when he could no longer bear to watch the injustices, he agreed to part ways with Eliyahu, as long as Eliyahu would explain his actions.

"The benevolent but needy woman was destined to die that very day," Eliyahu enlightened him. "I prayed that her cow should die instead of her.

"The miser," he went on, "was not aware that beneath the ruins of his damaged wall lay a treasure chest full of gold and jewels. I wanted to prevent him from discovering the fortune.

"You should know that all of Hashem's deeds are just and fair. Don't assess facts at face value."

With these words, Eliyahu disappeared, and R' Yehoshua realized that he was simply incapable of comprehending Hashem's complex plans.

(Rabbeinu Nissim Gaon, *Sefer Ma'asiyos*)

Unraveling the World

*N*OT ONLY TZADDIKIM had questions. The *malachim* did, too!

When the Romans tortured R' Yishmael to death, even the angels broke down and cried out in incontrollable anguish, "This is the Torah and this is its reward?" (as recited in *Yom Kippur Mussaf*). Even from their position in the World of Truth, they questioned Hashem's justice.

The Master of the universe answered them sharply: "Be quiet, or I will return the world to '*tohu vavohu* — astonishing emptiness'!" What did Hashem intend to teach them with this retort? Was this an answer to the question they dared to ask, or was it an angry rebuff?

Rabbi Shlomo Kluger, the *maggid* of Brody, explains with a perfect *mashal*:

The King and the Tailor: A Mashal

There was once a king who wanted a garment woven with gold and silver threads. He hired a competent tailor who did a wonderful job. The king was delighted to wear his unique, majestic garment. The king's ministers were jealous of the acclaim this tailor received and devised a plan to destroy him. They went to the king and accused the tailor of taking many of the gold and silver threads for himself.

The king summoned his tailor for interrogation.

"Is it true that you cheated me and stole many of the expensive threads? I demand that you account for all the threads I gave you!"

The honest tailor replied, "Every thread can be accounted for, but there's only one way to prove my innocence. Let's take your garment apart. I will separate every single thread that I wove together. We will count the threads, and you will see for yourself that I sewed every single one into the garment."

This is what Hashem answered the angels, explains Rabbi

Kluger. "I would have to unravel the whole creation of the world to prove to you the truth of My ways. I must go back to the creation of the world and lay out before you every event and every act that ever transpired so that you will see all the 'threads,' and then you'll understand. Every episode is woven together with the one before it and the one after it, and you can't possibly grasp it."

Sometimes, however, a *gadol* can get a glimpse of the Divine reasoning that eludes us. The following story illustrates just such a case:

Prolonged Life

Gadi* was a highly intelligent and talented teenager who possessed strong willpower and high aspirations. He grew up in a secular but somewhat traditional home in the city of Haifa.

When he finished his military training, he served in the army, but he always felt unsettled, a certain lack of fulfillment. Seeking more meaning in life, he ended up in the *heichal* of Yeshivas Nesivos Olam on HaShloshah Street in Bnei Brak. There he began to *shteig* in Torah study, sitting on a bench alongside boys who had been religious from birth.

With his strong motivation and sharp mind, he made huge strides in his studies. After one year he was already considered one of the most exceptional boys in the yeshivah. Everyone prophesied a golden future for him, but Providence had other plans. He suddenly fell ill with a cancerous growth, and, sadly, he passed away a few months later.

This was a horrendous tragedy. A boy had climbed mountains with such strong resolve and self-sacrifice, and he had passed away in the prime of his life, just as he reached the top. His mentors and friends were devastated.

Rabbi Yosef Bruk, the *rosh yeshivah*, wished to eulogize him at the funeral, but the very same day his voice became totally hoarse. He called Rabbi Chizkiyahu Mishkovsky, *mashgiach* of Orchos Torah, and asked him to deliver a *hesped* at the *levayah* instead of him to pay the boy his due respect.

Rabbi Mishkovsky knew this was a weighty but sacred undertaking, and although he would have preferred to decline, his conscience would not allow it. It was an extremely sensitive situation. What could he say to comfort secular parents and siblings who had witnessed with their own eyes the tragic end?

He decided to consult Rabbi Chaim Kanievsky to advise him on the right words to choose. The *gadol* instructed him as follows:

"This boy was surely destined to die at a younger age, but Hashem saw deep inside his heart that tiny seedlings of *teshuvah* were beginning to blossom. He therefore bestowed him with a gift of additional years of life. In this period, he became a *ba'al teshuvah* and a *talmid chacham*, and he merited to die as a *ben Torah* after his soul was purified with *yissurim*. This is exactly what you should say at the *levayah*."

Rabbi Mishkovsky was stunned. He himself believed these words 100 percent. But how on earth would secular Jews who had been raised without pure faith believe it? The whole way to Haifa he nervously anticipated the reactions to his speech.

Rabbi Mishkovsky delivered the *hesped* word for word, as Rabbi Kanievsky had instructed. Afterward, Rabbi Noach Hertz, who was present at the funeral, grabbed his arm and led him to the bereaved father. "Let's see what he has to say about your speech!"

(Rabbi Noach Hertz himself had become a *ba'al teshuvah* as a young man. As an air force pilot, his plane had been forced into enemy territory. He was captured, and, while he was in captivity, his leg had to be amputated. After his miraculous release, he became a *ba'al teshuvah* and a full-fledged *talmid chacham* who established a respected family.)

Reb Noach approached the father with Rabbi Mishkovsky. It was obvious that the father was overwhelmed with emotion. But his response was surprising.

"You don't know how right you are!" he exclaimed, waving his finger at Rabbi Mishkovsky. "Several years ago, my son was conscripted into the army, and he was assigned to enter Lebanon in a tank with other soldiers. Suddenly the commander approached him and screamed at him, 'Who told you to get into this tank? You are not supposed to be here. Come out immediately.' For no apparent reason, he led my son to a different tank right behind the other one and ordered him to take his place inside."

The father continued with tears in his eyes, "A short while later the first tank was hit by a shell, and all the soldiers were killed."

Rabbi Kanievsky's words had been proven true in such an open fashion, to the letter!

In another story, Reb Chaim Volozhiner was able to see the incredible future that appeared as a terrible misfortune:

A Far Better Fortune

Reb Moshe was a prominent wealthy Jew, a charitable person who went out of his way to perform acts of kindness. He was held in high esteem by all of his community. But to the dismay of the whole town, he lost his entire fortune, leaving him totally bankrupt.

His family and friends couldn't grasp it. How could such a thing happen to an upright, generous person like him? They began to ponder about what could be the cause.

Reb Chaim Volozhiner heard about the discussions, but said nothing about the tragedy.

With his business in ruins, Reb Moshe now had free time. He began to learn. He would enter the *beis midrash* and delve into the Gemara for hours on end. He suddenly discovered the delights of learning. He realized that he had a head for Gemara, and with time and effort he became a great *talmid chacham*.

He became known as Rabbi Moshe Soloveitchik, none other than the head of the prestigious dynasty of Brisk, grandfather of the Brisker Rabbi, Rabbi Chaim Brisker, and of the Beis HaLevi.

Reb Chaim Volozhiner later explained that as a prominent

ba'al tzedakah, Reb Moshe did not yet have the merit to become such a great *talmid chacham*. He had to lose his wealth in order to grow in Torah.

Second-Guessing Hashem

*U*NFORTUNATELY, WHEN WE'RE suffering, we're not always interested in seeing our situation as part of a larger context. We just want the suffering to end. However, like R' Yehoshua, we may be blind to what our suffering is accomplishing. Yet even if we were to acquire a glimpse of Hashem's knowledge, our limited human minds would be unable to deal wisely with what we perceive. As the adage goes, "A little knowledge is a dangerous thing." This *mashal* from the Chiddushei HaRim illustrates this point:

The Language of the Birds: A Mashal

There was once a wise man who understood the language of the birds. He would sit in the fields under the trees, listening attentively to the birds chirping, making note of important information.

One day Yankel approached him and questioned him regarding his strange behavior. "What do you do in the fields every day?"

"I listen to the conversation of the birds, and I pick up vital knowledge," the man divulged.

Yankel was impressed. "Wow! If only I understood them, too. They could reveal to me so many secrets that would make my life a success. Please teach me this wisdom!"

The wise man refused. "This wisdom is a very dangerous tool," he warned. "It can cause you great harm. You'll regret having studied it."

But Yankel insisted and pleaded until the wise man reluctantly agreed to teach him.

Yankel learned diligently, and after a few weeks he was ready to go out to the fields and practice his new skill. He listened carefully to the chirping of the birds, and he heard them whispering, "Next week, Yankel's warehouse will catch fire, and all his produce will burn!"

Yankel was horrified. He quickly emptied out the entire warehouse, and indeed a week later the warehouse went up in flames and he was spared a major loss.

The next week he heard the birds singing that there would be a drastic rise in the price of silver. He hastily purchased large quantities of silver and made a fortune selling it a while later at triple the price. And so it went. Luck smiled on him and his fortune grew.

Then one day he heard the birds whispering, "Yankel is going to die." He was shocked. He ran in hysteria to the wise man who had taught him the wonderful secrets and he cried, "What should I do now?"

"I warned you that you'd be sorry," the man told him. "Had you lost your produce and not become rich by making a fantastic profit on the silver and so on, you would have had your share of heartache and you wouldn't have had to die."

This was a *mashal* that the Chiddushei HaRim saw played out in real life with one of his chassidim:

When Poverty Is Precious

A wealthy Gerrer chassid fell into difficult times, and he had to declare bankruptcy. He began to suffer pangs of poverty, and he and his wife couldn't bear it. He went to his Rebbe, the Chiddushei HaRim, to ask for advice and a blessing. He mentioned that he had a wealthy brother from whom he could borrow money and try to set himself up again.

The Rebbe listened to his sorry plight, deep in thought. Finally he told him, "Don't ask your brother for a loan. Hashem will help you."

Months passed and the chassid's situation didn't change. His wife urged him to go to the Rebbe again. She couldn't fathom why the Rebbe had advised against asking for help. His brother would only be delighted to comply. He would surely have offered help on his own initiative had he known their situation. The chassid again traveled to the Rebbe and poured out his heart. He explained that his wife was broken and despondent. The Rebbe once again shared his pain, but he still advised against asking for a loan.

But his wife felt she was breaking under the burden, and she nagged her husband to approach his brother. When he could no longer bear her complaints, he confided in his brother regarding his financial struggle and his brother immediately offered him a loan. He took the money and invested it carefully.

Within a short time he was able to stabilize his affairs, and the pressure in their home diminished. Times seemed to be better again until one day the chassid discovered that he had a serious illness. The doctors gave him just a few weeks to live.

His wife realized that the predicament arose from failing to heed the Rebbe's words. She sent a message to ask for a *berachah* on her husband's behalf.

The Chiddushei HaRim explained sadly, "I saw that the poverty he endured was a *kapparah* for him. With *emunah* and endurance, the difficult times would have passed eventually. But now that you have interfered, I can't change the decree anymore."

Everyday problems assaulted this chassid and his wife, and, like most people, they just wanted their troubles to go away. Rather than seeking the message in the pain, accepting it, and trying to alleviate it through *tefillah* and *teshuvah*, they looked for a quick method to improve their lot. This is like a person who asks for a painkiller to treat his appendicitis. He might numb the pain, but ultimately, without surgery, the condition that underlies the pain could cost him his life.

This is what the Chiddushei HaRim was telling the chassid's wife when he said that he couldn't change the decree.

But not always is it possible to receive clear instructions from a *gadol*. Not always is there a person who can answer our question of why, why, why? Only stark, steadfast *emunah* can support us. Hashem's calculations are far too complex and intricate for us to begin to understand them. Our only recourse is to rely on the One

Who knows everything from the creation of the world until the end of time. Knowing that He loves us and cares for us more than we love and care for ourselves, trusting that He can save us in a split second, we can put aside our questions, pray for help, and lean on His strong, supportive arms.

A person without *emunah* will never, ever achieve contentment. There will always be something that will mar his enjoyment, even if he attains wealth and honor. A believing Jew, on the other hand, can always be joyful, no matter what he goes through.

> Michoel was informed that he had won ten million dollars in the lottery. He was on the way to obtain the check, full of excitement. With his mind preoccupied by dreams and plans, he didn't notice the lamppost, and he walked straight into it, injuring his forehead. While the paramedic bandaged his wound, his thoughts flew elsewhere: the *tzedakah* he would give, the ease with which he could marry off his children, the new home for his family... He didn't even feel the pain.

Without *emunah*, every bump and scrape makes us flinch. With *emunah*, however, we sail through life just as Michoel sailed through his momentary pain. Our thoughts are directed to another world, where we are paid far more than ten million dollars for every challenge we accept with trust in the Ribono shel Olam and His infinite love.

Chapter 6
Asking the Right Questions

When a person acknowledges that his suffering is from Hashem and he accepts it, the remainder of the suffering will be held back. It will be canceled!

(Rabbeinu Yonah, Sha'arei Teshuvah)

*D*ESPITE ALL WE know, when we experience the pain of *yissurim*, still we may ask "*lamah*" — why is this happening? That question, however, will never lead us to serenity. A far better option is to change the Hebrew word's punctuation and turn it into "*l'mah*." For what?

Lamah — why — demands an explanation. It asks the impossible: that Hashem reveal to us His Divine wisdom in creating our circumstances. In contrast, *l'mah* — for what — is a constructive question: "If the situation I am in now is so demanding, difficult, and unexpected, what does Hashem want from me now? What is He asking of me?"

A *pasuk* helps us to hear Hashem's voice in our troubles: "*Kol dodi dofeik pischi li* — The sound of my Beloved One is knocking. He said, Open [your heart] to Me" (*Shir HaShirim* 5:2). He is calling us, beckoning us to come closer. This is no stranger at the door: it is our beloved Father. When challenges arise, it's time to open the door for Him, accept that it is all from Him, and do some thinking.

Ask Him, "What do You want from me, Tatte?" He will help us

discover what He really wants, and He will help us make amends if we are truly sincere.

The truth of this statement is often difficult to discern. We may feel we are indeed responding wholeheartedly to the wake-up call, taking on *kabbalos* and doing extra mitzvos, and yet still suffering. In this case, we have to realize that everything we are doing is to our credit. None of it is wasted. Salvation is a process, and everything we do to come closer to Hashem helps move the process along. When "suddenly" everything resolves, the resolution is not sudden at all. It's the culmination of everything we've been doing.

Undoubtedly, if our troubles are not yet over, then our training course is not yet complete. We still have obstacles to overcome before we arrive at the place our soul needs to be. We need to hold on. For sure, the additional merits we continue to accrue will help us persevere.

Hashem's Torah and mitzvos are not only a merit for our salvation, but a balm in our times of trouble: "*Tzar u'matzok metza'uni mitzvosecha sha'ashu'ai* — Distress and anguish have overtaken me, Your mitzvos are my delight" (*Tehillim* 119:143). This *pasuk* exemplifies the Jew's reaction to distress and anguish. Rather than languishing in his pain and worry, he can open a Gemara and enter the world of Rava and Abaye. "*Toras Hashem temimah meshivas nafesh* — The Torah of Hashem is perfect, reviving the soul" (ibid. 19:8). Or he can put aside his troubles and enjoy helping someone less fortunate than him. There is nothing that can lift a person's mood more than the pleasure of giving and helping someone in need.

When a person realizes that he has taken on himself new commitments that he would not have adopted without Hashem "knocking on his door," he should be filled with joy. He can feel confident that "these mitzvos that I am doing now are what Hashem wanted from me. He takes a personal interest in me and cares about *my* personal *avodah!*"

The reward a person will get for mitzvos he does despite his distress is surely magnificent. Instead of moaning over the "why" of his situation, his potential greatness has been activated by the "what for." He has sought the opportunities for growth and meaning in his plight, and, in doing so, has answered Hashem's knock on the door.

A Circle of Compassion

*T*HERE IS AN amazing *Zohar* brought in the *sefer Ohr Tzaddikim*:

When HaKadosh Baruch Hu has mercy on a person, He sends him a gift. What is that gift? He will send his way a poor or needy person for whom he can feel compassion so that he will help him. At that moment, he himself is deserving of Hashem's compassion, and Hashem helps him. In this way he merits salvation even though he did not deserve it.

(*Zohar, Bereishis* 104a)

This is an eye-opener. When a person is in great distress, he might feel that he is almost incapable of thinking of anyone else. He needs a big *yeshuah*, but perhaps he is undeserving. In this case, the Ribono shel Olam gives him a different route to access his *yeshuah* in the form of a person who needs his help. If he chooses to grab hold of this gift, he will arouse Hashem's compassion for him and bring his *yeshuah* within reach.

If a person internalizes this "secret," he will assist people in need despite his distress and he will do it with the greatest joy. Rather than a burden, he will view it with gratitude as a custom-made opportunity from Hashem.

This idea is found in the following *pasuk* (*Tehillim* 41:2): "*Ashrei maskil el dal b'yom ra'ah yemalteihu Hashem* — Fortunate is the person who contemplates the needy on the day of evil; Hashem will deliver him." When a person is experiencing his own troubles, and he is having a particularly difficult day, and yet he gives of his time and money to a needy or ill person, Hashem will surely save him.

Pursued by Kindness

A major *askan* from London traveled to the Knessiah Gedolah of the World Agudath Israel in Vienna, wishing to meet the Chafetz Chaim there to ask a *shailah*. His wife felt that his time was too preoccupied with his work for the *klal* and it was affecting their home life. Should he give up his volunteer work?

He approached Rabbi Akiva Schreiber, who was hosting the Chafetz Chaim, and requested a meeting. Rabbi Schreiber suggested that he join them for breakfast.

Before the *askan* even had a chance to raise his query, the Chafetz Chaim began reciting Psalm 23 of *Tehillim*. When he came to the words "*Ach tov vachesed yirdefuni kol yemei chayai* — Only good and kindness shall pursue me all the days of my life," he asked, "Why does David HaMelech use the word *yirdefuni*, 'pursue'? This is a word that is used to describe troubles, not kindness.

"When a person feels overloaded with all the kindness he is performing for other people, the *yetzer hara* will come and persuade him to give it up: 'It's spoiling your *shalom bayis*! It's taking away from the time you need for yourself and your children!'

"He should pray, 'May I be pursued only by the good and kindness that I do, and not by troubles.' Hashem will answer his prayer, and the kindness he does will take the place of troubles that he would have had to endure."

The *askan* realized that the Chafetz Chaim was talking directly to him, and his question had been answered. He believed he was attending to the *klal's* needs, and he was; but at the same time, he was helping himself and his family even more.

Chazal (*Midrash Rabbah*, *Rus* 5:9) comment on the *pasuk* "She said, 'The name of the man whom I helped is Boaz'" (*Rus* 2:19). Boaz had extended a great kindness to Rus. Why did she say she helped Boaz when the opposite was true?

R' Yehoshua teaches, "The kindness that the needy person does for his benefactor is greater than what the benefactor does for the needy person."

The *chesed* we do is for our own benefit. The wonderful sense of gratification generated by helping others is a healing balm for the *yissurim* in our lives.

Hashem Doesn't Owe You Anything

*T*HERE IS ONE danger in undertaking *chesed* as a response to our troubles. That is the possibility that we might come to feel that Hashem now owes us a *yeshuah*. The reality is very different. We are not entering a business transaction with Hashem in which we do a mitzvah and He pays us back for it. We are helping another Jew out of compassion, and we hope that Hashem will respond to our deed with compassion, *middah k'negged middah* — but only He knows if the *yeshuah* we are seeking is truly the compassionate response to our situation.

The starting point for every request from *Shamayim* is to know that nothing is "coming to us." This is a powerful lesson with powerful results. In the following story, Mrs. Miriam Gabbai relates how she learned this vital lesson from a *gadol hador*.

A Way to Arouse Heavenly Compassion

The house was quiet. It was 11 p.m., and my husband had gone to sleep already. I didn't follow suit because I knew that any attempt at sleep would be futile. I was too distressed.

Sadness was a stranger to me. I had always been a happy child and an optimistic adult. I married very young — I wasn't even seventeen yet — and went to live in Tzefas, where I taught and later became the principal of a school that focused on outreach. How I loved my students! How I loved to teach them about Shabbos, Chanukah, and *Chumash* and see their pure, innocent eyes light up with understanding.

I loved our life in Tzefas. My husband is a *talmid chacham*, a kindhearted person, and a gentle soul, and our home was a haven of Torah and spiritual growth. But as one year went and the next one came and I still wasn't blessed with children, I started wondering if something was wrong. And so began my journey of infertility.

With the blessings of our *rav*, we moved to Yerushalayim. *"Meshaneh makom, meshaneh mazel"* (*Rosh Hashanah* 16b), he advised us. Change your place, change your mazel. My husband immersed himself in his Torah studies with my blessings and encouragement.

Three years after our move and ten years after our wedding, there was still no change. I had consulted with the best doctors in the country, and even traveled abroad for help, but I had nothing to show for it.

I lay in bed, thinking that I had to do something, but what? Impulsively, I went downstairs, stood on the street, and hailed a taxi. "To Shaarei Chesed, please," I said. "To the home of Rabbi Shlomo Zalman Auerbach."

As the car approached the tzaddik's house, I saw a small light shining through the window. My spirits lifted. Perhaps Rabbi Auerbach was still up?

I paid the driver and walked up the rickety steps leading to the apartment. Tentatively, I knocked at the door, hoping against hope that someone would open it.

And someone did. Not just someone. The tzaddik Reb Shlomo Zalman himself. "How can I help you?" he asked courteously, opening the door wide and showing me inside.

I couldn't speak. I could only cry. The tzaddik waited patiently, silently, while I cried and cried. Finally, through my tears, I managed to tell him how I longed more than anything for Hashem to bless me with a child.

"It pains me to see your distress," the Rav said gently, and I felt a surge of hope. I would get a *berachah* from the tzaddik, and all would be well.

However, his next words shook me to my core.

"But HaKadosh Baruch Hu doesn't owe you children," he declared in a strong voice. "HaKadosh Baruch Hu doesn't owe anyone anything." Then he began enumerating on his fingers the gifts not owed: "He doesn't owe you children, health, life, money... He doesn't owe you anything," and with that he turned over both hands, empty.

I was devastated. I felt that all hope was gone, plummeted, dashed. Feeling completely crushed, I tried to gather my composure and leave the house. I respectfully backed away toward the door, and as I reached for the handle, I heard Reb Shlomo Zalman's voice once more.

"HaKadosh Baruch Hu doesn't owe you anything, but if you give others what you don't owe them, Hashem will give you what He doesn't owe you. Whoever shows mercy to Hashem's creations will be shown mercy from Above. Hashem acts toward people *middah k'negged middah*."

At these words, I felt my hopes rise again. I thanked the rabbi from the bottom of my heart and left.

Then and there, outside the tzaddik's apartment in Shaarei Chesed, I promised Hashem that I would give His children all my time, my money, and my energy. The next morning I started volunteering in the maternity ward of Bikur Cholim Hospital. I acquired a cart, decorated it with ribbons, and made my rounds among the new mothers, distributing candy and other goodies.

I soon realized that the happy new mothers didn't need me to cheer them up. I started making the rounds with my decorated cart in the more somber wards: oncology, hematology, urology, and others. I am a naturally upbeat person, and Hashem had blessed me with a way of imparting some of my cheer to the patients. A year after I began my volunteer rounds in the hospital, the impossible happened. Hashem blessed me with a baby boy. Almost five years later, Hashem blessed me once again with twin girls.

Throughout it all, I never gave up my volunteer work. I didn't want to let go of my mission: to do what I am not obligated to do.

Today my son is married with a baby of his own. My twin girls are seventeen years old and are a source of endless *nachas* to me. My joy knows no bounds.

Neither does my volunteering. Three times a week I go either to Shaare Zedek or Hadassah Ein Kerem to do my rounds, sometimes with my mother joining me. I go from floor to floor, from bed to bed, with my trademark cart heaped with candy, chocolate bars, rice cakes (the most popular item), cookies, drinks, magnets, and balloons. I visit Jew, non-Jew, Orthodox, non-Orthodox, it makes no difference. They are all Hashem's creations, and they are all recipients of my compassion.

As I bring comfort to the patients, I feel Rabbi Shlomo Zalman Auerbach at my side, encouraging me. A smiling portrait of the tzaddik is proudly displayed in my hallway, and I have never lost sight of his message: Hashem doesn't owe you anything. But if you give others what you don't owe them, Hashem will give you what He doesn't owe you.

The Chafetz Chaim, in his *sefer Ahavas Chesed* (Vol. 2, Ch. 5), quotes the Gemara's statement, "R' Yehoshua says: Whoever does *chesed* on a regular basis will merit children who are wise, wealthy, and versed in *aggadah*" (*Bava Basra* 9b).

The Chafetz Chaim remarks, "I personally witnessed many who tried this *segulah*, and it worked for them."

The Nugget of Gold Inside the Challenge

A woman once went to see Rabbi Binyamin Zilber, known as "Rav Binyamin HaTzaddik," a *talmid* of Yeshivas Novaradok and a member of the Moetzes Gedolei HaTorah in Eretz Yisrael, in his home in Bnei Brak. She unburdened herself, relating her feelings that with so many sudden problems and difficulties one after the other, she felt that the Ribono shel Olam was distancing Himself from her. Something was wrong.

He comforted her with the most genuine and calming words.

"If everything would be going completely 'right,' then you would have to be concerned."

Within our troubles and challenges is a precious nugget of gold: the motivation to call upon Hashem, to lift up our eyes and reach out to our Father for help. What seems like a curse is actually a blessing, because as long as we're in need, we will never forget Hashem.

Meforshim explain that this is the meaning behind the punishment of the snake that tempted Chavah in Gan Eden. He was consigned to eating the dust of the earth, and as a consequence of his endless supply, he would never run out of food and never have a need to connect to Hashem.

Chavah, on the other hand, was given the challenge of raising children, and Adam received the challenge of earning *parnassah*. Ever since then, infinite prayers have ascended to Heaven due to those two challenges. Hashem bound mankind and Himself permanently together with these "punishments."

That is the way Rav Binyamin HaTzaddik saw the troubled woman's plight: You are lucky. You are Hashem's beloved child. If He didn't want to have anything to do with you, then you should worry. Right now, nothing is wrong. Things are going just right. Make the most of your close connection!

Too Much for Me

EVEN WITH THE most sincere desire to accept our *yissurim*, we often have a preconceived idea of exactly how much we can be expected to handle. One thing goes wrong, and we're able to smile and move on. Another thing goes wrong, and we may have to work a little harder, but we're still able to accept it and keep going. At some point, however, we encounter the "straw that breaks the camel's back." We ask Hashem, "Just how much am I expected to take?"

In this story related by Rabbi Ephraim Wachsman, we discover that our burdens in life are measured precisely, right down to the final straw:

He Just Couldn't Handle It

At the end of Shacharis on a Shabbos morning in the town of Kotzk, someone came running inside the shul shouting, "There's a terrible fire in the middle of town! Reb Yosef's store is burning down!"

Reb Yosef heard the commotion, and when he realized his store — and his entire fortune — were at stake, he fainted on the spot. His friends revived him, but he just fainted again. This went on several times until the Kotzker Rebbe walked over to him and whispered in his ear, "It's a mistake. It's not your store."

On *motza'ei Shabbos* he went to investigate, and indeed it was a different store. His store stood intact and unscathed. Everyone acclaimed the Kotzker Rebbe's miraculous powers.

The Rebbe set them straight. "I didn't perform any miracle, and I didn't have *ruach hakodesh*. I simply saw that he couldn't handle the situation. I realized that his store couldn't have burned down, because Hashem doesn't give a person a test that he can't handle."

Moreover, Rabbeinu Bachya (on *Devarim* 22:8) teaches that not only are we equipped for the tests Hashem sends our way, but also that we have agreed to them in advance:

Every single person was created willingly with his full consent. At the creation of the world, Hashem showed him what sort of life he would lead. He was informed of every single affair and every single event that would take place in his lifetime. He was told how many years he would live, when and how he would die. He was shown how much *parnassah* he would have: whether he would live comfortably or be needy, whether he would be independent or dependent on others. So Chazal explain that all of Hashem's creations were created knowingly and willingly...

And every single person, having seen every *nisayon* he would endure, was satisfied. He agreed and gave his full consent.

Every hardship we endure was already destined for us. We were informed about every one, and we willingly agreed to undertake it. We understood that this will bring our *neshamah* to perfection. It was custom made for our soul, at the exact dose that we would be able to withstand and the precise measurement we need to complete our *avodas Hashem* (see *Rashi, Tehillim* 147:17). There is no mistake. We saw it and we wanted it.

Accepting *yissurim* with love can bind us to our Father like no other mitzvah can. No other self-perfection can compare to its power to refine and purify our *neshamos*.

The Vilna Gaon's daughter passed away a day before her *chuppah*. That night his mother came to him in a dream.

She told him, "My son, if you would know what you accomplished when you gladly accepted this tremendous tragedy, you would have danced at her funeral with greater joy than you could have danced at her wedding!"

Those whose souls are attuned to Olam HaBa, even while their feet are still planted firmly in Olam HaZeh, understand even without a visitation from the other world that our tears in this world will be our *simchah* in the World to Come. Rabbi Aharon HaKohen, the Chafetz Chaim's son-in-law, related the following story:

A couple was getting married in Radin, and there was a terrible snowstorm. There was no way the orchestra could get to the wedding. At the *chuppah*, in place of music, some *bachurim* banged pots and pans together. The Chafetz Chaim called me to come and watch from his window and he remarked, "Just look at this *chasunah* without music! There is something tangibly missing in the atmosphere. That is how Olam HaBa looks for a person who didn't suffer *yissurim*."

(*Chesed L'Avraham* 42)

Our *yissurim* are our music in Olam HaBa. In fact, R' Yishmael says, "If forty days pass and a person didn't suffer any *yissurim*, he has received his reward in this world and he loses his Olam HaBa" (*Arachin* 16b). One who has no *yissurim* is extremely unfortunate!

What Constitutes Yissurim

THE QUESTION IS, what sort of suffering is considered *yissurim*? The Gemara there gives several examples:

R' Elazar says that if a person has a suit tailor made, and he tries it on and it doesn't fit properly, this is reckoned as *yissurim*.

R' Shmuel bar Nachmani says that if you ask for hot water and you were poured cold water or vice versa, that is *yissurim*.

Mar the son of Ravina says that if you mistakenly put on your shirt inside out, that is *yissurim*.

Rava's famous definition is even less bothersome than the previous examples: If you put your hand into your pocket to take out three coins, and you mistakenly take out two coins, that is *yissurim*.

If these minor mishaps are considered *yissurim*, then why is it necessary to experience severe suffering? Rabbi Eliyahu Eliezer Dessler explains with a parable.

A Precious Burden: A Mashal

A king once went on a cruise in his private luxurious liner. One day, a terrible storm broke out. The king grabbed a life jacket and dived into the sea, taking hold of a piece of wood to float on. When the storm died down, he swam with all his might toward an island he saw in the distance. He reached the shore and collapsed in exhaustion.

A kind native found him unconscious. He brought him to his home on the desert island, fed him, and revived him. The king spent the rest of the day sitting by the shore, trying to signal to passing ships to come and rescue him.

Finally a ship arrived, and, using only sign language, the king persuaded the native to accompany him to the palace. Now he could reward the native for saving his life.

He took the native down to his cellar and opened the heavy metal door of the treasury. They walked into a room full of trunks brimming with diamonds, pearls, and precious stones. The king handed the man several rucksacks and indicated with hand motions that he could fill them up with as many treasures as he wanted. The king left the room, locking the door behind him, and promised to fetch him in a few hours.

The native was horrified. Why was he being locked in this dungeon and forced to do slave labor? Is this how the king wanted to show his gratitude? He was determined not to lift a single stone. He rested on the floor and closed his eyes to take a nap.

Suddenly he heard footsteps. The king was approaching. He quickly picked up some stones and stuffed them into one of the bags.

The king bade him farewell, and he went out into the
street with his bag on his shoulders.

At least I took the small stones, he thought to himself. *If I
had taken big stones, the bag would be heavy.*

He looked around, and, to his surprise, a fellow native ran
toward him. He was so glad to be able to break his silence
and speak to someone in his language. He related to him
the whole story. His friend was shocked.

"Do you realize how much every one of these stones is
worth? You have missed an opportunity to be wealthy for
the rest of your life! What a fool you are!"

(Michtav MeEliyahu, "Tzaddik V'Ra Lo")

A person despises any minor hardship. He wants to live in peace.
If he only realized that each small bit of *yissurim* is worth a fortune, and that after 120 years, he would reap a fortune from each
setback, each drop of pain and each problem, he would treasure
these burdens and carry them diligently and gleefully. The bigger
the "stone," the greater its worth.

Chazal's Mathematical Formula

ALONG THE SAME lines, Rabbi Dessler explains
another statement of Chazal regarding *yissurim*
(Michtav MeEliyahu, Vol. 3, pp. 14–15). Chazal
say, "A mitzvah that is done with a little hardship is worth a hundred times more than a mitzvah done easily"
(Avos D'Rabbi Nassan 3:6). This means that when someone en-
counters a little *tza'ar* in doing a mitzvah, it's as if he has done
the mitzvah one hundred times. He is rewarded as if he has done
a hundred mitzvos.

This is when he does the mitzvah with one measure of *tza'ar*. If
he does it with two measures of *tza'ar*, he gets paid for doing ten
thousand mitzvos (100 × 100) even though he did only one.

For example, a man tries to raise money for *hachnasas kallah*,
and the donor he is trying to telephone is unavailable. This measure of *tza'ar* makes his mitzvah worth 100 mitzvos. If he tries to
dial again unsuccessfully, his mitzvah, which is now worth 100,

will be worth 100 × 100, which equals 10,000, for the second measure of *tza'ar*. One should actually be much more excited about doing mitzvos with difficulty than without!

When a person has *yissurim* — he has a headache, *tza'ar gidul banim*, health problems, difficulty with *parnassah*, or he is degraded or belittled — but he continues to do mitzvos with joy, the value of each mitzvah grows dramatically with every drop of *tza'ar*. He does a few mitzvos, and he gets rewarded for doing billions!

The real query a person will have in the next world is not "Why did I have *yissurim*?" but "Why didn't You give me more *yissurim*?"

Rabbi Mordechai Miller, the principal of Gateshead Seminary, offered this illustrative scenario: After 120 years, a blind person is shown his portion in Olam HaBa and he sees how each mitzvah he did, despite his handicap, became worth billions of times more. He is asked, "What was your most precious possession in life?" He answers, "My blindness."

The following story shows us a stark picture of the preciousness of a mitzvah done despite unimaginable obstacles and risks. The story was related by the renowned Maggid Rabbi Yaakov Galinsky, of the Hadera Yeshivah, in the name of Rabbi Yitzchak Shlomo Ungar, the rabbi of the Chug Chasam Sofer community in Bnei Brak:

Retrieving an Immeasurable Merit

Eliyahu* was a Hungarian teenager who was separated from his family in the first few minutes of their arrival at the concentration camp. How lucky for Eliyahu that Reb Baruch,* the man who slept alongside him on the hard wooden plank, was a tzaddik whose every word radiated holiness. He infused Eliyahu daily with powerful doses of *emunah*, which did more to keep him alive than the meager bread rations.

One evening, after they lay their exhausted heads on their wooden bunks, Reb Baruch turned to his young friend. "Pesach is fast approaching," he said. "We're going to have to make a Seder. That's not even a question. We have plenty of *maror*. Bitterness is our lot. But I don't see how we can possibly find a way to bake matzah here in the middle of Auschwitz."

Eliyahu peered closely at his friend. It was difficult to see him in the darkness of the barracks, but he was sure that there were tears in his eyes. Could it be that Reb Baruch was literally crying over the mitzvah of matzah despite the unbearable suffering that they were experiencing day after day?

"Reb Baruch, my friend, I will see what I can do. No promises. But if there's a way to bring you matzos here in Auschwitz, then you'll have a *kezayis* of matzah this Pesach."

And Eliyahu put his mind to the challenge.

Every morning, after roll call was taken and daily rations dispersed, Eliyahu was marched off to work at one of the nearby factories. In the same complex of factories was a huge warehouse of wheat. Sometimes the prisoners were sent there to clean the room. It was almost impossible to steal the wheat. The guards, knowing how hungry the prisoners were, kept a close watch on them. Stealing was forbidden; the penalty was death. But when your soul is flying out of its earthly confines, begging for a reminder of holy days long gone, anything is possible.

While at work in the storehouse, Eliyahu managed to remove sufficient wheat to make enough matzah for both him and Reb Baruch. During his short break, he snuck off to the side and, using two stones that he found, pounded the wheat until it had become coarse flour.

He hid the flour in a corner of the vast room and the following day mixed it with the majority of his water ration to make a paste that resembled dough in name only. And who would ever have imagined baking matzah on a metal slab of machinery that was used to manufacture airplane parts? Yet, at the end of the day, Eliyahu held two *kezeisim* of matzah in his hands, one for him and one for Reb Baruch. His heart rejoiced. Life was beautiful even in Auschwitz if a Jew was capable of eating matzah.

Slipping the matzos under his uniform, Eliyahu pressed them against his chest with his arm, doing his best to appear nonchalant, as he approached the gate leading back into the camp. There was a sentry standing there searching every inmate for contraband. Something in Eliyahu's manner raised his suspicions.

"What are you hiding under your uniform?" the guard yelled at him.

Eliyahu raised his arm for a second, to show the guard that there was nothing there, but to his shock and horror, the matzos slipped from beneath his arm and fell to the ground as if in the slowest of motion. Two beautiful pieces of *ahavas Hashem* falling — falling — to the ground, and the guard was laughing, overjoyed that he'd caught him in the act.

Lifting his club, he slammed it across Eliyahu's back, sending him sprawling to the floor, the matzos crumbling as they scattered. The guard showered him with a beating, until Eliyahu's weakened, bleeding body gave way. He fainted, sprawled forlornly on the floor, crumbs of matzah surrounding him.

The guard turned his attention to one of the other prisoners. Eliyahu lay there for quite a while until he finally came to. One of his fellow prisoners rubbed his face with water from a puddle on the floor, and he sat up, the world spinning around him. With his last remaining strength, he gathered as many crumbs as he possibly could — the matzah crumbs for which he'd risked his life — and returned to his barracks and Reb Baruch.

Reb Baruch was waiting for him in tense anticipation. His holy face lit up when he caught sight of his friend.

"Do you have the matzos?"

Eliyahu nodded, but his swollen, bruised face told Reb Baruch that something had gone miserably wrong.

"What happened?"

Eliyahu opened his fist and showed his friend the pile of crumbs. Then he explained what had occurred on the way into the camp and how the two *kezeisim* for which he'd endangered his life were now one.

Reb Baruch immediately set about treating his friend's wounds, but his heart was pained when he realized that his dream had been shattered. Then he dared make a suggestion.

"Eliyahu," he appealed, "I'm begging you with every fiber of my being. Please let me be the one to eat the one remaining *kezayis*. Please!"

Eliyahu shook his head. "Out of the question," he said. "I put my life in danger for this matzah, the guard beat me for this matzah. Now you want me to give it to you?"

"Eliyahu," Reb Baruch entreated, "in all my life I have never missed eating matzah at the Seder. How can it be that I will miss it now?"

"I'm sorry, Baruch, my dear friend, but I just can't give this to you. I need it for myself."

"Eliyahu, I know the Haggadah by heart. I will recite it in its entirety for you. I will even say *Shir HaShirim* with you, word for word, only please give me the *kezayis*!"

Still Reb Eliyahu demurred.

Now Reb Baruch stood up. His eyes were blazing with an inner fire, making him look like a heavenly angel.

"Eliyahu, I will give you the reward of this mitzvah if you allow me the privilege of eating the *kezayis* matzah. I have lost my family, I have lost my home. But I'm not willing to lose this mitzvah also. I'm begging you with all my heart!"

Thus they arrived at a compromise.

Reb Baruch would recite the Haggadah from beginning to end.

Eliyahu would repeat it after him word for word.

Reb Baruch would eat the matzah.

And Eliyahu would receive the reward for the mitzvah of eating the matzah.

That was the deal they made.

What a Seder it was! The words of the Haggadah came alive as the two men discussed the story of *yetzias Mitzrayim* into the late hours of the night. And finally it was time for the matzah. Reb Baruch ate it, consuming every bite with a look of pure delight on his face. They sang the Hallel in an undertone and almost broke into a dance when they reached the words "*L'shanah haba'ah biYerushalayim*."

The next morning, when they went out to work, Reb Baruch was still in heaven. As he went about his work, he recited the Shema with eyes tightly closed and even said *She-*

moneh Esrei. When he reached Hallel, Reb Baruch couldn't control himself. Without thinking of the consequences, he let his voice rise in spiritual ecstasy. But the Nazi guards didn't appreciate spiritual ecstasy. As Reb Baruch opened his heart to his Creator, one of them raised his gun and shot him for having the nerve to pray out loud. He collapsed and died on the spot.

Eliyahu survived. At the war's end, he left bloodstained Poland forever and moved to Eretz Yisrael, where he built a new life for himself. He married, raised a beautiful family, and became a prominent member of the Chug Chasam Sofer *kehillah* in Bnei Brak.

Many years passed. One night, as Reb Eliyahu lay sleeping, he had a visitor. Face glowing like the sun, Reb Baruch had come to him to make a request.

"Reb Eliyahu, do you recall how you allowed me to eat your matzah on that Seder night all those years ago on condition that you receive the reward?"

Reb Eliyahu remembered. How could he have possibly forgotten? The events of that night and the day that followed it were forever burned into his memory.

"You should know that as soon as I was shot, I was taken directly to Gan Eden where only holy *neshamos* that were killed *al kiddush Hashem* are allowed entry. Now after so many years I've come to beg you for a favor."

"What's that?"

"Please grant me the reward of that *achilas matzah!*"

Reb Eliyahu was taken aback.

"I have received reward for all the mitzvos I did during my lifetime, except for that one mitzvah! I'm begging you, my old friend, to please release that *sechar* into my hands as well."

Reb Eliyahu was shocked by the request, by the audacity of his old friend.

"Reb Baruch, how can I possibly give you the reward for this mitzvah? I endangered my very life gathering the wheat, grinding it, baking it. I took a terrible beating for my bravery — a beating that almost killed me. How can you ask for such a thing?"

"But I was the one who convinced you to bake the matzah in the first place. I counted the weeks and kept a reckoning of the Jewish calendar. If not for me, you would not have known it was Seder night. And I'm the one who recited the Haggadah, and I led the Seder."

"Yes, you did, but it was I who put my life in danger to make it happen. I'm sorry, but I don't want to give up the mitzvah. We made a deal."

Reb Baruch's face took on a look of abject disappointment, but he said no more. Reb Eliyahu awoke deeply disturbed by what had just transpired. Had he made the right decision? Was he wrong for withholding the reward for a mitzvah for which he had put his life in danger? He understood that he would have no peace until he knew the answer.

Reb Eliyahu decided to consult his rabbi, Rabbi Yitzchak Shlomo Ungar, the rabbi of the Chug Chasam Sofer community and *rosh yeshivah* of Machaneh Avraham. Rabbi Ungar listened carefully to the entire story before replying.

"Reb Eliyahu," he said, "this isn't a question for me. This is a question for a Rebbe. Go to the Rebbe of Machnovka, and he will advise you. Come back and tell me what he says."

The Rebbe, Rabbi Avraham Yehoshua Heschel Twersky, asked Reb Eliyahu to tell him the entire story. After weighing all the sides, the Rebbe looked Reb Eliyahu in the eye and said, "Truthfully, *al pi yosher*, the correct course of action, you should probably yield to Reb Baruch."

Reb Eliyahu was taken aback.

"*Al pi yosher! Al pi yosher* I definitely don't have to give him the reward. My question was whether or not I should choose to act *lifnim mishuras hadin* and do more than what's expected of me!"

"Reb Eliyahu, let me explain. Your friend is not alive anymore. Whatever mitzvos he was able to accomplish while in this world is all the reward he has in the next world. But he did one additional mitzvah for which he's not receiving any reward, and there's nothing he can do about it, because he has no opportunity to do mitzvos anymore. He's no longer alive. That door is closed.

"But you are still alive. You can wrap tefillin around your arm and build a succah and fast on Yom Kippur. You can *daven* every morning and wear tzitzis. You can give charity and perform acts of kindness. So many mitzvos. So much reward! And you have children, and they also do mitzvos for which you also receive reward! Don't you see how fortunate you are?

"That's why I'm telling you that *al pi yosher* you should give in to him in this case."

Reb Eliyahu fell silent for a while and then said, "If the Rebbe feels that's what I should do —"

"And you should do it with a complete heart, because it is the right thing to do! You'll be able to eat many more matzos in your life, but for him that was his final matzah.

"Now there's something else that I want you to do," the Rebbe went on. "Take these keys."

He held out a key ring to Reb Eliyahu.

"Go into the nearby *beis midrash*, open the lights and the *aron kodesh*, and then tell Hashem the entire story. How you met each other in the camp and how you were the best of friends and how he convinced you to be *moser nefesh* to bake those matzos. Tell Hashem everything! About that final Seder and how Reb Baruch recited the Haggadah and how you made a compromise that he would eat the matzah but that you would get the reward. And then, tell Hashem that you are choosing to give up that reward. Of course, the reward for baking the matzos with incredible *mesirus nefesh* remains yours."

Reb Eliyahu took the keys and followed the Rebbe's advice. Standing before the open *aron kodesh*, he poured out his heart to Hashem. He relived that terrible time in the camp, but also relived the incredible *mesirus nefesh* that he'd undertaken for the mitzvah of matzah on Pesach: granting the reward of eating the one *kezayis* to his friend, who had been killed so close to liberation without the opportunity to do any more mitzvos.

When he finished telling Hashem everything, he felt relieved, as if a great weight had slipped off his shoulders. He closed the door of the *aron kodesh*, flicked off the lights in the big room, and locked the doors behind him. He returned the keys to the *gabbai* and left the shul to go home.

When he reached his house, he found that he had no strength left and needed to lie down. Seconds later he was sleeping. The next thing he knew, he was dreaming again.

Reb Baruch was there, face shining with a tremendous light. So happy, so light, so filled with joy. He had come to thank him and tell him that his request had been approved.

Then he disappeared.

And Reb Eliyahu understood.

He understood that he need not feel pain anymore when he envisioned the sight of Reb Baruch being shot in cold blood right in the process of singing Hallel with such tremendous devotion. He was surely to be envied, not pitied.

He also understood that a human being can't possibly comprehend the reward in Olam HaBa for one mitzvah — especially for a mitzvah done with *mesirus nefesh*.

(*V'Higadeta, Shemos*, p. 180)

Reb Baruch had to wait more than thirty years until he was permitted to return to earth to retrieve the reward of *one* mitzvah. He pleaded for the reward of that one mitzvah, although he had already earned the most coveted place in Gan Eden.

Let us try to work out how much *mesirus nefesh* went into this mitzvah. Perhaps it was the most precious mitzvah he ever performed.

From the very first day in Auschwitz he took care to keep count of the Jewish calendar so that he would know when it was Pesach. He persuaded Eliyahu to bake the matzos. He waited with such anticipation for his friend to return with the treasure. He was devastated when Eliyahu came back with only one *kezayis* and was prepared to give away his reward just to be able to eat the matzah. He made a Seder in secret and ate the matzah with love and devotion, even as his heart was pounding in fear that the Nazi guards may spot him and kill him and his friend. Finally, still feeling the elation of being able to perform the precious mitzvah of eating matzah in the concentration camp, he *davened* Hallel with such fervor that he couldn't contain himself and was murdered for it.

How many measures of *yissurim* went into that mitzvah? Rava says that taking out the wrong coin from one's pocket is equivalent to one measure of *tza'ar*; therefore, this mitzvah must have been worth thousands of measures of *tza'ar*. Since Rabbi Dessler explains that each measure of *tza'ar* multiplies the reward of the mitzvah by one hundred, the value of this mitzvah is too great to calculate. No wonder Reb Baruch didn't want to lose it!

We tend to enjoy doing the easy mitzvos that come our way and shy away from those that cost us too much time, effort, or money. We see, however, that this is misguided. We should be pursuing the mitzvos that, because of the *tza'ar* involved, grow geometrically in value, placing immeasurable fortunes into our heavenly accounts.

If Yissurim Are So Good, Why Do They Stop?

THERE IS STILL one significant question that remains unanswered.

If Olam HaBa is only acquired through *yissurim* and they are so beneficial for us, then how can it be that by accepting them with love, we can cause Hashem to cancel the remaining *yissurim* due to befall us? When a father takes his son to the hospital for a lifesaving operation, he won't cancel the procedure because his son expresses his understanding that the pain is for his benefit. The operation is still needed, and it wouldn't be a kindness for the father to cancel it.

Hashem does what is best for us even if it hurts us and even though it hurts Him more. Is it really possible that He would refrain from doing what is most beneficial for us just because we accept it with love?

The Sfas Emes asked the same question concerning our conquest of Eretz Yisrael. The Gemara says that three things are acquired through *yissurim*: Torah, Eretz Yisrael, and Olam HaBa. When the Jews left Egypt, Hashem's plan was that they would journey through the Wilderness and enter Eretz Yisrael in only three days. But due to the sin of the spies, they had to wander for forty years. The Sfas Emes asks: If Eretz Yisrael can only be acquired through *yissurim*, how could they have been ready to enter the Land after only three days?

He answers that had they accepted the *yissurim* they experienced during those three days with love, the level they would have reached would have equaled all they attained through their forty years of suffering. More suffering would have become unnecessary.

This is what Rabbeinu Yonah writes (*Sha'arei Teshuvah* 4:12): When a person acknowledges that his suffering is from Hashem and he accepts it, the remainder of the suffering will be held back. It will be canceled!

Rabbi Shalom Arush, author of *The Garden of Emunah*, explains that this is so because the person who accepts suffering with love and faith in Hashem reaches a tremendously high level. His suffering need not continue, because he has already fulfilled his mission.

Often, *emunah* only takes over when a person is in desperate straits and thinks, *It's all in Hashem's hands.* But what about the everyday irritations that are also considered *yissurim*? The child who annoyed us, the bus we missed, the garment that was ruined, the loss of money — the list is endless.

If a person experiences an inconvenience, and he doesn't have the presence of mind at that moment to say, "This is from Hashem, I am not going to get nervous," nothing will happen. He will feel irritated, and his life will continue. But he has missed a chance to pass the test Hashem sent his way. He missed the chance of Hashem holding back more serious suffering since he would have accepted his challenge with love.

So much good would come to each of us and to the world if every person would utilize life's minor disturbances to acquire *emunah*. This is the reason they are sent to us. If the Gemara lists minor inconveniences as *yissurim*, then they are not really so trivial. They are opportunities to earn tremendous reward and save us from more difficult trials. It's worthwhile to pay attention when inconveniences surface and make an effort to react with *emunah*.

The Gemara states, "One who rejoices in the afflictions that befall him brings salvation to the world" (*Ta'anis 8a*). This includes the minor setbacks that the Gemara describes as afflictions. To reap the rewards of *emunah*, we don't have to be heroes of faith who risk their lives to bake matzah or weather years of childlessness. Just by facing each small setback with serenity and faith, we have the opportunity to bring salvation to the world.

Conclusion

* Let's not ask why! Let's rather ask: What does Hashem want from me?
* Use the gift of giving to revive our spirits and arouse heavenly compassion.
* Remember that every measure of difficulty is a very precious commodity and it multiplies our reward one hundredfold.
* Accept small inconveniences and annoyances with love so that they will serve in exchange of obvious *yissurim*.

Chapter 7
Don't Give Up

There is one Ba'al HaBayis in this world. All you have belongs to Him. If He left you alive, then He hasn't given up on you. So you are not allowed to give up!

(Chazon Ish)

*W*HAT HAPPENS WHEN we bear a burden that seems too heavy for us? Sometimes a person gives up. Even a great, learned person can find himself believing that his worries, sadness, and problems will never dissipate, that Hashem will never again be close at hand. Certainly, those who emerged from World War II all alone in the world, with unspeakable horrors emblazoned in their memories, would seem perfectly justified in saying that their losses were simply too great to bear.

This was the lot of Rabbi Yaakov Galinsky. When the war began to rage across Eastern Europe, he was learning in the Novaradok Yeshivah in Bialystok. He was sent to Siberia with 150 *bachurim* when the Russians occupied eastern Poland. Rabbi Galinsky survived, but his entire family perished. After the harsh years in Siberia were over, he found himself without any living relatives.

He married, and after much wandering, he arrived with his wife and two small children in Eretz Yisrael. Although he began a new life in Bnei Brak, the memories of Siberia and his late family members continued to haunt him. He went to visit the Chazon Ish for *divrei chizuk* to help him recover from his traumatic experiences, and the Chazon Ish told him a story:

The Red Wallet

In a small village not far from the town of Kovna lived a couple who barely managed to feed their hungry children. One day the mother decided that she and her husband would put together a small sum of money, and she would travel alone to the marketplace in Kovna to buy and sell merchandise.

She set out on her way and arrived on a busy market day. She discovered that she had a flair for business. With her knack for choosing interesting, well-priced merchandise and convincing buyers to pay a good price, she had soon filled her red wallet with enough money to feed her family for many weeks to come.

As she set out to go home, disaster struck. The wallet went missing. She screamed out to the crowd, "My purse has been stolen. Help!"

Her fellow Jews tried to help her search for it. Finally, one kind man who was asking around the marketplace about the wallet found a Jew who had seen it lying on the ground. Believing that it was *hefker*, he took it. *Even if it belongs to the woman, I don't have to give it back*, he told himself. *She lost it in a public marketplace filled with non-Jews, and therefore she despaired of finding it. According to the halachah, the money belongs to me.*

The frantic woman called the man immediately to *beis din*. They went together to the rabbi of Kovna, Rabbi Yitzchak Elchanan Spektor. The rabbi listened patiently to both sides of the story, and then he asked the woman, "Tell me, does your husband know that the purse is lost?"

She laughed. "Of course not. He gave me the money and sent me here to Kovna. He is waiting for me to return home. I have no way to contact him."

Reb Yitzchak Elchanan turned to address the man. "The money belongs to her husband. He doesn't know it's lost, and therefore he didn't despair of finding it. According to the halachah, you must give it back."

The Chazon Ish explained to Reb Yankel, "There is one

Ba'al HaBayis in this world. All you have belongs to Him. If
He left you alive, then He didn't give up on you. So you are
not allowed to give up."

Leave the Calculations to Hashem

HEN A PERSON gives up on Hashem's salvation,
the next thing he is apt to do is try to figure out
how to save himself. He thinks he has a better
idea, something more practical and realistic than
what Hashem requires of him. He knows he should give one-
tenth of his earnings to *tzedakah*, but his common sense tells
him that this will leave him without enough money to pay his
bills. He knows he should use a superior level of *hechsher*, but
his common sense tells him that with so many children to feed,
he needs to buy the cheaper option, even if the *hechsher* is ques-
tionable. He knows he should learn every day, but his common
sense tells him that he won't keep his job if he doesn't put in
those extra hours at work.

The Midrash (cited in *Rashi*, *Bereishis* 4:25) relates an interesting story that illustrates the power of *emunah* to move us past the
predictable results of our own calculations and ensure that we play
our role in Hashem's plan:

Lemech had two wives, Adah and Tzilah. They were
afraid to have more children because they knew of the
curse Hashem had given Kayin: he would have seven generations of offspring and then they would perish. Lemech's
children were the seventh generation. His wives wanted to
save themselves terrible anguish of seeing this curse coming to fruition with their children. They also knew that a
flood would soon drown all the inhabitants of the world. Why
bear children who were doomed? They decided to part from
Lemech.

Lemech could not change their minds. Finally, they
agreed to accompany him to pose their dilemma to Adam
HaRishon, the *gadol hador*. The wise sage Adam listened to
their argument.

"True," he said, "Hashem has cursed Kayin and, true,

there will be a flood. But you can't interfere with Hashem's *cheshbonos*. You do what's right, and Hashem will do His part."

They accepted his words, but they challenged him: "If this is so, then why are you still living alone after 130 years, still sitting in repentance?"

Adam took their words to heart. He immediately reunited with his wife, and they had a child who they named Sheis.

Tzilah then had a daughter named Na'amah. Although all the sons of Lemech did indeed perish, Na'amah lived to a ripe old age.

From Sheis descended Noach, whom Hashem chose to start the world again after the flood. Noach survived with his three children, his daughters-in-law, and his wife: Na'amah.

With a curse bearing down on their children and a world-destroying flood on the horizon, who could blame Lemech's wives for their assessment? Yet their despair didn't take into account what Hashem knew lay ahead: that from their *emunah*, their desire to follow Hashem's will, the entire world would be rebuilt.

In the midst of our deepest troubles, we may feel that Hashem is nowhere to be found. We search for His comfort and guidance, yet still feel lost and alone. At such times, the most self-defeating thing we can do is quit the search. Hashem is waiting for us to find Him, and when we do, the reunion is sure to be filled with the fiery emotion of long-lost loved ones.

Seek and Find

Ten-year-old Pinye walked through the Siberian forest with his father in the heavy snow. They had to keep moving or their legs would certainly freeze.

Rabbi Schreiber was deep in thought. He didn't know how long his frail body would survive. He felt that his end was near. His wife had given birth a short while ago, and she was ill and weak. Who would look after their young child and his newborn baby brother in Siberia?

He tried to find the right words to prepare his son. He needed words that would give him strength to survive and live as a Jew — words to last him a lifetime. He longed to ensure that his brilliant son would continue using his mind to learn Torah, as the two of them had been doing during their arduous journey through the freezing forests.

"Pinye," he said, "do you remember what happened that time you played hide-and-seek with your friends back at home in Poland?"

Pinye recalled immediately how disappointed and hurt he had felt that evening. He had found a fantastic hiding place that he was sure would take quite some time for his friends to find. He waited and waited until it was dark, but his friends didn't come. Finally, he stepped out of his hiding place and realized that his friends had gone home. They hadn't even bothered to search for him. He arrived home and fell into his father's arms, bursting into tears.

The memory was vivid in his mind.

His father's words interrupted his thoughts. "Do you know, Pinye, sometimes Hashem wants to see how loyal we are to Him, so He hides and waits to see if we will come looking for Him. He watches us carefully and longs for us to carry on our search, not to give up and leave Him. He continues to hide and to wait, so that we can prove our loyalty."

"If we look for Him, confident that He is there watching us, we will always find Him in the end. The time will come when we will be able to fall into His warm embrace and tell Him how our fiery love for Him didn't allow us to give up. Listen to what *Shir HaShirim* tells us: '*Im timtze'u es dodi mah taggidu lo shecholas ahavah ani* — When you find my Beloved, what will you tell Him? That I bore all the travails for love of Him' (*Shir HaShirim* 5:8).

"It might take a long time to find Him. We may call to Him, and it will seem as if He is not answering us: '*Bikashtihu v'lo metzasihu kerasiv v'lo anani* — I searched for Him and I could not find Him; I beseeched Him and He would not answer me' (ibid. 5:6). But if we carry on searching, He will send us signs to let us know that He is still with us, and in the end we will find Him.

"My son," Rabbi Schreiber whispered, hugging his son close to him and looking him straight in the eyes, "don't ever give up, even if He has been hiding for so long. You know what it felt like to be abandoned and betrayed. He will always be there waiting for you, watching you and longing for you to continue your search and prove your loyalty. You will never be alone. One day you will fall into His embrace and express your mutual love."

A few days later, Rabbi Schreiber passed away. The ten-year-old orphan watched as fellow Jews assured he had a Jewish burial. Not long after, his mother left this world, and Pinye buried her with his own bare hands. He was left an orphan, with an infant baby brother to take care of in the wilds of Siberia.

But his father's words gave him the strength to persevere until, finally, he could leave Siberia. The words accompanied him in Teheran and then in an antireligious kibbutz where he and his brother were placed upon reaching Eretz Yisrael. He was forced to eat *tereifah*, his yarmulke was snatched away, his *peyos* were cut off. The other boys gave in slowly, but not Pinye and his brother, whom he shielded.

One day the children went on a trip to the Kosel with their guardians. Pinye slipped away from the group and motioned to a *chareidi* Jew to help him. The Jew looked at the bareheaded boy without *peyos* and preferred not to interfere. Pinye begged him, "Save me!" He began to repeat the Gemara *shiurim* he had reviewed with his father in the forest.

The Jew was shocked. He promised the boy that he would devise a plan to rescue him. And he was true to his word.

The reunion of Pinye and his Father was truly intense. Pinye grew up in Batei Ponevezh to become an outstanding *talmid chacham*. He raised a generation of prestigious *talmidei chachamim* who are *marbitz Torah v'chesed* today in Yerushalayim and Bnei Brak.

"*Mayim rabim lo yuchlu l'chabos es ha'ahavah* — Many waters cannot quench the love" (*Shir HaShirim* 8:7). When our love of Hashem burns like a tremendous flame, it can never be extinguished. Even if it seems as if Hashem has disappeared, we will remain loyal until we find Him. Even if we have no one in the world to guide us, no one to turn to for help, even if we are alone in Siberia, or in the clutches of heartless, ruthless people, Hashem observes us from His hiding place and guides us toward Him, where He waits to embrace us tightly.

Gam Zu L'Tovah — All Is for the Best

*T*HE WELL-KNOWN INCIDENT involving Rabbi Akiva (*Berachos* 60b) presents us with a template for dealing with misfortune upon misfortune. In this story, Rabbi Akiva traveled through the forest with a donkey, a candle, and a rooster, each of which were to provide him with a necessary service on his journey. When he arrived at a town at nightfall and found no one willing to offer him lodging, he was forced to spend the night in the forest. That was the first "disaster" to which he responded with *emunah*: "Everything Hashem does is for the good."

As his troubles mounted, he maintained the same response. The candle by which he planned to learn blew out. A cat ate his rooster, and a lion devoured his donkey. As people sometimes say, "Everything that could go wrong did go wrong." But Rabbi Akiva didn't see it that way. In his eyes, it was all from Hashem, and therefore it was all good, even if the troubles just kept mounting despite his *emunah*.

Of course, he soon found out that his troubles were blessings. He heard the screams of the townspeople as soldiers invaded the village and went on a rampage, looting and killing. His hidden spot in the woods would have easily been discovered had he not been stricken with "trouble after trouble." Had he complained to Hashem about his terrible luck rather than accepting each mishap with staunch faith, he might have forfeited the salvation that was predestined for him.

When a person is struck with one disaster after the other, he sometimes feels that this gives him permission to give up on Hashem. "I gave Him a chance, but instead of coming through for me, He just keeps giving me more challenges. I'm done!"

But if we cling to the belief that Hashem is doing what is the very best for us, we will merit the salvation that is already on the way. These are only the final tests before the massive salvation.

The least productive reaction is to start making *cheshbonos*:

"There's no hope."

"I'm being punished."

"Why is this happening to me?"

In the midst of our troubles, it's not the time to ask questions or make *cheshbonos*. Just hold on and say, "*Gam zu l'tovah*. It's good. Hashem will help me. He's my Father."

When we have *emunah* without *cheshbonos*, Hashem won't make *cheshbonos* in deciding whether or not to help us. Our staunch *bitachon* will *force* Him to help us. And just as Rabbi Akiva's extinguished candle, dead rooster, and devoured donkey became part of his salvation, so too will the troubles we've already endured show themselves to be part of our salvation.

In the story below (from *Be'er HaParashah*), we see this concept in action as an *erev Shabbos* "traffic jam" turns into the vehicle of a *yeshuah*:

Shabbos Is Coming!

Reb Yaakov Yosef HaKohen of Polnoye, also known as the Toldos Yaakov Yosef, was traveling with Reb Nachman of Horodenka to Mezibozh to spend an uplifting Shabbos with the holy Baal Shem Tov. Although they had left early Friday morning after *davening vasikin*, by noon it seemed that there was only a slim chance that they would make it to Mezibozh before Shabbos.

Anxiously, they urged the wagon driver to travel faster. He sped up, and the wagon began to overtake the other carriages on the road until finally they reached the front of the line. But a shock awaited them. Riding in the front carriage was the governor of the entire district, and it was against the law to overtake the governor. They were forced to slow down and inched along behind him.

The Toldos Yaakov Yosef was agitated. Reb Nachman, however, reassured him. "I have worked on myself my whole life not only to accept that everything is for the good, but to believe that from the very misfortune, salvation will surely spring forth."

The Toldos Yaakov Yosef replied, "If only that were so. Let's see if your *emunah* will prove itself true today."

As they neared another village, the travelers slowed down even more. It was market day, and the resulting traffic forced the travelers to inch forward at a snail's pace. But then the villagers realized that the governor's carriage was passing through. They pulled to the side respectfully in order to make way. The wagon driver of the Toldos Yaakov Yosef and Reb Nachman didn't let the opportunity slip by. Keeping as close as possible to the governor's carriage, he was able to freely bypass all the village traffic.

Eventually, both wagons reached a crossroads where they parted ways. Finally traveling at full speed, the Toldos Yaakov Yosef and Reb Nachman reached Mezibozh one half-hour before Shabbos. Reb Nachman's outlook of *emunah* had proven correct.

Day Follows Night

*R*EB TZADOK EXPLAINS another marvelous principle in his *sefer Ohr Zarua LaTzaddik*:

Hashem established a law of nature in the functioning of the world. When one goes through *yissurim* but longs for salvation and trusts that Hashem will surely help him, he will merit a salvation that is the opposite extreme of his difficulty.

It's a law in chemistry — Newton's third law: "For every action there is an equal and opposite reaction." Everything in this world has an exact opposite.

Darkness is always followed by daylight. In the same way, the dark, difficult times we experience are only a preparation for the bright daylight — the *chasadim* Hashem is waiting to give us — which will come to us in the same measure as the darkness. We reach that daylight by longing for it.

This is the meaning of the words "*Samcheinu kiyemos inisanu* — Gladden us with the [same measure of] joy as the days You afflicted us" (*Tehillim* 90:15). Reb Tzadok promises that every single instance of *yissurim* represents a special gift that lies in store for us. So however difficult our situation, we can be assured that the same measure of *chasdei Hashem* is on its way.

Life is like the Ferris wheel at the amusement park. Sometimes we're up and sometimes we're down. But one thing is guaranteed: if we're at rock bottom, we are starting our ascent and will soon reach the top, just as surely as morning follows evening. But if we give up hope, we're stopping the wheel and preventing it from turning.

First the Decay, Then the Blossom

*W*HEN OUR LIFE seems to be falling apart all around us, think about the growth of a seed. A person plants a seed, and it begins to fall apart and decay in the soil. Nevertheless he continues watering the decomposing seed. Suddenly, one day, the seed begins to sprout. Out come the leaves and the sturdy stalk that starts to flower and produce fruits.

What would happen if the gardener would look at the rotting seed and decide to stop watering it, quite sure that nothing will ever grow from it? What would he lose?

Hashem is "*matzmiach yeshuos*" — He makes our salvation grow specifically from a rotting seed, specifically from the situation that is so bleak and hopeless, as long as we nurture the rotting seed with water called "*emunah.*"

If you look at your hopeless situation and say, from the depths of your heart, "Ribono shel Olam, I believe that from this desperate situation, You are going to bring the *yeshuah,*" you are watering your decaying seed and will soon witness its sprouting. You will be amazed time and time again to watch your *yeshuah* sprout forth out of what appears to be a hopeless cause.

But if you give up, and you stop watering the decaying seed, you are throwing away your salvation!

Appeasing the Beloved Child

*N*OT ONLY ARE *yissurim* often the very vehicle of our salvation, but they also create an *eis ratzon* — a time of favor for us to make requests of Hashem. We can learn this concept from an explanation of Rashi on a *pasuk* in *Mishlei*. The *pasuk* says, "For Hashem admonishes the one He loves, and like a [loving] father He mollifies the child" (*Mishlei* 3:12).

Rashi writes:

> What is the meaning of "He mollifies the child like a father"? He loves his son and wants to be kind to him, and He will appease him after He strikes him. Therefore, if we have been punished harshly, Hashem will very soon show us extra-special kindness and mercy.

The Vilna Gaon takes this explanation further:

> When He removes His rod, He wishes to fulfill his [the child's] every wish and He comforts and appeases him. Therefore, don't despise *yissurim*, since if He afflicts you with *yissurim*, you are certainly very dear to Him, like a favorite son, and when the *yissurim* are over, He will appease you and fulfill your wish.

These are all the vast blessings and benefits that come to a person who accepts that *yissurim* are from Hashem and are for his benefit. As we struggle with our challenges and reach out to Hashem for help and comfort, we create a very special *eis ratzon* to ask for a very special wish that we yearn for — and He will give it to us.

The best demonstration of this principle can be seen in the generation after the Holocaust. The *gedolim* predicted that there would be an extraordinary outpouring of blessings coming down to the world after the terrible persecution that *Klal Yisrael* had suffered.

Rabbi Shmuel HaLevi Wosner once spoke at a *siyum* of a prestigious *kollel* and expressed wonder at the flourishing of yeshivos and *kollels* in our generation. He recalled that when he married and lived in the town of Pressburg, there were perhaps two *yungeleit* out of the thriving Jewish *kehillah* who sat and learned the whole day. There was no such thing as an *avreich* receiving a monthly stipend to learn from morning to night. It didn't exist in Vienna or Budapest either. Neither was there the affluence that now enables wealthy Jews to support the yeshivos and *kollels*.

The sudden burgeoning of full-time learning is an outpouring of Hashem's love for us, to soothe us after the great afflictions of the Holocaust. So, too, individuals who experience *yissurim* should be comforted knowing that Hashem is eager to mollify them and fulfill their wishes at the very first moment the afflictions are no longer beneficial for them.

Whether we accept them or not, whether we understand them or not, *yissurim* will enter every person's life. If we give in to despair, we abandon the exquisite gifts these challenges can bring. Instead, we can view *yissurim* as the seeds of our own personal salvation. Then, indeed, Hashem will take our pain, worries, and sadness and coax from them a beautiful, sturdy, fruitful tree: the fulfillment of our fondest hopes.

Chapter 8
Ban Blame and Fear

Don't think of the suffering that you already endured and don't think of the worst that can happen. Take one step at a time. Concentrate on surviving the moment.
(Rabbi Mendel Futerfas)

*M*OST BELIEVING JEWS are capable of occasionally summoning encouraging thoughts of *emunah* when they feel themselves sliding into despair. However, human nature provides many counterforces to our best spiritual efforts, and these forces can quickly erode our belief that Hashem is with us.

Fortunately, forewarned is forearmed; we can prepare ahead of time to conquer our negativity by knowing what to expect and knowing how to protect ourselves from the inner voices and outer forces that pull us down.

Blame and Self-Persecution

*B*LAMING OTHERS FOR our troubles and harboring guilty feelings totally drain and exhaust a person. Guilt and blaming are the antithesis of *emunah*. No one is responsible, no one is to be blamed — other than the One Above!

What if we know we made mistakes? We can take a lesson from

Waze, the system that many people use to guide their way on the road. It works like this:

- First it shows us where we are presently located.
- Next, we enter the address of our destination, and it immediately calculates a route to get us there.
- If we make a wrong turn or veer off the recommended course, the navigator plans a new route instantly, showing us how to get to our destination from where we are now.

Significantly, there is one thing Waze never does. It never blames us. It never says, "What on earth did you just do? Now it's going to take an extra fifteen minutes to get there. How could you be so inattentive?"

We sometimes make wrong turns in life. But Hashem has already planned an alternate route. He has given us all the tools we need to find our way, and He was quite prepared for our mistake. So there's no reason to eat ourselves up with guilt or to blame anyone else.

We can start now to get to our destination. We're on the right track.

The following story on this subject is a poignant childhood memory heard from Rabbi Yitzchak Meir Levine:

Done by Man, Decreed by G-d

Rabbi Yitzchak Meir Levine, a son-in-law of the Imrei Emes, and his brother Rabbi Pinye Levine sat shivah in Warsaw with their family members after their younger brother passed away suddenly. The family was devastated and could not be comforted. Although nobody expressed it, the mourners' consciences gnawed at them. They felt that the tragedy could have been prevented. No words of *chizuk* could change their mood or lift their spirits. Some of the guests' intrusive questions regarding the young boy's passing rubbed salt into their fresh wound.

One day during the shivah, a hush suddenly fell over the room: the Beis Avraham of Slonim was ushered inside. He uttered just a few powerful words — "*B'yadayim iz oich min* haShamayim." Something a person brings about with his own two hands is also decreed from Above.

He related that Reb Yechiel, the rabbi of Moush, a devoted follower of Reb Mordche of Lechowitz, had once witnessed a tragic accident. When the person who had caused the accident fell into a deep depression, Reb Yechiel encouraged him with those words.

This was enough to infuse a new spirit into the mourners, helping them accept their loss from Hashem Yisbarach.

Many years later, Rabbi Yitzchak Meir Levine approached the Nesivos Shalom in Eretz Yisrael and revealed to him that they had been stunned when the Beis Avraham had uttered the very words needed to revive their souls although no one had even mentioned to him how they felt. He admitted that until this very day this principle still gave him strength, and he felt tremendous gratitude to the Beis Avraham.

Here is another story, related by Rabbi Yaakov Galinsky and recorded in *Be'er HaParashah*, that conveys a similar, equally inspiring idea:

Where Was the Nebulizer?

Rabbi Michel Feinstein had a daughter who suffered from asthma as a young girl. There was always a supply of oxygen inhalers around the house to help her breathe in case of an attack.

One day she had a serious attack, and they frantically searched in the cupboard, on the shelf, in the bedroom — all over — but they couldn't find any of the inhalers. They quickly called an ambulance, but by the time help arrived she had breathed her last breath.

As they began to get ready for the *levayah*, someone found three nebulizers under her bed. Reb Michel and his wife were devastated. They could not be comforted. At the shivah, Rabbi Yaakov Galinsky reminded Reb Michel of a very important principle they had both learned in Lomza Yeshivah: A person is obliged to do *hishtadlus* for the future. He must make inquiries before he makes a *shidduch*, before he makes an investment, or before he undergoes any medical procedure. But after something has transpired, one should never feel remorse for the past. He should never question, "Why didn't I do this or that?" Expressing anxiety over what would have happened if only I had or had not done such and such is *kefirah*.

The Ribono shel Olam is the One Who gives us the sense to make decisions and Who leads us in the direction we are supposed to take. We are obligated to take precautions and make the greatest effort we can. But once something has happened, *hishtadlus* does not exist anymore. We must accept Hashem's will with faith.

Once Reb Michel was reminded of this, he was able to acknowledge that it was pointless to regret not searching under the bed. He recognized that the tragedy, as preventable as it seemed, was Hashem's will.

Rabbi Elimelech Biderman tells another story along these lines:

J Would Have, J Should Have...

Reb Leibke Gloiberman, a close disciple of Reb Yisrael of Stolin, suffered from an inflammation in his leg. He was informed by his specialist that his leg had to be amputated in order to save his life.

At the end of the operation, his son overheard one of the doctors remark that the surgery could have been prevented by using a different treatment. He was shocked. Not wanting to distress his father, he kept the information to himself.

A short time later the information accidentally leaked out and reached Reb Leibke's ears. "The operation was a mistake," someone told him. "Your leg shouldn't have been amputated!"

Reb Leibke didn't lose his composure for even one moment. He shouted without hesitation, pointing to his ears, "Woe to my ears that hear such words! I heard with these very ears from my Rebbe, '*Wolt ich solt ich iz apikorsus!*' 'I would have, I should have' is heresy.

"If my leg was amputated, then it had to be amputated;

the surgeon is mistaken. The proof is that it was amputated! Because that is how it had to be *min haShamayim*."

As Reb Leibke so deeply understood, regrets are simply a lack of *emunah*. In fact, if a person wants to gauge his level of *emunah*, he can do so by counting the number of times he finds himself saying, "If only— ? Why did I— ? Why didn't he— ?"

Fear: The Flip Side of Regret

FEARING THE FUTURE is just as destructive as regretting the past. They are two sides of the same coin, and that coin is the currency of Olam HaZeh only. People who don't feel Hashem's love and trust in His goodness become tangled in knots when trying to make decisions. They foresee every possible negative outcome and worry about every possible risk, no matter how likely or unlikely it may be. They are the people who can't rest easy when their children are away from home: Why haven't I heard from him today? Why doesn't she answer her cell phone? What if he's gotten into an accident? They're afraid to take a risk in business: What if I lose money? What if someone grabs my idea and does it better than me?

All of these worries paralyze a person and fill him with anxiety. Yet underlying these fears is the sense that we're out there on our own, hanging above an abyss on a narrow rope that can snap at any second. What a different feeling it would be to instead sense that we are being held securely in Hashem's embrace, sustained by His unlimited bounty and carried moment by moment on the road we are meant to travel.

Rabbi Mendel Futerfas, a Lubavitcher chassid, influenced many with his spiritual encouragement and sound advice. In his youth, Reb Mendel was imprisoned in Siberia, where he endured indescribable afflictions in subzero weather conditions. Many years later, while living in Eretz Yisrael, people would ask him how he had the strength to persevere. He would relate the following story with a remarkable message:

The Tightrope Walker

I grew up in a small town in Russia. Once, there was great excitement in town; a tightrope walker was to stage a grand performance. On the designated day, throngs of townspeople turned out to watch the event.

The town's topography was perfectly suited for a tightrope walker's exploits. It had a range of mountains separated by heart-stopping chasms. The performer nimbly scaled a mountainside, carrying with him a coil of heavy rope. He expertly tied one end to a sturdy rock and then threw the other end across a yawning ravine, into the waiting arms of his assistant, who firmly affixed it to a sharp mountain peak. He was now ready to begin.

All eyes were on the stuntman as he placed his first foot on the swaying rope. There was an audible gasp as he took a second step, then a third and a fourth, his brows furrowed and lips pressed together in concentration. The spectators held their breath as he slowly and steadily made his way across, knowing that one misstep would send him plunging to his death. For an agonizing few minutes he forged ahead, step after careful step, until, finally, he took that final step to safe, solid ground.

A resounding cheer went up from the crowd as the tightrope walker raised his arms in victory. The cheering quickly died down, though, as it became clear their hero had something to say. "Do you want me to walk back?" he shouted, his voice booming across the mountains.

"No!" the audience yelled back as one. Who could live through that torturous experience again?

In response, the man smiled broadly and then turned around and boldly placed his foot on the rope. He pressed his lips together determinedly as he made the dangerous journey all the way back to his starting point.

Once again, the crowd cheered in admiration until he quieted them down with another question. "Do you believe I can do this with a wheelbarrow?" he asked.

As if on cue, an assistant wheeled a wheelbarrow right in front of him.

"Yes!" shouted the audience enthusiastically. Their faith in him had increased, it seemed, seeing that he had made this journey and emerged in one piece — twice.

"Good!" The man nodded approvingly. "Now would anyone like to volunteer to be *inside* that wheelbarrow?"

This time, a stunned silence met his words. *Inside* that wheelbarrow? Much as they believed in him, this was something else.

Yet, to their amazement, one lone voice rang out in the crowd. "I'll do it!" said a little girl, her eyes shining with excitement.

There was an awed silence as the little girl made her way through the crowd, ignoring concerned spectators who whispered to her as she walked past them, "Don't do it, little girl! Don't!"

Up the mountain she climbed and into the waiting wheelbarrow she clambered, looking unperturbed as it reached the mountain's peak and started making its way across the frightening chasm below. The crowd watched in agonizing suspense as the tightrope walker wheeled the brave little girl safely to the other side, whereupon it broke out in thunderous applause.

After the pair descended the mountain, one person pushed his way to the crowd until he reached the performer and the little girl. "How could you do that?" he asked the little girl. "Weren't you afraid?"

The girl slipped her small hand into the broad hand of the man standing at her side. "I wasn't afraid," she replied simply, "because he is my father."

(Rabbi Elimelech Biderman's Haggadah shel Pesach)

"That is how I survived those years in Siberia," Reb Mendel explained. "I knew my Father was standing right behind me, guiding me every moment. With this thought in mind, I felt secure. Although I was walking a tightrope, I knew that as long as I was in His hands I would never fall.

"I do remember, however, that I wasn't completely satisfied with the answer. I was driven to ask the tightrope walker a question, too. I pushed myself forward and asked him, 'How did *you* do it? How could you make that terrifying journey with your daughter's very life in your hands?'

"He replied, 'I'll tell you my secret. I never look back, and I never look forward at how far I still have to go — and I never, *ever*, look down. I take one step at a time and concentrate fully on that step, which I know, with my skill and practice, I *can* accomplish.'

"I told myself," Reb Mendel concluded, "'Don't think of the suffering that you already endured and don't think of the worst that can happen. Take one step at a time. Concentrate on surviving the moment.'"

If we have a major problem, we must ask ourselves, *Do I have the strength to endure one more day?* Yes? Then we can use our energy to survive just one more day. Tomorrow we will have the courage to get through still another day. If we concentrate now on this very moment and don't waste energy on being nervous about the future, we will be calm in the knowledge that Hashem will certainly take care of everything.

Real Life Emunah
The Happiest Woman on the Planet

We have learned how to master emunah.

We have learned that emunah can solve our problems even miraculously.

We also know that true faith always eliminates stress, worry, and anxiety.

The following is an interview with a woman who suffers physically, but her emunah is so steadfast that this does not dampen her happiness.

Whoever stands close to her can feel an inspirational sensation of kedushah, kirvas Elokim, and true contentment that permeates the air around her.

"Hashem tzaddik yivchan — Hashem tests the righteous" (Tehillim 11:5) — R' Yochanan said: The flax dealer will not bang damaged flax since it will burst, but when his produce is perfect, he will bang it hard. Why? Since this will make it better. Similarly, Hashem does not test the wicked. Why? Because they will not be able to withstand it. Who does He test? The righteous, as it says, "Hashem tests the righteous."

HaKadosh Baruch Hu loves His righteous children. Sometimes He lifts up a neshamah very high, and the tzaddik then illuminates the whole world. Mrs. Tammy Karmel was diagnosed with ALS at the age of forty-six, shortly after her youngest child was born. This is her story:

It began very subtly. Weakness in my limbs, fatigue, and an inexplicable limp in my right foot. I was a busy mother of seven children, two of whom are married with children of their own. I was giving classes on parenting, *shalom bayis*, and *avodas hamiddos* and was doing private counseling. My days were full, and I could barely find the time to schedule a doctor's appointment to consult about those little annoyances. But the annoyances grew bigger, and I had to give them their due attention.

An hour in the doctor's office led to several days in the hospital's neurological ward and the ultimate diagnosis. This was an illness that was not going to get better with time, only worse. And as of yet, there was no known cure.

My initial reaction was a talk with Hashem: "Where do You want me to go with this, Hashem? What would You like me to do now?" The answer was so clear to me: "Accept it, live with it, and don't worry. I will be at your side."

And I felt at peace.

It was Thursday night. Still at the hospital, I called up my children and told them to buy their favorite Shabbos treats.

"We're making a *seudas hoda'ah*," I said. "Hashem has done so much good for us. He will continue to help us all the way."

And that Shabbos we celebrated. My personal celebration was the fact that Hashem led me to this place at a time when I felt ready. The words of Avraham Avinu when he was given his greatest *nisayon* reverberated through my being: "*Hineni*. I am ready, Hashem, to do Your bidding."

Yes, for a fleeting moment in the doctor's office, I had felt sorry for my children, sad for them that their mother was to be confined to a wheelchair for the rest of her life, but the thought was fleeting. Using the tools I had accumulated over the years, I told myself, *This is the best for my children. It's best for the journeys their souls must make in this world. It's best for me and best for my husband.* Hashem had always answered my prayers for spiritual guidance in the past. And now, in turn, my response was, "*Hineni*. I am ready."

This is not to say I gave up hope. I *davened*, and continue to *daven* daily, that Hashem should provide a cure for this illness. I know that if He wants it, I can be on my feet tomorrow. Nothing is beyond His ability.

And I set about doing *hishtadlus*.

I once heard a *vort* that had a profound impact on me.

The Chafetz Chaim explains that Hashem allows bad things to happen to us only because we open our mouths and bad-mouth each other, giving license for the prosecuting angel in Heaven to open his mouth and bad — mouth us, too. If we would love every Jew, no matter who or what, and never see them in a bad light, we wouldn't speak about them in a bad light, and the prosecuting angel would be silenced forever. How much pain and suffering that would prevent!

With this in mind, I set out on a campaign as a *zechus* for my *refuah*. With the help of several wonderful friends, I spoke from London, where I was at the time, broadcasting my message via live teleconference to a large gathering of women in Yerushalayim, my place of residence. I set in motion a *shemiras halashon* campaign in which every participant — hundreds to date — commit to two *lashon hara*–free hours each day. Participants call a hotline number where a woman teaches one or more halachos of *shemiras halashon* daily. Each participant is given a fifteen-minute slot in which to call so that for twelve hours throughout each day, people are listening to the halachos.

I also had a booklet written which is titled *CPR* — Cultivating Personal Relationships — in which the root cause of *shemiras halashon* is explored. In a three-step program, readers learn how to get out of this rut. First, we must know that we're addicted to this *aveirah*. Then we must realize how destructive it is. And, finally, we must learn to rid ourselves of the triggers before they give rise to action.

I hope to spread awareness of this program worldwide. I am campaigning for groups to get together, watch the accompanying video, and work through the CPR booklet program. All this is part of my spiritual *hishtadlus*.

On a physical level, I do everything I possibly can to seek a cure for my condition. When I heard about a neurological naturopath who had seen my medical notes and believed I had a highly treatable form of Lyme disease, I flew to London from Eretz Yisrael and spared no expense to consult with him and be treated with intravenous antibiotics for a month. When that course of treatment failed, I flew to the United States to consult with the top specialists in the field. All along, I knew that whatever would come of my *hishtadlus*, I would embrace Hashem's will, whatever that would be. I knew that whatever would happen, He was there for me, holding my hand.

Indeed, I've seen Hashem's endless kindness time and time again. My daughter was of *shidduch* age, and I was wondering who would want to marry someone whose mother has such a dire prognosis. Well, at a *shiur* I gave on *emunah*, I mentioned my daughter a few times and how she helps me on this journey. One woman sitting in the audience thought to herself, *I wonder who is going to be the lucky boy to marry this special girl?* Her son turned out to be the lucky boy, and my daughter, a very happy *kallah*!

I feel blessed. Until my diagnosis, I had lived in a small, not very comfortable apartment, albeit in Yerushalayim. Now Hashem has orchestrated that I live in a beautiful, spacious apartment.

Hashem is looking out for me. My friends and my family have been so very supportive all the way through. My children, too, are completely fine with the situation. They don't view me as a *nebach*.

My six-year-old daughter had a friend over one day. I imagined that she would circumspectly avoid the room where I was reclining. Instead, she brought her friend into the room and proudly introduced me to her. "This is my mommy," she said. "Her feet and this hand, here, are naughty. They don't behave and don't work like they should. This other hand, here, is a little bit naughty but also good, because it can still move a little bit — see?" Her friend was quite impressed by her explanation. I even more so.

I believe that part of why my children are so accepting of my situation is that from the very beginning I was matter-of-fact about it. There are no secrets in my home, no hushed whisperings, no false promises that everything will be hunky-dory by tomorrow. We don't cling to false hopes, but at the same time there is no crushing fear or anxiety about the future. I tell my children that this is the situation, and that Hashem will help us through it. I accept Hashem's will, and my children have learned to accept it, too.

When I got my wheelchair for the first time, I settled into it quite matter-of-factly. Walking had become so difficult for me, and I was grateful for this means of transportation. My son, in turn, casually wheeled me to my friend's house, down the street, in full view of everyone. Part two of my journey had arrived and we were ready to traverse it.

And then came part three. My hoist. "We're having a ride come to our house!" I announced to my children. "Just wait and see!" When the sizable, convoluted contraption arrived, I demonstrated how it works and they gleefully took turns taking rides. Today my children and grandchildren enjoy the privilege of being strapped on my lap and being transported from room to room. My hoist is no secret, and there is no shame as I wave to them from my view up above. It came as a matter of course, a natural evolution of the circumstances.

I am often asked what gives me the *kochos hanefesh*, the spiritual strength, to face this enormous challenge with equanimity. And the answer is that it didn't happen overnight. It was a long, arduous process, and I am grateful that Hashem gave me this *nisayon* after I had acquired the tools to deal with it. Otherwise I would have been a total wreck!

I have had my fair share of challenges in life — don't we all? By nature, I am not the "*rebbetzin* type." I am a fun-loving free spirit who likes to socialize, appreciates nice things, and knows how to have a good time. In my school years, I was no goody-goody — not by a long stretch. I was the life of every party and drove my teachers berserk. I was not one to take life too seriously.

But life has a way of taking you seriously, making you stop and think. At first, with no tools to combat the obstacles that persistently popped up, I felt very down. I felt cheated of what I believed life owed me. I felt frustrated and resentful. And I knew I had to find a way to get out of this rut.

I was always one to engage in direct dialogue with Hashem. Since I was a child, I was in the habit of telling Hashem exactly how I feel. And now, when things became tough, day after day, I would put money into a *tzedakah pushka* and offer up a silent prayer: "Hashem, I want to give You *nachas*. Let me be a good daughter to You, a good wife to my husband, and a good mother to my children." (I often quip that were I to have brain surgery, they'd find this plea etched in my brain!) I combed through the local Jewish library and read many *sefarim* and books on Jewish thought and *mussar*. Among others, Rabbi Avigdor Miller's and Rabbi Ezriel Tauber's books helped me immensely.

Hashem answered my pleas. He led me on the path I had so begged for. I took a B.A. in parenting and started giving parenting classes. I also started practicing marriage counseling. My teachings became ingrained in my belief system, and I found myself a changed person. It almost caught me by surprise when one day I woke up and discovered that Hashem had answered my prayers on each of the counts I had so begged for: to be a good daughter to Him, a good wife to my husband, and a good mother to my children.

And then came — this.

I was ready. I felt privileged that Hashem had chosen me to go on this unique, incredible journey together. Hand in hand, He was walking me through this. It all felt so miraculous to me. Here I was, little me, seeing Chazal's words come true before my very eyes: "[Hashem says:] Open for Me an opening the size of an eye of a needle, and I will open for you gates through which wagons can pass" (*Shir HaShirim Rabbah* 5:2). I had been begging Hashem all these years to help me do His will, and now that I was faced with this incredible challenge, it almost seemed effortless for me to accept His decree. It was nothing short of miraculous!

Of course I have my difficult moments, moments of pain, of being uncomfortable, of feeling helpless as I watch others do what had always come so easy to me. But it's just that: a moment. It doesn't come with the accompanying drama: "I can't bear this pain, I will not be spoonfed, why me?" My moments of hardship are all very technical. It happens, and then it's behind me. I am by nature a dramatic person — ask anyone who's seen me on stage — and I marvel daily at my 180 degree miraculous transformation. Hashem has rewarded me disproportionately for the effort I put into trying to do His will.

One night, I was sitting by my baby's crib when I discovered that I could no longer reach my hand through the slats and stroke her face. I could have been utterly crushed. In what sense was I a mother if I couldn't even stroke my baby's face? But with this tool under my belt, I was unfazed. I knew that my inherent worth as a mother wasn't contingent on my ability to keep house, carry my baby in my arms, or stroke her cheek. My worth was measured by the manner in which I was doing Hashem's will. If Hashem wants me to mother my children with my limited capacities, then this is how I will mother my children. I am not less of a mother or a person because I can't do what I can't do, but I am a better mother and a better person when I embrace Hashem's will with love.

I have never appreciated the value of life like I do now. Every second that I am alive, that I can breathe, speak, say amen to a *berachah*, appreciate Hashem's glorious world, is so precious to me. My illness has robbed me of my physical capabilities but I can still accomplish so much spiritually, which is all that matters.

Rabbi Avrohom Yehoshua Heschel told me in an overseas telephone conversation from the United States: "Hashem has chosen you to atone for *Klal Yisrael*." Those words make me feel special and privileged. I am not being punished; on the contrary, Hashem felt I was worthy to carry this awesome burden on behalf of His beloved nation. I don't think *Why me?* Just the opposite; I feel, *Wow; me!*

Rabbi Ezriel Tauber said to me, "*Tamim tiheyeh im Ha-*

shem Elokecha — You must be simplistic with Hashem, your G-d" (*Devarim* 18:13). We must accept His plan for us with unsophisticated, blind, trusting faith — no questions asked. Just like the *Avos* and *Imahos*, I should say, "*Hineni.* I am ready to serve You."

After that conversation, I was bothered by the fact that I could accept my situation wholeheartedly — but only up to a point. Being on a respirator? That I couldn't deal with. I was vexed to no end. Why could I say *hineni* to everything but a respirator? And then, about two hours later, the thought struck me, and I was calmed. I couldn't say *hineni* to a respirator because I wasn't in need of a respirator! Hashem gives me the strength to cope with each challenge as it comes. He doesn't give me a challenge when I am not yet ready to cope with it.

What a waste of time it is to fret. Today I have the emotional stamina to deal with whatever comes today. Tomorrow Hashem will give me the stamina to deal with whatever comes tomorrow.

When I tell the attendees at my *shiurim*, "I am the happiest woman on this planet!" I see their disbelieving expressions turn into smiles as I continue, "You think I would lie to you? Not at this stage, when I could be facing the heavenly tribunal sooner than I'd like." And it's true. I'm in a happy, content place. In a technical sense, too, I no longer have to make impossible demands of myself. I don't have to struggle to cook and clean with my muscles in a weakened state. My condition has deteriorated to the point where there's no way I can keep house, and everybody has stepped up to the plate to take over. I feel completely at peace.

In my classes, I tell my attendees the four principles that have led me to reach this place of inner peace. First of all, the *ratzon*. You must have a strong will, a burning desire to be close to Hashem. If you really want it, Hashem will come toward you as you walk toward Him. If you feel you're lacking the *ratzon*, then *daven* for it. Hashem may not always grant our requests for physical needs, because they may not be beneficial for us, but in spiritual matters, Hashem always answers our prayers.

Second, the *middah* of *hakaras hatov*, gratitude. Recognizing the good in my life — and thanking for it — instead of grumbling at any perceived injustices, has completely transformed me. While in the past I used to compare and complain, I am now immensely grateful for every *chesed* Hashem does for me, and there are many. Rabbi Avigdor Miller's books *Rejoice O Youth!* and *Sing You Righteous* helped me view life through an entirely different lens.

Hashem also sent people in my life to teach me this remarkable trait. I once visited Rachel Broncher, whose teenage daughter had been involved in a serious car accident and was lying comatose in the hospital. I was expecting to meet a strained, tearful woman but instead I met a person brimming with gratitude. She was grateful to the superior medical team for treating her daughter; she was grateful for the support of the community. In the darkest of the night, Rachel saw only good. Two weeks later, her daughter was out of the hospital, well on the road to a complete recovery. I am sure that Rachel's deep faith and optimism had a lot to do with the miraculous outcome.

Yes, even in the most trying of circumstances, there is much to be grateful for. I am grateful that I have the privilege of inspiring so many women with my *shiurim* — who would ever have believed I would be doing this? When the muscles in my throat contract as they should and allow me to chew and swallow my food, I am grateful. I am grateful I am not in the hospital, not on a respirator. I'm so grateful I'm alive!

Third, being in control of our thoughts.

Can we actually control our thoughts? Yes!

Our train of thought works much the same way as those old-fashioned movies in which a roll of film was wound around a reel. The front end of the strip was attached to a second reel, and when both reels were set in motion, the roll of film unwound from one wheel and was wrapped around the other. As the reels turned, a projector's light shone on the segment of the film currently moving from one reel to the next, highlighting that scene. Our thoughts are like that roll of film, except that we can choose which parts of the movie on which to shine the projector and which will remain shrouded in darkness. Contrary to popular belief, we are in control of our thoughts. Fear for the future? Anxiety? Don't shine the projector's light on it! Don't give it life, don't lend it color! Instead, let it reel on unnoticed, unseen. Yes, it can be done!

Obviously I have my moments of anxiety. My daughter is getting married in a few months. What condition will I be in then? Sitting? Reclining? What will be should my throat muscles that control my breathing and swallowing decide to retire?

But I don't lend those thoughts color. I hurry them along onto the next reel, out of sight and out of mind. I will not let those unwelcome thoughts make themselves comfortable inside my mind.

Finally, recognizing our self-worth. Too often, we measure our actions by other people's standards. We live our lives following a simple, conditional rule: If other people think well of this, it is good. If other people look down at this, it is bad. If other people equate a beautiful house and well-behaved children with success, we feel like failures when our houses are in disarray and our children don't turn out the way we hoped.

But in truth, there is only one yardstick to go by: what Hashem wants from us. Is a beautiful house on Hashem's list of priorities? Does Hashem want us to have well-behaved children, or else? Our self-worth doesn't depend on our physical accomplishments, only on our own (and not our spouse's or our children's) spiritual achievements.

Training ourselves to think this way is hard work, but the reward is extraordinary. It extracts so much frustration from our lives. I could feel sad, angry, and humiliated when other people have to help me do the most elementary tasks, but

I don't. I know that external achievements don't define my true self.

May tomorrow bring only good tidings for all of us.

Please daven for a refuah sheleimah for Yocheved Tamar bas Ita Baila. To listen to two daily halachos on the shemiras halashon hotline, call 076-599-0069, access code 178904. To learn more about the CPR program, or to order Tammy's videos of her very inspiring shiurim, contact Esti Lefkowitz +972-2-537-5957 or the author.

Chapter 9
Emunas Tzaddikim

The tzaddik decrees and Hashem fulfills his decree.

(Kesubos 103b)

$\int$ O FAR, WE have been working on fortifying our faith in Hashem. We have learned about ways to access our faith, to feel Hashem in our lives, and to take comfort in Him during times of trouble. The holy tzaddikim that Hashem has sent to dwell in our midst provide another avenue of relief, because their blessings and guidance are more powerful than we can imagine.

When a person rises to a level of such purity that nothing stands between him and Hashem's will, we can be sure that his advice has been distilled from the purest sources. We can be sure that his *berachos* draw their power straight from *Shamayim*.

The Tiferes Shlomo of Radomsk writes in his *sefer* on the festivals: "*Emunas chachamim* is one of the most fundamental principles of our faith. A Jew who doesn't believe in the tzaddikim should not consider himself a Jew!"

What exactly does *emunas chachamim* entail? It means believing that:

- when a tzaddik decrees, Hashem will fulfill the decree, even if it requires a miracle.
- a tzaddik has the power to annul a Divine decree. (*Moed Katan* 16b)

Believing these principles is an essential part of believing in the Torah. We can understand this by considering the circumstances around the giving of the Torah.

We celebrate the day of *mattan Torah*, the festival of Shavuos, on the sixth of Sivan. But according to R' Yose (*Shabbos* 87a), nothing actually happened on that day. Hashem had informed Moshe that the people would have three days to prepare for the receiving of the Torah, but Moshe felt that they needed one more day. He therefore postponed *mattan Torah* for one more day. Hashem agreed. Thus, according to R' Yose, the Torah was given on the seventh of Sivan.

The concept of *emunas chachamim* was established, according to R' Yose, on the sixth of Sivan, the day Hashem deferred to the will of the tzaddik Moshe Rabbeinu. In this way, *emunas chachamim* became the very basis for our acceptance of the Torah the following day.

When Hashem gave us His Torah, it was as if He gave to the *chachmei Yisrael* His sole authority to govern the world.

This authority does not rest in Moshe Rabbeinu alone. When Hashem created the world, He dispersed the *neshamos* of the tzaddikim throughout the ages, so that each generation until the coming of Mashiach would have its leaders. In every generation, the *gedolim* are as great as Moshe Rabbeinu was in his generation.

There is just one condition for the powers of the tzaddikim to become effective. That is *emunas tzaddikim*. The fulfillment of their blessings depends very much on how strongly we believe. The following story proves this point.

Sefarim or Sirim

A woman approached Rebbetzin Kanievsky, frantic for advice and a blessing. She was close to giving birth, and the doctors had told her that the baby was lying in a breech position; she would need to have a caesarean section. The *rebbetzin* told her, "Check all the *sefarim* in your apartment and make sure they're right side up. If you see anything that is upside down, turn it over. This is a tried-and-tested *segulah* that should help turn the baby to the right position."

The woman thanked the *rebbetzin* and hurried home to implement her suggestion. However, for some reason, she'd misheard the *rebbetzin's* Hebrew instructions, and thought she'd told her to check her "*sirim*" — her pots. She enthusiastically opened her pot cabinets and drawers and made sure to turn all her pots and pans the right way. She even opened her Pesach cabinets to check on her Pesach pots, because the *rebbetzin* had clearly told her to check *all* of her pots.

The *segulah* worked. Within a day, the baby turned, and there was no need for surgery. In her great delight, the woman related the story to several of her friends, who began to laugh as they realized that she had confused *sefarim* with *sirim*. The woman went back to the *rebbetzin*, who confirmed that she'd indeed spoken about *sefarim*.

The *rebbetzin* related the story to her husband, Reb Chaim, who responded by telling a story from the Gemara in *Pesachim* (42a):

One year, prior to Pesach, R' Masna gave a *derashah* in his town. He quoted R' Yehudah, who teaches that when women knead the dough for the matzos, they should use *mayim shelanu*. The women who heard his speech misunderstood his words. They didn't realize he was referring to water that had been pumped the night before and left overnight (*mayim shelanu* is water that rested overnight), and thought he was saying it was best to use water that belonged to him (because *mayim shelanu* can also mean "our water").

The next morning there was a long line of women outside Rav Masna's house, clamoring to receive some of his water.

Rabbi Yisrael Salanter asks: Why did the Gemara relate this story? Doesn't it show the women's ignorance?

On the contrary, explains Reb Yisrael, the Gemara is praising the exceptional *emunas chachamim* of these women. Even though they didn't understand why they suddenly had to use Rav Masna's water, they hurried to comply with his instructions.

Reb Chaim explained to his wife that certainly in the merit of this woman's blind faith in the *rebbetzin*, the *segulah* worked for her, despite the fact that she had misunderstood and done something entirely different. He writes in his *sefer*

Orchos Yosher that even if a *gadol* himself makes a mistake, or the person misunderstands what the *gadol* says, the blessing still takes effect as long as the person has strong and unwavering *emunas chachamim*.

The Power to Receive

*W*E LEARN MORE about the necessity of believing in the tzaddik's blessing from the way Yaakov blessed his children. The Torah tells us that shortly before he passed away, "*Vayischazeik Yisrael vayeishev al hamitah* — Yisrael exerted himself and sat up on the bed" (*Bereishis* 48:2). The *Da'as Zekeinim MiBa'alei Tosafos* explains that Yaakov Avinu knew that his end was near, but he didn't want his children to consider his final words to them as the deathbed gift of a dying man who wasn't completely lucid. So he exerted himself to summon his last remaining strength to sit up on the bed.

Reb Simcha Zissel Ziv of Kelm asks: What difference did it make what they would think? He answers that a blessing, even of a tzaddik like Yaakov Avinu, only takes effect if the recipient believes that the tzaddik has the power to give that blessing. If we don't believe in the blessing, it has absolutely no power!

Ultimately, the recipient is the one who has the power to ensure that the *berachah* is fulfilled. The tzaddik is only the conduit.

That, says Reb Simcha Zissel, is why Yaakov sat up. He wanted to be certain that his children would believe his *berachos* came from a lucid mind so that he could be certain that they would take effect. In other words, when we receive a blessing from a tzaddik, it is our *emunah* that "the tzaddik decrees and Hashem fulfills his decree" that allows the blessing to come to fruition.

A Walking Miracle

The *bachurim* learning in the Klausenberg yeshivah in Union City, New Jersey, loved and revered their Rebbe, Rabbi Yekusiel Yehudah Halberstam. That was why everyone was overjoyed when they learned that the Rebbe planned on taking up residence in the yeshivah building. Living in the Rebbe's proximity was an experience they would relish for the rest of their lives.

Until that point, there hadn't been an elevator in the yeshivah building. Now, in honor of the Rebbe's arrival, an elevator was installed — to be used solely by the Rebbe and the yeshivah staff. It was not to be used by the *bachurim*. That rule, however, didn't mean that the *bachurim* gave up on using the elevator. After all, who wanted to trudge up numerous flights of stairs to the sixth floor when there was a perfectly good elevator just waiting to be used?

One day, an enterprising *bachur* invented a brilliant device that could be used by anyone to open the elevator door. Within a very short time, many of the yeshivah's *bachurim* were equipped with the device: a piece of wire six inches long, which fit easily into their pockets and into a cavity in the door that could be manipulated to open it. This wire enabled them to use the elevator, although they knew it was against the rules.

Berel was a *bachur* learning in the yeshivah. He was conscientious and reliable and enjoyed helping his fellow *bachurim*. The *hanhalah*, seeing what a golden heart he possessed, requested that he take charge of the yeshivah's *bikur cholim* society — a responsibility that entailed visiting any *bachur* who wasn't feeling well, making sure he had the proper medicine, and bringing him food if he was hungry. Berel excelled at his task and went about it in the most caring manner.

The year 5736/1976 was a leap year, and Shushan Purim Katan fell out on Shabbos. This inspired a grand celebration that enveloped the yeshivah from the beginning of Shabbos until its departure. *Shalosh seudos* was spent with the Rebbe amid spirited singing and dancing. By the time the boys had *bentched*, davened Maariv, made Havdalah, and eaten *melavah malkah*, it was close to two o'clock in the morning.

Berel was extremely tired. His entire body ached and he longed for bed. But as he was about to make his way up the stairs to his dorm room, he remembered that one of the *bachurim* was ill and decided to check up on him and make sure that he had everything he needed.

Maybe he's hungry, Berel said to himself. He went down to the kitchen to see what he could find to bring his fellow *talmid*. In the kitchen, Berel came across a *bachur* making fries and asked him if he could spare a plate for their ill friend. The *bachur* agreed, and Berel left the kitchen, plate in hand.

At that moment a thought entered his mind: *Why should you have to climb so many flights of stairs when you are involved in a mitzvah?*

Berel decided to use the elevator-opening device right then and there. From the lit-up number 2 on the panel above the elevator door, Berel could tell that the elevator was presently on the second floor. He made his way to the second floor, plate in hand, device in pocket, accompanied by a friend who planned to join him.

It was very dark on the second floor. There was a reason for this: the second floor was where the Klausenberger Rebbe slept. The staff kept the hallway dark so that the Rebbe would be able to rest peacefully. Berel pulled the device out of his pocket and inserted it into the indentation above the door. The elevator door opened, but the light inside the little cabin didn't turn on. Berel was not surprised by the darkness because the elevator's lightbulb had burned out a short while before and had not yet been replaced. He therefore stepped into the elevator and suddenly, with no warning at all, found himself plunging through the air at breakneck speed.

Berel had not known that the elevator was broken. Though the number on the panel said 2, the elevator had in fact been on the third floor. When he stepped into the shaft, he went into a terrifying free fall.

He landed a few seconds later in a foot-high pile of dust. He began choking, but he couldn't escape the dust because both of his feet were completely shattered and his spine burned with pain.

"Berel," his friend shouted down into the elevator shaft,

"Are you alive? Answer me!"

But Berel couldn't answer his friend. He was completely submerged in dust and pain. His friend raced down the stairs to the first floor and used his own elevator-opening device to get the door open. Then he and a bunch of *bachurim* jumped down the relatively small gap into the bottom of the shaft. They lifted up their friend and stood guard over him until the ambulance arrived.

The ambulance drove Berel to the nearest hospital, where the emergency-room doctors X-rayed his injuries and declared that his feet were shattered. They predicted that he would never walk again.

But this was of minor significance compared to his life-threatening spinal injury. A vertebra had broken, and its sharp end was pressing on his spinal cord. All of this information was heaped upon Berel before his parents had even arrived from their home in Monsey.

When they finally got to their son's bedside, he strained his voice to beg them, "Call the Rebbe, call the Rebbe."

It was 3:45 a.m. but that didn't matter. They made the call.

The Rebbe, upon being woken up and apprised of the situation, rose and went to immerse himself in the *mikveh*. Then he called Berel's parents at the local hospital.

"You must move your son immediately," he told them. "Take him to the Hospital for Joint Diseases, where they are experts on every single joint in the human body. They are better equipped to help bring your son to a *refuah sheleimah*."

Berel's parents thanked the Rebbe for his advice and told their son and the doctors what the Rebbe had said. The doctors were horrified and stated their opinion with vehemence.

"There is no way in the world that this boy can be moved right now! His spine is in such bad shape that if he is moved, he will very likely die! He needs to remain here in the hospital in traction for the next nine to twelve months. After that we may be able to operate."

Berel's parents called the Rebbe again and told him what the doctors had warned.

"The X-ray is wrong," the Rebbe responded. "You must move your son immediately. *Auf mein achrayus* you should take your son to the other hospital. I take full responsibility for his recovery!"

When Berel heard that the Rebbe wanted him to be moved, he insisted that his parents follow the Rebbe's advice.

"I am already over eighteen," he said through teeth that were tightly clenched with pain, "and I insist that I be taken to the hospital the Rebbe recommended! I will sign any document they want, but I insist on obeying the Rebbe's words!"

And so, against the doctors' protestations, Berel was transported by ambulance to the next hospital. As he was wheeled out, the doctors exchanged pitiful glances as if to say, "Who knows if he'll make it there alive?"

"Every time there was a jolt," Berel later recalled, "I felt as if my *neshamah* was about to leave my body! The pain was phenomenal and I could hardly breathe! But it didn't matter in the slightest. The Klausenberger Rebbe had promised to take full responsibility for my recovery and I trusted him implicitly. I knew that the best course of action was to follow his directive."

When they arrived at the hospital, the doctors took another X-ray. Berel was later given a chance to compare the two X-rays.

"They were slightly different," he said. "But it was a difference that determined life or death!"

In the new hospital, the doctors examined him from head to toe. They concurred with the doctors in the former hospital that his shattered feet precluded his ever walking again. But when it came to his spine, they felt that the damage was much less serious than the original diagnosis. According to their interpretation, the vertebra was not putting pressure on the spinal cord.

For the next few days, Berel was given intensive treatment by the hospital's dedicated staff members, who went out of their way to help the young man reclaim his health. Miraculously, Berel was able to leave the hospital one week later with a brace on his back to support his spine. He was in a wheelchair, but the fact that he was alive, considering the first prognosis, was nothing short of a miracle.

Purim arrived three weeks later, and Berel informed his parents that he wanted to spend the holiday at the Klausenberg yeshivah in Union City. "How can you possibly travel anywhere?" they said. "Look at you. You're in a wheelchair, you aren't mobile, you're in such pain. Please stay home!"

But Berel wouldn't listen.

"I have to go see the Rebbe," he told them.

In the end they gave in, knowing their son and his determined nature. Besides, he had already wheeled himself to the front door and was threatening to hitch his way to the yeshivah.

"Fine, I'll take you to Union City," his father offered.

Since the elevator was still out of commission, the *bachurim* carried their friend up to the fourth floor, where the Rebbe's Purim *tisch* was taking place. When Berel was rolled over to the Rebbe, he kissed the Rebbe's hand.

The Rebbe looked his *talmid* in the eye and said in Yiddish, "*Auf Purim host du zich git farshtelt, a tug nuch Purim vest du schoin gehen auf de eigene fuss.*" (The wheelchair is good for a costume, but you will walk the day after Purim.) In Berel's mind, there was no question that it would be so.

He handed the Rebbe his *kvittel.* "You should know," the Rebbe told him, "you were already in the next world and were saved by a *teshuvah* (a halachic ruling)."

Berel would later learn what the Klausenberger Rebbe meant by those cryptic words. He was informed that the Rebbe had left the *mikveh* and opened a *Maseches Chullin*, stopping at a *sugya* that dealt with the halachos of an animal that has become *tereifah*. If the animal has the sort of defect that would cause it to die within twelve months, it is a *tereifah*. If it can live for longer than twelve months, it is kosher.

The Rebbe sat and wrote the ruling that if an animal falls, it will not necessarily die within twelve months, and therefore it is not a *tereifah*. It is kosher. The Rebbe's ruling, decided down on earth, had been accepted in the *beis din shel ma'alah* and had changed Berel's status so that he could live!

The morning after Purim, Berel woke up filled with anticipation. This was it. The big day. Today he was going to walk again. Though his feet were shattered, Berel didn't allow that to stop him. After all, the Rebbe had said that he would walk that day.

Without allowing himself to think too deeply into the consequences, the young man stepped out of bed and found to his dismay that his feet refused to hold him. The next second he hit the floor with a tremendous thud. The pain hit him like a tidal wave. The bright side was that there was carpeting in the room and no one had heard the noise. He really wouldn't have wanted his parents to come rushing to his room in alarm. Still the pain was unbearable, and it took him half an hour before he was able to move without feeling like he was about to faint in agony.

Finally, Berel managed to raise himself to his feet and pull himself back into bed. Maybe he had misunderstood the Rebbe. Maybe the time had not yet arrived for him to walk again.

No, he told himself firmly. *I heard the Rebbe. There is no question. If the Rebbe said I will stand on my feet today, I will!*

Ever so cautiously, he rose from the bed. This time, he put his weight entirely on his hands and kept his feet off the ground. Slowly and with infinite care, he rested one foot slightly on the ground, then the other. First for thirty seconds — and then for one minute — and then two. Leaning on the headboard of his bed, he tried to take one step and then another one, until he reached the dresser.

For several hours, the young man fought the pain like a superman, continuously placing one foot after the other on the ground, taking it bit by bit, a little at a time, back and forth, as the Rebbe's words reverberated through his mind: "The wheelchair is good for a costume, but you will walk the day after Purim."

It was the day after Purim and he was walking. Like an old man, but still. He kept at it for hours. Finally he was able to stand without holding on to the furniture. A few hours later he was able to move from one spot to another without feeling like his entire body was on fire. Though it sounds almost impossible to believe, Berel walked from his bedroom to the kitchen that same day. He had never ceased trusting in his Rebbe and believing that he would be able to do exactly as he had promised.

A few short weeks after the doctors thought he would never walk again and would quite possibly die, Berel was able to walk unassisted, his shattered feet recovering against all odds. It was a miracle, plain and simple. And yet, Berel didn't find it miraculous. After all, the Klausenberger Rebbe had taken full and complete responsibility, and in his mind that could mean only one possible outcome.

As Berel later heard from Reb Boruch Tessler, a medical consultant whom the Rebbe had alerted in the wee hours of that fateful morning, the Rebbe had said, "Berel will make it. He's a *melumad b'nissim* — someone who is experienced in miracles."

R' Chanina ben Dosa was a *melumad b'nissim* because his *emunah* in the Ribono shel Olam was such that nature and miracles were one and the same. Likewise, as we see from Berel's story (heard from Reb Berel Rosenberg himself, who today lives in Kiryat Sanz in Netanya), *emunas chachamim* against all odds results in miracles.

Believing in People

ON A DIFFERENT level, our belief in any of the people in our lives — our children, spouse, friends, coworkers — brings out the blessings that they can give to the world. Pessimistic and critical assessments do just the opposite, squelching others' talents, eroding their confidence, and preventing the flow of positive energy.

Children, especially, are keenly aware of how much they are valued. Even if we don't express our feelings in words, the faith deep in our hearts gives them the ambition and motivation to flourish. The more we honestly believe in our child or in any person, the more we are enabling their success.

This, too, is *emunah*. Hashem has made each of the people in our lives exactly as they must be. He has placed them in our lives for our benefit. From some people, we grow: we refine our *middos*, stretch our capacity to give, develop empathy, compassion, and patience. From some, we may learn by their example. We may be inspired. Not only does our faith in others bring out the best they have to give; it also brings out the best in us.

Part 2:

Emunah
Benefits

Chapter 10
Emunah and Middos Tovos

I never, ever heard of a case where a person was mevater and he lost out. A person who gives in always wins.
(HaRav Eliezer Menachem Mann Shach)

Painting Pictures

WORKING ON *EMUNAH* refines our character until our personality shines and radiates every possible *middah tovah*. The Chazon Ish once remarked about Rabbi Yechezkel Levenstein the *mashgiach* of the Yeshivos of Mir/Ponevezh, "Some people have *emunah* in their heads, others in their heart, but Reb Chatzkel has it in his hands!" When a person is so keenly attuned to *emunah*, it informs his actions in every circumstance. This manifests itself in extraordinary *middos tovos*.

We reach this level simply by following the Torah's directives on how to treat our fellow Jew. When anger is roiling inside us and we don't know which way to turn, the *mitzvos bein adam lachaveiro* point the way. Trusting in Hashem's directions for living in His world will never steer us wrong. In the incident below, related by Rabbi Mattisyahu Salomon the *mashgiach* of Lakewood Yeshivah, we see how these mitzvos can prevent senseless hatred from erupting.

The Shopping-Cart Move

The Schwartz* family's newly purchased apartment was a few minutes' walk from their present residence. This would definitely make the move easier. But the advantage was useless when Mr. Schwartz's car broke down on moving day.

The family had hired movers to transport major appliances and heavy furniture. But they felt it didn't pay to use the service for all their other belongings when Mr. Schwartz could easily transport them down the road. Now that they couldn't use the car, there was a major flaw in the plan.

Mr. Schwartz stood outside his house wondering who might be kind enough to lend him his vehicle for just a few hours.

"Good morning," he heard as someone tapped him on his shoulder. He swung around to meet face-to-face with Mr. Cohen* on his way home from Shacharis. Mr. Cohen was to be his new next-door neighbor.

"Oh, hello, Mr. Cohen. We're moving today, and of all days, my car has just broken down. Perhaps you could lend me your car for a few hours?"

This actually seemed like a reasonable request, especially since the previous week Mr. Cohen's wife had used the Schwartzes' car to travel out of town for the day.

Mr. Cohen looked uncomfortable. "Well, mm — I'm so sorry, but I need my car today," and he abruptly walked off.

It was 9 a.m. The moving truck would be arriving any minute; the car dilemma would have to wait. The next two hours were hectic until the broad-shouldered worker slammed shut the door of his truck and drove down the road with all the furniture, boxes, and cases he could manage to cram inside.

Without any choice, Mr. Schwartz began to load the remaining packed articles onto the shopping cart they normally used to transport their groceries home from the local supermarket. As he walked up the path leading to his new front door, he caught sight of Mr. Cohen watching him from his front window. The Cohens' silver Subaru was parked neatly just outside his home. *Interesting,* he mused. *He told me he needed his car today.*

The trips back and forth that Mr. Schwartz made that day seemed never-ending. He had not imagined how strenuous the move would be — especially without his car. A few hours later, he passed Mr. Cohen's home for the twentieth time, sweat streaming down his face, and again he noticed Mr. Cohen observing him from the window. Now his neighbor smiled and waved to him. Mr. Schwartz felt quite annoyed as he realized that the silver car was still standing idly beside the pavement. He felt hot, tired, and humiliated, and the sweet smile made him feel even hotter.

The next morning there was a knock at the Schwartzes' new residence. Mr. Schwartz paled when he discovered none other than Mr. Cohen standing at his doorstep holding a cake. His innocent smile made Mr. Schwartz cringe. But he was totally unprepared for the words to come.

"Welcome!" Mr. Cohen announced. "It's a pleasure to have neighbors like you. Do you know, I was watching you all yesterday afternoon and I marveled at the cart you used. It's so convenient. Perhaps you could lend it to me today so that my son can make a big purchase for our upcoming bar mitzvah?"

Mr. Schwartz felt faint. He didn't even have the strength to slam the door shut in his neighbor's face. What nerve! What downright brazen behavior!

Will Mr. Schwartz run, angry and offended, to tell his wife all about their rude, selfish neighbor? Will this be the start of a cold, strained relationship between the two families?

How does the Torah demand us to respond in such a situation? It commands us, *"Lo sikom* — You shall not take revenge" (*Vayikra* 19:18).

There is another commandment: *"V'lo sitor* — Do not bear a grudge" (ibid.). Rashi explains, "When a person refuses to lend us an article and then he, too, requests a favor, we may not say, 'Okay, I'll help you even though you didn't lend me what I requested yesterday.' We are expected to remove any ill feelings completely from our heart, and lend the person the article."

Is this humanly possible? Isn't it natural to feel hurt, wronged, or insulted? We're not made of stone. We might think that these mitzvos are voluntary, for pious people. But they are not. They are obligatory. Are we expected to act like angels?

There is a way to be in control of our human feelings. All our emotions are controlled by our thoughts. Once a person trains himself to think in the correct way, he can direct himself away from anger, frustration, and insult.

There is a positive commandment to help us out: "*B'tzedek tish-pot amisecha* — With righteousness you shall judge your fellow" (ibid. 19:15). We are obligated to use our imagination to paint a bright picture when the facts appear dark.

This is the real picture of what was taking place as Mr. Cohen appeared to be delivering insult after insult to his new neighbor:

Avrumi Cohen's mother was scheduled to go into the hospital for an angiogram and possible treatment to open her blocked arteries, which were causing severe angina. Her heart specialist had arranged the urgent procedure for her since her condition was serious. The appointment was scheduled for 1 p.m. Her devoted son Avrumi had arranged for her to take a taxi from her home in another town to his house, from which he would then take her to the hospital.

At twelve o'clock Avrumi was ready and waiting apprehensively by the window for his mother to arrive. She had no mobile phone, but she had given him a call before she left home. She should be arriving any moment. The minutes ticked by, but there was no sign of Mrs. Cohen. He began to get nervous. If they didn't leave now, they would miss the appointment. The specialist had warned them that she could suffer a heart attack in her situation.

He dialed the road service to discover that there had been a terrible accident causing enormous traffic jams. He began to imagine his mother, with her weak heart, in a stuffy car in the heat of the day, certainly a bundle of nerves. This alone could bring on a heart attack. The slightest sound of a car outside made him go running to the window to see if it was his mother. This went on for almost two hours until his mother finally arrived.

He noticed Mr. Schwartz passing by, but it had slipped his mind completely that he had wanted his car. He genuinely smiled and waved to him, not even thinking that there was anything strange about him pushing a shopping cart.

The moment his mother arrived, he informed the hospital and they agreed to give her a different date in two weeks' time. Mr. Cohen knew it was a risk to her health to wait so long, and for the next few hours he worked frantically until he succeeded in getting the procedure scheduled for two days later. He went to bed that night physically and emotionally drained.

Meanwhile, his wife had prepared a cake for the new neighbors and asked him to deliver it on his way to work. Mr. Cohen's mind was completely out of focus after the strenuous nerve-racking day he had endured. Mentioning the shopping cart was simply a poor attempt to make conversation while his mind veered elsewhere.

In this scenario, there's nothing for Mr. Schwartz to be angry and insulted about. On the contrary, the Cohens really did want to welcome the Schwartz family warmly. Avrumi Cohen would have lent him his car if he hadn't needed it urgently that day.

Doing Ourselves a Favor

TO BE *DAN l'chaf zechus* is a gift directly from the Master Inventor Who created human beings and designed human nature. This mitzvah, as well as not seeking revenge and not bearing a grudge, are just a few of the mitzvos that comprise the Torah's "instruction manual" to living happily and securely. These mitzvos, although they focus on the other person, are for our own benefit.

In the midst of our anger and humiliation we might think, *Why should I give him the benefit of the doubt? He deserves a piece of my mind!*

Rather than trying to punish the other person, we should focus on protecting ourselves from the terrible consequences we will inflict on ourselves by seeking revenge. Every doctor and psychologist today agrees that harboring insult, ill feelings, and anger is detrimental to one's health.

We are not only doing ourselves a favor by heeding the Torah's commandments, but we are also enriching our own quality of life by living peacefully. Hatred kills our own peace of mind. In addition, maintaining the peace earns us tremendous reward in this world and in the next.

Judging favorably is a mitzvah like any other that might involve spending time and money. The Chafetz Chaim observes that people are willing to spend money on buying an *esrog* or writing a *sefer Torah*. They are willing to spend time to fulfill the mitzvah of *hachnasas orchim*. He explains that a person should be just as willing to invest effort and money in keeping all the mitzvos related to living in harmony with our family, friends, and neighbors. Instead of arguing and fighting over petty sums of money, dedicate that money to the mitzvah of promoting peace. It's certainly just as significant as any other mitzvah.

Judging favorably also saves us from violating the hundreds of Torah prohibitions involved in speaking *lashon hara*. Instead of allowing negative thoughts about people to occupy our minds, we can switch channels and think of all their positive traits. Every positive thought is a mitzvah, and we can mark it as such by preceding our positive thoughts with the following words:

הִנְנִי מוּכָן וּמְזוּמָן לְשֵׁם יְחוּד קוּדְשָׁא בְּרִיךְ הוּא לְקַיֵּם מִצְוַת עֲשֵׂה שֶׁל וְאָהַבְתָּ לְרֵעֲךָ כָּמוֹךָ, לֹא תִקֹּם, בְּצֶדֶק תִּשְׁפֹּט עֲמִיתֶךָ, לֹא תִטֹּר, לֹא תִשְׂנָא אֶת אָחִיךָ בִּלְבָבֶךָ.

Behold, I am ready and prepared for the sake of HaKadosh Baruch Hu to fulfill the positive mitzvos of "Love your neighbor as yourself," "Do not take revenge," "With righteousness you shall judge your fellow," "Do not hold a grudge," and "Do not hate your brother in your heart."

Then we can let our imagination run wild. We can turn the whole situation around and look at it from a positive perspective. As we do this, we shouldn't forget to imagine our dear Father sitting on His heavenly throne smiling at us, gleaning *nachas* from our effort. Wouldn't we rather give Him *nachas* than cause Him the pain of seeing His children fight?

Does the story need to be true? Not at all! Once we have painted the picture, we have fulfilled our obligation. It might very well turn out to be true. Rabbi Akiva was *dan l'chaf zechus*, as the Gemara relates (*Shabbos* 127b; *She'iltos, Shemos* 40), when his employer refused to pay him after one year of labor, and every detail he imagined was precisely correct. At the very least, our storytelling proves to us that there are possible circumstances in which the other person might be completely innocent.

Rabbi Chaim Zaid, a well-known *kiruv* speaker in Eretz Yisrael, relates the following:

Bull's-Eye

About a week before Yom Kippur, I was invited to speak in Herzliya. I had never lectured in Herzliya before, and I wasn't familiar with the area. I got off the train, headed to Sokolov Street, and looked for the shul where I was to deliver the lecture. I walked up and down the street several times but couldn't find the place.

It was a quiet street with few passersby, so I had no one to ask. Finally, I saw a man sporting a weird kind of ponytail divided into two braids exiting a building. "Good morning," I greeted him courteously. "Do you know of any *beit knesset* in the area?"

Instead of answering politely, the man yelled at me.

"Get out of here! You people stick your noses everywhere!" He went on to let me know exactly what he thought of the *chareidim*, their rabbis, their lifestyle, and their clothing.

My instinctive reaction was to return his aggression. I was at no loss of words to let him know just what I thought of *his* dress and *his* lifestyle. But I hastily checked myself. *Yom Kippur is in a few days' time,* I thought. *I'm going to look at him as a fellow Jew who deserves to be treated with respect. Chazal tell us that even Jews who are distant from Yiddishkeit are as full of mitzvos as a pomegranate is filled with seeds (Eruvin 19a).*

Feeling only love toward him, I stepped forward, gave the surprised guy a hug, and said to him, "You have no idea what a tzaddik you are! You are a unique individual!"

Astonished, the man stuttered and stammered, "Look — I wasn't attacking you personally, you know. You're okay. I was just talking about people in general."

"I have no doubt about that," I said.

"Let's try to find the *beit knesset* together," he offered.

We found it on the third floor of a nearby building: a shul called Ohr L'Yisrael.

I thanked him, and then said to him, "How about coming in to join the lecture? You'll hear some nice things. Come on in and enjoy yourself."

And the man with the two braids, warmed by my hug of moments before, agreed to attend a Torah lecture.

He sat there for a full hour, seeming to enjoy every minute. Before parting, he said to me, "This lecture gave me just the boost I needed. I was in a lousy mood today, and when you stopped me on the street I let it all out on you. I was actually hoping you'd insult me back so that we'd get into a good sparring match, and I'd give vent to all my annoyance. But instead, you hugged me and actually complimented me, which totally threw me off. Why on earth did you do that?"

"To be honest, I was very upset at first," I said to him, "and my initial reaction was to insult you back. But then I remembered that I'd noticed you stepping out of the dentist's office, and I decided to judge you favorably. *Poor guy*, I thought. *The dentist probably told him that he needs to have all his teeth replaced and it's going to cost him fifty thousand shekels. No wonder he's in such a bad mood.*"

The man looked at me, dumbfounded.

"You're Eliyahu HaNavi!" he said in total awe, and with trembling hands he withdrew the dentist's bill from his pocket showing a sum total of fifty thousand shekels for tooth implants!

"I'm not a *navi*," I said to him with a smile. "I'm simply a son of HaKadosh Baruch Hu, just like you are, and He has instructed us in his Torah to judge everyone favorably, to love every Jew, to care for each other. Come, I highly recommend that you learn more about His Torah."

Then and there, I enrolled him in an Arachim seminar for *ba'alei teshuvah*.

When a person tries to concentrate on another's good points, he can actually elevate the other person. And as we see from this story, when we try, Hashem helps us make a winning guess and hit the mark!

Winning Favor for Yourself

THE MORE WE judge others favorably, the more Hashem judges us favorably. Even if we absolutely don't deserve it, the defending angels begin to sing our praises.

Each time a person closes his mouth and refrains from derogatory speech, the accusing angels are forced to close their mouths and are unable to prosecute the person even if he committed serious *aveiros*.

The Baal Shem Tov explains that when a person dies, his *neshamah* goes up to the *beis din shel ma'alah*, and he undergoes a trial. He is shown a video of all the years of his life. Every action, word, and thought unfolds before his eyes. It's all real and vivid. Then he is asked to judge all he has just seen, thereby determining his own verdict.

He is in the World of Truth and can only say the truth. If he was accustomed to judging favorably during his lifetime, his *neshamah* will automatically have only good things to say, even concerning his own wrongdoings. But if he was accustomed to criticizing and condemning people's actions, he will judge himself the same way.

A Perspective on Jealousy

BA'AL BITACHON KNOWS that Hashem gives him all he needs; there is no purpose or need to feel jealous of others. But it's not always so simple to combat pangs of jealousy while observing other people's success. One important fact can help us steer our thoughts away from jealousy: what we observe is only a sliver of the full picture, as the *mashal* below from the Zhidichover Rebbe illustrates:

Conversation Between Angels: A Mashal

One day the Chief of Dreams met the Chief of Success. They began to chat about the events of the day. "So what have you been doing today?" the Chief of Success asked his friend.

"You don't know what I did last night," the Chief of Dreams replied proudly. "Mr. Reich declared bankruptcy, and the authorities came into his home to take away all his furniture. He was left without a bed to sleep on! He lay a mattress on the floor, and when he finally fell asleep, I painted him the most fantastic dream. He saw his best friend coming to offer him an enormous loan, which he invested successfully. He soon had the whole sum to pay back his debts, save his house, and climb out of his predicament."

"Is that what you did? You are very cruel!" said the Chief of Success. "You allowed him to feel elated for a few seconds, and then he woke up to find himself lying on the floor in a bare room. Reality slapped him on his face!"

"And you are so innocent and kind?" the Chief of Dreams retorted sarcastically. "You allow a person to taste success his whole life. He feels respected for his intelligence, for his wealth, for his wonderful children. He lacks nothing.

"Then, in one split second, everything is taken away from him. He leaves the world of falsehood for the World of Truth, where he is not respected for his wealth and intelligence, and not even for his wonderful children. These were all gifts. No acclaim is given for free gifts. You are cruel! You deceive people for a whole lifetime!"

(*Ateres Tzvi Derash*)

Some people do go through life with luck and good fortune smiling at them. Others don't begin to achieve esteem and success. But it's all an illusion. There comes a time when success is of no worth at all. Only effort is valued. Life is one big dream, and it makes no sense to be jealous of another person's dream!

The Talmud (*Pesachim* 50a) relates that when R' Yosef, the son of R' Yehoshua, passed away, his *neshamah* soared up to the World of Truth. He saw the proceedings of the next world and then came back to life. R' Yehoshua asked him, "What did you see in the World of Truth?"

He responded, "I saw an upside-down world. Those who were respected in this world were at the bottom, and those considered simple here were highly respected up there."

R' Yehoshua said to him, "You saw a clear world."

So much of what we crave and so much of what we admire is nothing more than an illusion that pops like a soap bubble the moment we leave this world. On the other hand, the challenges with which we struggle become our true, eternal wealth. For example, sometimes parents may invest an incredible amount of effort in helping their child succeed. Yet their toil goes unnoticed as the child barely advances. It is for that particular child that they will be awarded the greatest respect in the World of Truth.

Jealousy, anger, worry, feelings of resentment, and revenge are all destructive *middos* that we strive to shed in the course of our lifetimes. With *emunah*, we have the perspective that not only helps us to restrain ourselves from these traits, but renders them foolish in our eyes. We know that no one can do anything to us, for us, or against us. It's all Hashem.

Making Peace

*W*HAT SHOULD A person do if he has been wronged or hurt, and there is absolutely no way to be *dan l'chaf zechus*? The person who hurt him might be someone he sees often, and now, each time he catches sight of him, the wound reopens.

Once again Hashem guides us, through His "instruction manual," on how to respond: "*Lo sisna es achicha bilvavecha* — You shall not hate your brother in your heart" (*Vayikra* 19:17). Chazal say that if a Jew avoids speaking to an acquaintance for more than three days because of hatred, he has transgressed this mitzvah (*Sanhedrin* 27b).

To prevent this stewing in anger, the Torah advises us how to erase our vengeful, angry emotions. The *pasuk* continues, "You should surely reprove your fellow." Along these lines, the following straightforward words of the Ramban on the verse are the key to mending many broken relationships:

> Don't hate your fellow Jew in your heart when he did you an injustice. Go up to him and confront him: "Why did you do this to me?" Don't bear his sin by covering up the hatred in your heart and not approaching him to tell him how hurt you feel, because when you explain to him how he offended or wronged you, he will probably apologize, or regret his actions and admit his mistake. Then Hashem will forgive him.
>
> If you bear the hatred in your heart, you will transgress the sin of hating your brother in your heart, and you will also bear his sin, since you didn't give him the chance to apologize.

By confronting the person who offended you, the Ramban says, you will rid yourself of your offended feelings. You won't have reason to seek revenge or bear a grudge. Instead, you will be able to live in peace. This is a mitzvah rewarded faithfully by Hashem, because only He knows what was in your heart and how much self-control you had to exercise to resolve your grievance.

How many feuds could be resolved if only the offended person would realize that approaching the other person is not just a courageous act; it's a mitzvah. Once the conversation is opened, a large percentage of feuds could be resolved quickly and quietly.

It's Not Beneath You

*N*O ONE CAN count himself so great as to be exempt from fulfilling this mitzvah. Some people think, *He did me a terrible injustice. He should come and ask me for forgiveness. I don't need to go to him!*

This outlook is quite contrary to the Torah perspective demonstrated by Moshe Rabbeinu when a group of distinguished Jews, led by his cousin Korach, organized a revolt. He knew that his leadership was at stake and, with it, the Torah itself. All he had to do was beseech Hashem to put an end to these troublemakers, but that's not what he did.

The Midrash (*Bamidbar* 16:25) tells us that he went out to look for Korach. Why should he appease the one who had incited so many people with slander and ridiculed him in a most humiliating fashion?

And what was the point? Moshe knew that Korach wasn't interested in coming to terms with him. But Moshe put aside his dignity and all these logical arguments and went to appease Korach in order to restore the peace.

As he walked toward the tent of Korach, Korach's three sons saw him from the distance. The *gadol hador* was approaching, and they knew they were obligated to stand up for him in respect, but this would defy their father!

They chose to stand up.

At that very moment they were given Divine assistance to repent and were saved the fate of their father and his 250 followers. From their offspring, *Klal Yisrael* merited a great leader and prophet named Shmuel HaNavi, who was the equal of Moshe and Aharon.

It is well known that a person should ask for forgiveness on *erev Yom Kippur* if he knows he has offended someone. It's also a mitzvah to approach those who we feel have wronged us and give them the chance to correct their mistake, so that we can forgive with a whole heart (*Shulchan Aruch, Orach Chaim* 606:1).

May every Jew have the strength to fulfill the precious commandments between man and his fellow so that we can live in unity without animosity. This will certainly speed the coming of Mashiach and the Ultimate Redemption.

He's Just the Messenger

WHAT HAPPENS IF the offender isn't prepared to admit that he wronged us? We realize we have no way to receive compensation for the harm he caused us. How, then, can we deal with our angry and vengeful emotions? This is where our *emunah* is put to the test.

The *Chovos HaLevavos* brings a wonderful *mashal* in *Sha'ar HaBitachon.*

A powerful king who ruled over a large province was informed that one of his subjects was initiating a rebellion. After confirming that this was so, he ordered his chief adviser to have the rebel arrested to restore law and order. The adviser ordered his trusted chief of police to do the task. The chief in turn called one of his policemen and demanded that he travel to the home of the culprit and arrest him. The policeman arrested the man and took him to the local prison. The prison warden locked him in one of the cells.

The angry man began screaming at the warden and tried to beat him.

Will the prisoner gain anything by beating the warden? Will he gain anything out of pleading with him to let him free?

The warden is not the right address. He has absolutely no say in the matter. Neither does the policeman nor the chief. Even the king's chief adviser is only carrying out the king's order. How foolish is the man to think that there is any point in venting his anger on the warden, who has no power and is only doing his job!

Likewise, if we are wronged and there's nothing we can do about it, we must remember that this person is only Hashem's messenger. It's a waste of energy to let out our anger on a lowly messenger who merely carried out the task that Hashem appointed him to do.

We should turn to Hashem and say, "This is from You. Please help me." He will look after us, and we will have no need to harbor anger or find ways to take revenge.

However, when people cause us loss or harm, we do have the right to seek redress. The fact that our loss comes from Hashem doesn't mean that we shouldn't try to right a wrong. For instance, we are permitted to go to *beis din*, if we feel someone owes us money; such behavior does not mean our *emunah* is weak. (Of course, one should consult with a Torah authority first.) Similarly, if a teenager drives the family car too fast and skids, causing damage to the car, we don't just shrug it off and say it was meant to be; that youngster needs to be taught safety and discipline.

The problems arise when we fail to recognize the proper boundaries for our efforts.

A person approached the Chazon Ish and asked him a question: "How should I identify the borderline between taking action to get back what rightfully belongs to me and overdoing my obligation of *hishtadlus*?"

The Chazon Ish replied, "Have you ever hammered a nail into the wall?"

The man nodded. "Of course."

"Then you know that one must hold the nail in the right place and bang carefully with the hammer. As long as the nail is straight, you can pound it further. But if the nail gets bent, you must stop pounding it. You have to take it out. As long as things run smoothly in a natural way, you can take action. But if things begin to get crooked — you find yourself occupied the whole day running from one *din Torah* to the next, you can't learn, you can't sleep — then it's time to stop immediately! It's time to let the One Above sort out your affairs. It's not the right *hishtadlus*."

When the *hishtadlus* is flawed, even if a person wins the case and receives compensation, the money will be lost to sudden unpredicted costs. But if the money is rightfully his, the Ribono shel Olam will reimburse him through other means.

At times a person has difficulty letting go of his grievance because his dignity is insulted. *Who is he to speak that way to me?* he thinks. Or, *He can't get away with doing that to me. Who does he think he is?* His pride doesn't let him back down.

A famous story about David HaMelech proves that such pride has no place in a Jew's heart, even if he is a king.

David's son Avshalom betrayed his father and tried to take over as king. This resulted in major rebellion. Shimi ben Geira, the head of the Sanhedrin, brazenly cursed His Highness King David in public, pelting him with stones (*II Shmuel* 16:5–12). David's followers wanted to murder Shimi on the spot, but David didn't allow it. "Leave him alone," the king ordered. "This is from Hashem. I am not angry at him. Hashem — the Name of G-d that represents the attribute of mercy — is the One Who did this to me, so that when I accept it with love, it will be of tremendous benefit to me."

The *Zohar* writes that at that precise moment, when David behaved in this elevated manner and swallowed his humiliation with love and faith, he became the fourth leg of Hashem's chariot, along with the three *Avos*.

Only Hashem Guarantees Justice

*I*F WE FEEL that we are entitled to stick up for our rights and demand justice, we are totally correct. But can any human being guarantee us justice? Hashem can compensate us in a much better way than any of the people who wronged us.

It's natural and instinctive for a person to stick up for his rights. Animals behave instinctively. Many human beings behave instinctively, too, in order to protect themselves, but in doing so, they portray animalistic behavior.

When our natural instincts prompt us to take revenge, to display animosity toward a person who harmed us, we must bear in mind again the two words that close *Parashas Kedoshim* after the prohibitions against taking revenge, bearing hatred, and speaking *lashon hara*: "*Ani Hashem* — I am Hashem" (*Vayikra* 19:18). Even if you think that these commandments between man and his fellow are logical and for your benefit, that is *not* why you must perform them. Because then you might not want to fulfill them if you feel that it's not for your benefit. Hashem commanded you to fulfill them, even when you think it's not right, and Hashem will compensate you accordingly. You won't lose out.

If you bear in mind that you are behaving in a way that pleases Hashem, you won't be bothered by what your adversary gains. Furthermore, Rashi explains (*Vayikra* 19:14, 16) it's Hashem you are serving. He knows exactly what you've gone through, and He will reward you for your self-control much more than you would have received by carrying on the fight.

The Chafetz Chaim illustrates this point with a parable: A father gives each of his two sons a candy. The younger one swipes away the older child's candy. The older child tries to decide what to do. Should he fight for his rights?

He decides not to start a fight and instead goes to his father and says, "My brother took my candy, but I don't want to fight with him, so could you give me another one from your big bag of candies?"

Says the Chafetz Chaim, the father will be so delighted with his son's desire to maintain the peace with his brother that he'll reward him with ten candies. Likewise, when we turn to our Father for help instead of fighting it out with our adversary, we arouse His delight and affection, and He returns what we have lost tenfold.

As mentioned in the opening to this chapter, Rabbi Shach would say, "I never, ever heard of a case where a person was *mevater* and he lost out. A person who gives in *always* wins."

When we're not prepared to give in, we lose. There are no exceptions. The story below, related by the rav of Baghdad, the Ben Ish Chai, illustrates how our anger and resentment over others' affronts always boomerang against us.

Killing the Cure: A Mashal

There was once a king who would stroll the streets with his closest confidant. They would mingle among the people disguised as simple townsfolk so that the king could listen to the conversations of his people and get an inkling of what really transpired in their daily life.

One day, as they passed a hospital, the king suggested that they go inside to visit the patients. They entered the intensive care ward and came across a man writhing in agony. "What happened to you?" the king asked.

"I was bitten by a dog, and the bite became infected," the man answered. "The infection is spreading, and the doctors have given up hope."

"Is there no cure at all?" the king inquired.

"Yes, there is. They say that if I could eat the liver of the live dog that bit me, I could be healed."

"So why don't you do so?" the king probed.

The man replied sadly, "I was so angry with the dog that I killed him!"

As they exited the hospital, the king told his companion, "Today we learned a valuable lesson for life. A person sometimes get kicked or bitten, but if he reacts with an explosion of anger, he is killing himself."

The Ben Ish Chai expounds: A person can't imagine how many *tzaros* he is saving himself when he accepts the insults, kicks, and bites that he receives from people with love and faith. Instead of reacting wildly and angrily, he can accept that this is in place of greater suffering and that he might be saving his very life.

The following true story, which took place on September 11, 2001, with the attack on the Twin Towers, is a dramatic demonstration of the lifesaving power of letting go of a grievance:

Saved by a Broken Arm

The Kohn* family sent their daughter to a sleepaway camp for the first time in the summer of 2001. In camp, she slipped and broke her arm. Her parents were furious, and they threatened to sue the camp.

The camp director spoke to the Kohns' rabbi, who succeeded in persuading the father not to take legal action.

Shortly thereafter, on September 11, the office where Mr. Kohn worked in New York's World Trade Center went up in flames and collapsed, killing thousands of workers who were trapped inside. But Mr. Kohn had not gone to work that day. He had accompanied his daughter to the hospital to have her cast removed.

The Preferred Route to Purity

*W*HEN A PERSON takes a loss or is dealt an insult, he can certainly try to set the situation right in a peaceful, normal way. But if those means don't work, he has two choices: press harder, with aggression and anger, or accept the loss and move on. If he chooses the latter route, he can achieve a level of purity that otherwise he would only be able to achieve through suffering.

The Chida reaches this conclusion through a *mishnah* (*Avos* 1:17): "Shimon says: I grew up among wise men, and I did not find anything more beneficial for the body than remaining silent."

The Chida cites the Ramak, Rabbi Moshe Cordovero, who divulges a kabbalistic secret. There is nothing that elevates the soul and atones for our sins as completely as being humiliated with demeaning, angry words and remaining silent rather than respond-ing in kind. No amount of fasting or affliction can equal this atone-ment.

Shimon is telling us, "I grew up among wise sages, and I learned from them how illness, poverty, mourning, the death of children, and other difficult afflictions cleanse and purify our soul at great cost to our body. Yet suffering the pain of a verbal assault in silence provides the greatest purification with the least amount of physical pain."

A tongue-lashing, while humiliating and unpleasant, leaves us with our physical health intact. As soon as we realize that the an-ger and lack of self-control the other person displayed is his prob-lem, not ours, we can even forgive him for the attack.

When someone embarrasses us, we have an opportunity to en-sure ourselves of a pleasant, healthy long life by remaining si-lent. It is the great kindness from Hashem, as long as we are wise enough to make the most of it.

The Gemara relates that Rav Huna was deathly ill and Rav Papa came to visit him (*Rosh Hashanah* 17b). He noticed that Rav Huna lay lifeless, and he hurriedly instructed the family to prepare his shrouds.

Suddenly Rav Huna woke up and Rav Papa was terribly em-barrassed. Rav Huna calmed him. "You didn't make a mistake. My soul had already ascended to the heavenly court, where they began my court case. All of a sudden I was given an extra lease of life and was not judged according to the letter of the law, because I have always looked away from affronts against me."

A person literally earns added life by being *mevater*.

Along the same lines, the *Tomer Devorah* writes (Ch. 2):

> Sometimes it is decreed that a person must die. The an-gels of mercy come and plead that his life be spared. The heavenly court agrees to sweeten his verdict with illness. The angels of mercy beg again for mercy, and once more the verdict is exchanged for a loss of livelihood. But the an-gels do not stop beseeching for mercy since poverty is also unbearable. The last and final agreement is that his verdict will be sweetened in the best possible way: in the form of *elbonos*, insults, and someone is sent to insult him.

If this person had witnessed the goings-on in Heaven, he would be dancing for joy when the insult came his way. Rav Chaim Vital, talmid of the Arizal, would say, "One who has sense would look out for opportunities to be insulted or wronged in order to overlook it and earn extra life."

There are many stories exemplifying the tremendous power of overlooking insult. Here are a few of them:

A Small Price to Pay

Rebbetzin Hadassah Linder lived in the Knesset Yisrael neighborhood, near Batei Brodie in Yerushalayim. She was a much beloved figure in the city, known for her kindness, friendliness, and the good advice she freely dispensed.

The *rebbetzin* had a neighbor of unsound mind who was unable to take proper care of herself and was in a perpetual state of neglect. Her clothing was filthy, her nails were long and dirty, and an unpleasant odor hovered around her. The neighborhood children avoided her at all costs, while the adults nodded politely when they met her but then quickened their pace and hurried away.

One day the old lady collapsed and had to be taken to the hospital. With no next of kin to accompany her, Rebbetzin Linder volunteered to go along with her in the ambulance. When they arrived at the hospital, a nurse came toward them to admit the patient and open a medical file. With professional courtesy, she masked her distaste for the patient's repellant odor and asked the *rebbetzin* the standard questions: age, medical history, reason for admission, etc.

"And what is your relationship with the patient?" the nurse asked politely, pen poised, ready to mark the next answer.

The *rebbetzin* looked at the helpless patient and thought quickly. *If I say that I'm just a neighbor, that this poor woman has not a relative in the world, what kind of care will she receive? Who will so much as glance at her after I go home? Who will bring her a drink of water, feed her, smooth her pillow, brush her dirty, tangled hair? How can I leave her in this state?*

"I'm her daughter," the *rebbetzin* answered stoically, putting her arm around the frail, hunched shoulders.

The nurse took a long, hard look at the *rebbetzin* and then said pointedly to two of her colleagues passing by, "You see this patient in the wheelchair? She's *her* mother," and nodded at the dignified-looking *rebbetzin*.

The three of them sniggered. It was obvious that they had little regard for the woman who couldn't take proper care of her mother — and whose misfortune it was to have such a mother in the first place.

The *rebbetzin* bit her tongue and kept quiet. It would have been so easy for her to absolve herself of this undeserved shame. She could have recovered her dignity and earned the nurses' fullest respect if she would have just told them that she claimed to be the woman's daughter for the noblest and most altruistic of reasons: so that the poor soul would get some decent care. But she chose not to say anything and accepted the implied insult with grace.

Only after Rebbetzin Linder had seen her "mother" attended to by a team of doctors and comfortably settled in the hospital ward did she make her way home.

When she arrived home, she found her family members in a state of panic. "Oh, Ima!" they cried. "Don't worry, nothing happened — but something nearly did!"

It turned out that her son had been knocked over by a vehicle on his way home from cheder. Bystanders had been shocked when they'd witnessed the accident. Judging from what they'd seen, the boy should have been seriously injured. Yet he hadn't suffered a single scratch.

When the *rebbetzin* heard this, she turned pale as she realized that the accident had happened at about the same time that she had swallowed the nurse's sneering remark.

Who knows? she thought to herself. *Perhaps his life was saved in the merit of my having kept quiet in the face of insult, just as the Ramak has promised. Hashem, thank You for giving me the opportunity! A bit of hurt pride is a small price to pay for my precious son's life!*

Embracing an Insult

Reb Shlomke of Zhvil would immerse himself every day in the *mikveh* amid great *kavannos*. Ill people would come to him pleading for salvation when their doctors had given up hope. He would go to immerse himself in the *mikveh*, and when he left, he was able to work miracles, advising people with *ruach hakodesh*, defeating the laws of nature.

One day, as he was on his way to the *mikveh*, a Jew came and screamed at him, disgracing him in public. Reb Shlomke didn't utter a word until the Jew finished and walked away. He then told his students, "Going to the *mikveh* is virtuous, but being degraded is even greater. I do not need the *mikveh* today."

He turned around to go home without immersing himself that day.

Reb Shlomke's daughter was once critically ill. He saw with *ruach hakodesh* that all the gates of *refuah* and prayer were bolted. But he was aware that one *segulah* could still help: the *segulah* of overlooking insults.

He left his daughter's bedside and walked toward the home of an ill-mannered woman who owed him a significant sum of money. As soon as she noticed him approaching, she began to shout and berate him. He listened in silence, and as soon as the attack was over, he forgave her wholeheartedly.

By the time he returned to his daughter, there was already a positive change in her condition. Miraculously she recovered completely from her illness.

A Timely Reprieve

Rabbi Avraham Bardky, an illustrious *talmid chacham* who lived in Yerushalayim, suffered from diabetes and had to have one of his legs amputated. The day before his operation, he came to *daven* in the *beis midrash* and a Jew began screaming and shouting at him.

Reb Avraham felt hurt and embarrassed by the nasty comments, but he controlled himself and didn't reply. He offered up a silent prayer: "Ribono shel Olam, I could have answered back and defended myself, but I kept silent. I forgive him for the shame and hurt he caused me, and now, please send me a *refuah sheleimah*."

The next day, the doctors performed last-minute tests in preparation for the operation. After a consultation, they called the surprised patient and informed him that they had decided on a different form of treatment and the amputation would not be necessary.

Reb Avraham would relate time and again that he was saved from being disabled for the rest of his life in the merit of closing his mouth while being verbally abused.

The following true story took place recently in England and was heard firsthand:

Instant Yeshuah

Rabbi Elya Shein,* a respected *rosh yeshivah* in England, was in shul one day during summer vacation, a short while before the new Elul *zeman* was set to begin. All of a sudden, a man entered the *beis midrash*, and when he saw Reb Elya, his face turned red with rage.

This man had a son who had applied to study in Reb Elya's yeshivah, but for various reasons, the staff could not accept him. The offended father went over to the *rosh yeshivah* and began to yell at him. He did not suffice with voicing his disappointment about the rejection of his son, but went on to insult Reb Elya personally. There were many people present in shul at the time, and the vicious verbal attack caused Reb Elya immense embarrassment.

Despite being extremely hurt, Reb Elya did not respond. He realized that the wisest thing would be not to retaliate, so he remained silent as the man carried on ranting against him.

That night, Reb Elya couldn't fall asleep as the mortifying scene replayed itself over and over in his mind. He wondered what all the people in shul thought of him after witnessing his humiliation. He knew that the father had spoken out of pain, but he had gone way too far. Reb Elya tossed and turned as he contemplated what to do.

Suddenly, a thought occurred to him. He knew that a person who is shamed and does not answer back has a special power. The Gemara states (*Shabbos* 88b), "Those who are embarrassed and do not retaliate...about them the *pasuk* says, 'Those who love Him are like the sun when it shines forth in all its radiance' (*Shoftim* 5:31)." In addition, "The world exists only in the merit of those who close their mouths during an argument" (*Chullin* 89a).

He decided to use that *ko'ach* to bless someone. As soon as it was morning, he called up a young man who'd been married for six years and was still childless. The man shared a close relationship with Reb Elya and had recently confided in him that he and his wife had tried multiple treatments, all unsuccessfully, and the doctors had very little hope that they'd ever be parents.

Reb Elya told the *yungerman* that he had been shamed publicly but had refrained from replying. "I want to use this *ko'ach* to offer you my heartfelt *berachah* that you should be blessed with a healthy child very soon," he told his incredulous listener.

Nine months later, the young man became a father of a precious little baby girl. The joyous *kiddush* took place before Lag BaOmer.

This remarkable story took place in March 5776/2016:

"Murder" at the Cash Register

I stood in line at the checkout, patiently waiting my turn. I knew I had to behave myself, because in front of me stood my former principal. Although I had finished school many years earlier, as all good Bais Yaakov girls know, once a principal, always a principal.

Apparently, a man standing at the checkout adjacent to us recognized her, too. To my horror, he started yelling at her in front of all the shoppers.

"You know how much pain you have caused our entire family? You should know that you are to blame that my daughter has gone off the *derech*! You murdered her! You will have to account for that one day!"

There was a stunned silence in the store. My former principal turned white, then red, then left her shopping cart piled high with goods and walked out the door, accompanied by the high-volume verbal harangue.

As soon as she left, the silence morphed into hushed whispers. I couldn't bear to see or hear any of it, and I followed my former principal to the exit.

I tried to recall what happened while she had been principal. I knew there had been major politics going on; she'd left while I was still in school, but I had no idea what the particulars were. One thing I knew: she didn't deserve to be humiliated like this.

From afar, I saw her walking fast, as if trying to escape the nightmare. I caught up with her and, mustering up my courage, asked her, "Do you remember me?"

"Of course," she said, and mentioned my surname.

There was a short, awkward silence.

"I just want to tell you," I said, "that that man was probably in a lot of pain and that's why he spoke that way. But I don't believe him one bit. I remember you as principal. You were always fair, you believed in us, and we all respected you. You were our best principal, and I really admired you!"

By now, I was crying, I was so distressed at what I had just seen.

My former principal seemed unperturbed. "Don't worry," she said tranquilly, trying to calm me. "Don't cry, it's okay. I must have deserved this — it's a *kapparas avonos*."

I was astounded by her faith.

On impulse, I said to her, "Please, give me a *berachah*. I'm twenty-two years old, and I have two older sisters at home, one a divorcée and one single. You swallowed this insult with such equanimity. You must have a *ko'ach* to give a *berachah*. Please bless me that I and my sisters should find our *zivugim* very soon."

My principal blessed me warmly, and I left her feeling

strangely uplifted, considering that I had observed something so ugly mere minutes before.

One week after this incident, my older sister got engaged. Two weeks later I, too, was an ecstatic *kallah*.

(Heard from the girl involved)

When the Anger Isn't Yours

*E*VEN WHEN YOU use all of the strategies you've explored to keep the peace or restore it, you're not always able to succeed. Sometimes the other person is the one who is clinging to anger, even though you truly have done nothing to deserve it. When this is the case, there is still one more remedy to try: you can try to erase all feelings of resentment toward that person and fill your heart with respect and love for him.

"*Kamayim hapanim lapanim kein leiv ha'adam la'adam* — As water reflects a face back to a face, so one's heart is reflected back to him by another" (*Mishlei* 27:19). The other person's heart will spontaneously reflect the love and admiration you show him. The waves of love will radiate directly from your heart into his heart, and his feelings of anger will melt away. Think about it: isn't it difficult to stay angry at someone who thinks well of you?

When all is said and done, we can't control how other people feel about us, speak to us, or treat us. But if we accept it all as the will of Hashem and assure ourselves that it is all for our benefit, we will be able to control our own reactions. We will be able to refine our souls, turn insult into blessing, and see with ever-increasing clarity the workings of Hashem in our lives.

Chapter 11
Emunah and Parnassah

HAKADOSH BARUCH HU has promised to sustain every single human being, beast, bird, and insect that He created. As the *pasuk* (*Tehillim* 145:16) declares, "*Posei'ach es yadecha u'masbia l'chol chai ratzon* — You open Your hand and satisfy the desire of every living being."

No creature is left out of this guarantee. The Talmud teaches, "The newborn boy enters the world with a loaf of bread in his hand" (*Niddah* 31b); in other words, his portion is already prepared for him. Hashem takes personal care of every human being individually, and one person's portion can't detract from another's.

Why, then, does a person work for his livelihood? Hashem promised to take care of him, and his portion is already allotted him. No one else can take it away. So why spend hours working so hard?

The Ramchal explains (*Mesillas Yesharim* Ch. 21, "*Kinyan Ha-Chassidus*") that if not for Adam HaRishon, a person would be able to sit idly and receive his *parnassah*. Before Adam sinned, he had full access to the bounty of Gan Eden. Angels served him gourmet meals on golden platters. But after he sinned, Hashem told him, "*B'zei'as apecha tochal lechem* — By the sweat of your brow you will earn your bread" (*Bereishis* 3:19). The free ride was over.

The Ramchal goes on to explain that this is a "tax" that has to be paid. We are no longer allowed to rely totally on Hashem to do miracles for us. A person must do his part. This part is called *hishtadlus*.

But we must be absolutely aware that it is not our *hishtadlus* that brings us our income. The money we earn is determined each year on Rosh Hashanah (*Beitzah* 16a).

The exception is money that a person spends on *melamdim* for his children and expenses for Shabbos and Yom Tov. That is all paid back to him above and beyond the *cheshbon* of Rosh Hashanah. Besides these expenses, he will not receive a cent more than what was decided for him on Rosh Hashanah. No added *hishtadlus* whatsoever will bring him more money.

Imagine a huge water tank with a single tap. Irritated that it takes so long for the water to come out, a person takes another tap and inserts it into the tank so that more water will emerge. It might seem as if there is suddenly a bigger water supply, but the second tap doesn't create more water in the tank. In the end, the person will only have access to the amount that is there. Likewise, working harder won't bring in extra income, although it may appear to do so.

Rabbi Shalom Schwadron would compare a person doing *hishtadlus* to a child sitting next to the bus driver. The driver puts a fake steering wheel in front of the child and the child spins it around, certain that he is driving the bus. Like that child, we sit in the driver's seat, and we think we are driving.

"Tax" Advice

TO AVOID BEING thrown off course by the requirements we each have for a *parnassah*, we can keep the three points below in the forefront of our minds:

1. *Hishtadlus* is an obligation.
2. It's not the *hishtadlus* that brings us our *parnassah*. Rather, *hishtadlus* is like a tax we must pay before we can access our portion.
3. Extra *hishtadlus* won't bring any extra income.

Now we must learn how to apply those points. How much *hishtadlus* should a person do? If he does less than necessary, he will lose out. Hashem won't perform miracles for him, and he will lack funds. If he does more than necessary, he is wasting time and energy, since he won't earn one cent more than he is supposed to. Even if he manages to earn more, his increased salary will be spent on unpredictable expenses that he would not have incurred had he done the correct amount of *hishtadlus*. So what is the correct measure?

People try to reduce their taxes to the minimum. No one voluntarily goes to the tax authorities and offers to pay extra. Likewise, a person should do the minimum *hishtadlus*. Every person has a different minimum, depending on his level of *emunah*.

Let us take a look at the minimum of several tzaddikim in the following stories:

Zusha Is Hungry

Every morning, after Reb Zusha of Anipoli had recited his prayers and completed his customary morning regimen of Torah study, he would lift his eyes heavenward and say with complete faith and trust, "Ribono shel Olam, Zusha is hungry!"

On cue, the *gabbai* of the *beis midrash* would serve him a simple breakfast with which Zusha would satiate his hunger.

One day, the *gabbai* decided to go on strike. He felt personally affronted that Reb Zusha always addressed the Ribono shel Olam when it was he, the *gabbai*, who was bringing his meal. In a fit of irritation, he thought, *Tomorrow I will not serve Reb Zusha his breakfast. Let him wait for the Ribono shel Olam Himself to serve him if that's the way he feels about my faithful service!*

The next morning, as Reb Zusha was taking his daily walk to the *beis midrash*, he turned onto a narrow path, where a distinguished Jew was coming from the opposite direction. Absorbed in his holy thoughts, Reb Zusha didn't notice the important personage, and the two collided. The Jew in turn did not realize that he had bumped into the esteemed Reb Zusha, and he rudely reprimanded him for not paying adequate attention while walking. Reb Zusha, in his humble manner, apologized and continued on his way.

It was then that the Jew realized whom he had just chastised. Greatly mortified, he continued on his way home and asked his wife to prepare a lavish breakfast tray, which he took to the *beis midrash* to present to the rabbi as a form of atonement.

Meanwhile, Reb Zusha finished his prayers and morning-study regimen. As was his custom, he lifted his eyes heavenward and said, "Ribono shel Olam, Zusha is hungry!"

The *gabbai* who was wont to step forth at this time, breakfast tray in hand, stood motionless. *Let Reb Zusha see who is the one who makes sure he doesn't go hungry,* he thought cynically.

Just then, the door opened, and a dignified, well-dressed Jew walked in and presented the rabbi with a royally prepared breakfast tray, along with sincere words of apology. Reb Zusha accepted the tray and the accompanying apology, completely unruffled by the unlikely turn of events. He then proceeded to eat his breakfast as if nothing unforeseen had happened. After all, he had requested something of Hashem, and Hashem had not failed him, just as He had never failed him before.

The Wagon Driver's Decision

All was quiet in the large shul in Tzefas as the assembled eagerly anticipated the Alshich's *derashah*. The topic was *bitachon*.

"One who has complete trust in Hashem need not make any effort to earn a *parnassah*," the holy Alshich said with fiery intensity. "He may just sit in the *beis midrash*, absorbed in learning Torah, and Hashem will supply him with all his monetary needs."

The audience sat spellbound. Moshe, the wagon driver, took those words particularly to heart. *From now on, I will fulfill my lifelong yearning,* he thought. *I will abandon my wagon's reins forever and take up Torah study in the beis midrash. I am fully confident that Hashem will provide me with all my needs.*

Moshe resolutely kept his promise. He sold his horse and wagon, and from that day on, he sat in the *beis midrash*, reveling in the delight of studying Hashem's holy words. Although the cash from the sale was slowly diminishing, never once did worry about *parnassah* gnaw at him.

His family members trusted their husband and father. He had been their breadwinner up until now, and if he assured them with such certainty that Hashem would provide, then undoubtedly He would.

The days wore on, and the cupboards gradually emptied of food. The test was becoming tough, but the pious wagon driver continued learning, while assuring his family that they would soon witness how Hashem would help them.

Meanwhile, the non-Jew who had purchased Moshe's horse and cart was busy at work digging ditches and quarries. One day, as he burrowed, he came across earth as hard as rock. Upon investigation, he delightedly uncovered a massive chest full of gold, diamonds, and pearls buried deep in the ground. He loaded the treasure on his wagon, but suddenly the pile of rocks beside him gave way and toppled right on his head, killing him in an instant.

The horse soon grew restless and trotted back to town, pulling the wagon behind it. It was tired and hungry, and with no one to take care of the animal, it took the route most familiar to it. Eventually, it arrived, with the treasure chest on its wagon, at the home of its beloved former owner.

The children cried out in alarm when they noticed the horse approaching. Then, curiously, they opened the box in the wagon and discovered hundreds of gleaming gold coins and precious stones. There was enough to sustain the family for more than a lifetime!

The wagon driver was completely unsurprised with this turn of events. After all, he had known all along that Hashem would provide for them. Not so his fellow townspeople. Several of them approached the Alshich HaKadosh and asked him, "Why is it that when we tried to abandon all our monetary concerns and dedicate our days to Torah, we were eventually driven to seek a *parnassah* to feed our wives and children? How come Hashem came to the aid of this wagon driver through this astonishing occurrence, and not to ours?"

The Alshich explained, "Only those who trust Hashem

with a complete, simple, unquestioning faith are worthy of seeing Hashem's hand provide for them so openly. And only the wagon driver has that complete, unquestioning belief."

Who Deserves Mahn?

The Lelover Rebbe, Rabbi Dovid Biderman, once related a story of a Jew who resolved never to depend on another human being for assistance, since he wanted to strengthen his *bitachon* in Hashem.

For a while, the man kept his resolution. But one day, while walking in the street, he collapsed on the ground, weak from hunger. Barely conscious, he heard the wheels of a carriage drawing near from a distance. As it drew closer, he saw two *mechutanim* sitting in the carriage, merrily drinking *l'chaim* over a bottle of wine for the *shidduch* they had just concluded between their two children.

In his weak and vulnerable state, the man was afraid he would not survive much longer if he persisted in refusing to accept assistance. He gave a feeble cough to attract the travelers' attention. Indeed, the men noticed the hapless person on the wayside, and they helped him up on the carriage, where they served him food and drink and revived him.

Reb Dovid of Lelov commented, "What a shame! Had he refrained from coughing, demonstrating total dependence on his Creator, he would have been given *mahn* from Heaven, since Hashem had sent that wagon and its occupants just to test his faith."

The Golden Coin

The Admor of Ozorov, in his sefer *Be'er Moshe* (*Beshalach*), relates the following story, which he heard from his grandfather, Reb Aryeh Leibish of Ozorov:

Once, when Reb Menachem Mendel of Riminov went to Lizhensk to visit the Noam Elimelech, he noticed a gold coin lying on the road. He was about to pick it up when he stopped himself and said, *If Hashem wants me to have a gold coin, He can put it in my pocket. I don't need to stoop to pick it up.* With that thought, he continued on his way.

Later on, another person, also on his way to Lizhensk, passed that very same spot, noticed the gold coin, and pocketed it. When he arrived in Lizhensk, he encountered Reb Menachem Mendel of Riminov in the *beis midrash* and handed him the gold coin, saying, "I don't need this. Please do me the honor and accept it as a gift."

Reb Menachem Mendel marveled at this *hashgachah* and said, "If something is destined from Above, one need not do a single action for it to come about."

Reb Aryeh Leibish of Ozorov commented on this story, "If a regular person would have refrained from picking up the coin, he would have been a fool! One must certainly invest effort in order to acquire material needs. But for a person of the stature of Reb Menachem Mendel of Riminov, who was on an extraordinarily high level of *emunah*, it was a praiseworthy thing to do."

What Is My Level?

THE OBVIOUS QUESTION arises: How can a person define his level of *emunah* to know how to act in a manner that is praiseworthy and not foolish?

To Invest — or Not to Invest?

Mrs. Klein* merited marrying a prestigious *talmid chacham* who devoted his entire day to learning Torah. They lived on the income of an investment made for them when they married.

An additional sum of money was set aside for marrying off their children. Rabbi Klein used this money to lend out to people on a short-time basis. Mrs. Klein was bothered by this. She reasoned that they could invest this sum, and the dividends would multiply and ease things for them when they would start to make *shidduchim*.

Her pious husband explained to her that as soon as he would turn his mind to investments, it would take him out of learning and harm his growth in Torah. He assured her that Hashem would take care of marrying off all their children, and it wasn't worth his while to be occupied with this worry at the moment.

Mrs. Klein was proud to have the *zechus* to be the wife of such a devoted *talmid chacham*, but the question still bothered her. How could they know if this was really the right thing to do? Perhaps her husband could spend a few hours during *bein hasedarim* to inquire about how to best invest the money and it should not occupy him after that. Surely in the future, the burden of finding major funds to marry off a large family would disturb him more.

Who is right? We'll talk about that a little bit later.

Defining the fine line between *hishtadlus* and *bitachon* is very tricky!

Rabbi Eliyahu Eliezer Dessler sheds light on this troublesome issue:

A person should do the minimum *hishtadlus*, and Hashem will provide for him the identical sum he would have earned if he had worked very hard. But how can a person calculate how much is expected of him? How can he know where he is standing on the rungs of *bitachon* in order to determine how much of his burden he may throw off?

(*Michtav MeEliyahu*, Vol. 1, *Bitachon V'Hishtadlus*, pp. 188–189)

He explains the extent of a person's *hishtadlus* in three words. He should do as much *hishtadlus* as necessary so that he does not come to be "*toheh al harishonos*," to regret his prior actions.

The Winning Ticket

Rabbi Yosef Chaim Sonnenfeld lived a life of dire poverty. One night he had a dream where he saw the winning ticket of the upcoming lottery. The next day he remembered his dream vividly, including the winning number. He knew that this was a heavenly revelation, and he could go out and buy the ticket that day and it would put an end to his poverty for the rest of his life.

He imagined the happiness on his wife's face when he would come home with the bulging envelope. He joyously pictured himself being able to sit and learn day and night, without having to take responsibility at all to sustain his family.

But then he reminisced about the blissful feelings of *deveikus* he would feel when he entered the chamber of the King of kings to personally request Him to provide sustenance. Hashem never disappointed him. He would witness with his own eyes how He miraculously sent him his needs. The wonderful feeling of being totally dependent on his Father and experiencing daily how He cared for him — should he give all that up? No! What sort of life would it be to distance himself from his Father and not be able to feel daily His strong and loving arm around his shoulders?

Then and there he decided to refrain from going out to buy the ticket.

The next day the winning number was publicized. It was the exact number Reb Yosef Chaim had seen in his dream! The magnificent sum of money was handed to someone else. Did Reb Yosef Chaim feel even a morsel of regret? Absolutely not.

This is what a person must bear in mind when he makes his decision. He has to honestly and logically assess how he will react in the future if he lacks funds. If he is one hundred percent sure that he and his family will withstand the financial pressure in the future and not regret their earlier decision to refrain from spending time working, then he is truly on the correct level of *bitachon* and the measure of *hishtadlus* he is performing is correct for him. Hashem will help him and he will be successful.

Going back to our earlier story: If Rabbi Klein is sure that he wants to devote his time solely to learning at this stage in life, and he will not be mortified if he should need to go out to solicit major funds in the future, it is extremely praiseworthy for him to follow that path. But if he realizes that he will probably regret not making the investment he could have made, this measure of *hishtadlus* is required of him.

Why is regret to be so assiduously avoided? The reason is that regret is a powerful force for both the positive and the negative. For example, when a person does *teshuvah* with love, HaKadosh Baruch Hu transforms his sins done deliberately into *zechuyos* (*Yoma* 86b). This seemingly magical transformation happens because *teshuvah* causes the person to regret his sins to the core of his soul. He is full of remorse to the extent that he will never, *ever* do it again. Because the sins brought him to this higher level, they become merits.

The same applies when a person does a mitzvah and then regrets it. For example, he lends an item, and his friend damages it. He then declares, "I am *never* going to lend out my things again!" The mitzvah he did is spoiled by his regret.

This is the danger Rabbi Dessler refers to when he says that a person must take care not to come to regret his prior decision. It is with this principle in mind that a person should make an honest and logical calculation when working out where he is standing on the rungs of *bitachon*. After honest consideration, he will be able to determine the precise degree of *hishtadlus* he needs to do at the moment. As time passes, he can always reassess his position and change his mind without regretting what he achieved in the past.

Parnassah Without Worry

*O*NE OF THE heaviest burdens that seems to come with the obligation of earning a *parnassah* is the worry that accompanies the work. People in business fret ceaselessly about sales, customers, employees, the cost of merchandise, and the state of the market. People who work for others live in fear of displeasing the boss or being outshone by a coworker. Yet none of this is part of *hishtadlus*. This *mashal* from the Chafetz Chaim describes the futility of carrying these unnecessary burdens.

Yankel's Wagon: A Mashal

Yankel was riding his horse-drawn wagon when he noticed his friend Yossel trudging down the street with two heavy sacks on his back. "Yossel, climb aboard," he called, stopping the wagon. Yossel accepted the offer gratefully.

Several minutes later Yankel turned around and was surprised to see Yossel sitting bent over, with the two large sacks still strapped to his back. "Why don't you remove those bags?" he asked.

"Oh, Yankel, it's kind enough of you to take me," came the reply. "I don't want to burden you with carrying my bags, too."

The person who walks around with a heavy heart and aching shoulders from the burden of worrying about *parnassah* is like that foolish person who rides in the wagon and holds his bags on his shoulders. He doesn't realize that the weight of his *parnassah* is already being borne by the Ribono shel Olam.

Even though a person has an obligation to pay his minimum "tax," he has no obligation to take upon himself the worry, the pressure, or the responsibility for the results of his effort. He has to do his job, but he is not in charge. Therefore, he can remove the *entire* burden from his shoulders and leave all the worry to the Ribono shel Olam. Hashem is already carrying him, along with his burden. This is how the Gemara (*Megillah* 18a) explains the *pasuk*, "*Hashleich al Hashem yehavcha v'hu yechalkelecha* — Cast your burden upon Hashem and He will sustain you" (*Tehillim* 55:23). This applies to any *pekel*, any challenge Hashem has given him.

Sometimes we forget this as we look at our situation and plan our future. We make our assessments as if we have no one else to count on.

But we do!

Depending on Him for Everything

A *bachur* in the yeshivah of Kfar Chassidim approached his *mashgiach*, Rabbi Eliyahu Lopian, and informed him that he would like to leave the yeshivah and learn to be an accountant.

"Do you really want to give up learning Torah?" Reb Elya asked him.

"No, I do regret leaving yeshivah, but I feel it is my responsibility to be able to support my wife and children in the future."

"Who will guarantee that you will get married?" Reb Elya asked him.

"I believe that Hashem will send me my *zivug hagun*," he replied.

"And what makes you think that you will have children?"

The *bachur* was taken aback by the question. "Rebbe, I believe that I will get married and the Ribono shel Olam will grant me children."

"If you believe that Hashem will find you a suitable *shidduch*," Reb Elya replied, "and He will grant you healthy children, then you don't need to leave yeshivah now in order to learn a profession. You should believe that He will provide you with a livelihood in the future, too. That is not harder for Him than marrying you off and giving you children."

Working Too Hard

*I*F WE'RE DOING our *hishtadlus*, then certainly we should do it to the best of our ability. We should develop good skills or sell good merchandise, and give those we serve their money's worth. But it's easy to fall into the trap of working harder, at the expense of higher priorities, with the belief that we will be able to increase our income. This is a fallacy, which the holy Ruzhiner describes with a *mashal*:

Working for His Meal: A Mashal

A poor traveler once arrived in town and inquired where he could get a bite to eat at no cost.

"You see the apartment building over there, on the corner of that street?" The passerby pointed. "A very generous man lives there on the second floor. You can get fresh, delicious food from him all day, for free."

His mouth watering in anticipation, the hungry traveler trudged down the street and up the stairs, and knocked on the door. "Can I please get a free meal?" he asked the owner.

"Of course," the man said. "But in order to earn it, you first have to wash the floors of my house."

The traveler was taken aback, but as he didn't have much choice, he wearily took the cleaning supplies and began mopping the floor. Two long hours and a shiny floor later, the owner approached him grinning. "Your meal is waiting for you in the adjacent apartment."

The exhausted man dragged himself next door. Tantalizing aromas came out of the large dining room, where many people were eating to their hearts' content. Sitting down, he turned to the man next to him and asked him what work he'd done in order to get the free meal. His neighbor looked at him in surprise. "What do you mean? In this house, everyone gets food for nothing!"

That's when the traveler realized that the neighbor had tricked him. He could have received a free dinner without working so hard.

How many times does the *yetzer hara* entice us to invest more time in order to make some money? "Just skip this one Torah *shiur* or this one *tefillah b'tzibbur*," he whispers, "so that you clinch that deal." Or he'll persuade a woman, "Stay at work a bit longer in the afternoon. You need that extra money. The children will be fine alone at home."

But he is a swindler! It won't make a difference anyway, as Hashem has already decided on Rosh Hashanah how much money you are going to make this year. It's a waste of our most precious commodity — quality time — to work too hard for no greater return.

We are also advised by the *Chovos HaLevavos* to look for an occupation that suits our personality and talents. A person is not required, as part of his *hishtadlus*, to do a job that he finds terribly unpleasant. Hashem can send him a livelihood he will enjoy and even ensure that he works during the hours that are best for him.

Just What You Needed

ASHEM DOES NOT just provide for us. He provides for us in exactly the form and manner we require. We can count on Him to fulfill our every need, whether we are working for a living or fully casting our burden of *parnassah* on Him. One example of Hashem's made-to-order kindness can be found in the Gemara:

Rava, the *rosh yeshivah* in Bavel, loved helping fellow Jews, and he frequently hosted guests who sought a comfortable place to eat and sleep. One day, a respectable Jew passed by his home. He was obviously needy, although his mannerisms and mode of dress indicated that he had once been wealthy. He shamefacedly admitted his financial decline and said that now he did not even have money to buy food.

Rava asked him what he would like to eat and he said, "I have been accustomed to dine on roast chicken and aged, sweet wine."

Rava was taken aback. "Are you not embarrassed to ask for the finest and most expensive gourmet meal?"

The Jew answered, "I am confident that Hashem will provide me with the meals that I have been used to. He takes care of me, and if I must accept charity, then He will send me what I require in this manner, because also the charity comes directly from Him."

While they spoke, Rava's sister walked in unexpectedly, holding a tray laden with roast chicken and aged, sweet wine. She had not been to visit him for thirteen years, and at this precise moment she decided to come on a surprise visit with a ready meal for her distinguished brother.

Rava immediately honored his guest with the meal and marveled, along with his sister, at Hashem's clear message that He provides for every person according to his desires and needs.

(*Kesubos* 67b)

Here is a contemporary example:

The Exact Sum

The holy Reb Mordechai, the Admor of Zhvil, learned Torah in the Chayei Olam *beis midrash* in Yerushalayim along with other notable *talmidei chachamim*. Unfortunately, the stipend that the members of this *kollel* received was barely enough to cover the cost of bread and water. When Reb Mordechai's daughter became engaged to the Shomrei Emunim Rebbe, he didn't have the money to cover the wedding expenses.

As the date of the wedding drew near, Reb Mordechai's wife pleaded with her husband to try his best to raise the money needed, because it was impossible to prepare for the wedding as matters stood.

Reb Mordechai approached the treasurer of the *kollel* and requested a partial list of some of its wealthy overseas supporters with the hope that some of them would be glad to have a share in *hachnasas kallah*. The treasurer feared that whatever the donors would give to Reb Mordechai would be deducted from their donation to the *kollel*. However, because of Reb Mordechai's standing, he also didn't want to refuse him outright. He therefore gave him a list of former philanthropists who had been generous donors in the past, but were no longer wealthy.

When Reb Mordechai arrived home, it took his smart *rebbetzin* one glance at the list to grasp that the donors on the list were no longer able to donate and would certainly not be the answer to their predicament.

"There is no way that this list can help us," she told her husband.

Reb Mordechai wasn't moved by her pessimistic predications. "It's not up to me to finish the job. I simply have to do my *hishtadlus*, and with that I've discharged my obligation to raise the money. What difference does it make if I turn to people who were rich in the past or people who are rich now?"

"If all that you are going to do is some minor *hishtadlus*," his wife replied, "because you are prepared to rely totally on Hashem's bounty, then why make the effort to appeal to every name on the list? Choose one name and send a letter of appeal only to him. That is also sufficient to fulfill your obligation."

Reb Mordechai was pleased with her suggestion. "I'll do just that," he agreed.

He sat down and wrote a letter to the first man on the list, explaining that he was about to marry off his daughter, and he detailed his expenses, up to and including the cost of the wedding feast. In total, he needed twenty-five thousand dollars. He signed his name, Mordechai son of the holy Reb Gedaliah Moshe, *zt"l*, and sent the letter off to America.

As the date of the wedding approached, a messenger arrived from the post office and handed Reb Mordechai a check for exactly twenty-five thousand dollars from the philanthropist Reb Mordechai had turned to. The relief in Reb Mordechai's home was palpable. The next day, Reb Mordechai approached the treasurer of the *kollel* in his office and thanked him from the bottom of his heart for his help.

"Who on earth gave you such a generous sum?" the astounded treasurer stammered.

As soon as Reb Mordechai told him what had happened, the treasurer sent the *askanim* of Chayei Olam in America over to the home of the philanthropist. "If you've regained your former wealth," they asked, "why haven't we heard from you?"

The philanthropist hesitated. "I can tell you what happened," he finally said to them, "but only if you promise to keep this absolutely confidential."

Of course they were anxious to know the story, and immediately agreed to the request.

"Let me tell you what happened," the man began. "I have not regained my lost wealth. But I too, have a daughter who is about to get married. To our distress, the *kallah* was stricken with an illness. We were in a great dilemma whether or not we were obliged to tell the family of the *chasan*.

"I approached Rabbi Moshe Feinstein and explained in detail my daughter's situation. He told us that in this case we should not reveal anything. However, he advised us to earmark all the money that we had saved until then for the mitzvah of *hachnasas kallah*. He blessed us that in this merit, we, too, would be able to bring our daughter to the *chuppah* in health and happiness.

"When we returned home from Rabbi Feinstein, we were astounded to find a letter from the son of the Zhviller Rebbe in Eretz Yisrael waiting for us, and in it was a plea for *hachnasas kallah*! All our savings amounted to twenty-five thousand dollars — the exact sum that Reb Mordechai was requesting. We immediately sent the money."

This is the incredible power of *emunah peshutah*.

Everyday Heroes

*W*E MAY THINK that such miracles only occur to tzaddikim and leaders of our generation. This is not true at all. There are hundreds of *avreichim* today sitting and learning, not knowing how they will cover unexpected costs or marry off their children. Nevertheless, they continue to sit and learn all day with solid *bitachon*, and they witness miracles. In the following story of one *ba'al bitachon*, *hishtadlus* takes an unexpected form:

Half-hour Hishtadlus

A young *avreich*, Chaim Levine,* had managed to buy a small apartment in Eretz Yisrael a few years after he was married. Since he was a full-time member of a *kollel*, the couple's means were limited, but their home was full of joy. Both husband and wife were anxious to do all they could so that Chaim could devote as much time as possible to learning Torah. Unlike most other members of his *kollel*, Chaim didn't go home for lunch or supper; instead, he remained in the *beis midrash* to learn Torah until 10 p.m. five days a week.

One night, when he arrived back home, his wife showed him a letter from the tax authorities. Apparently, when they had bought their apartment a few years previously, they had neglected to pay the taxes due on the purchase. Over the years, the interest on the amount, plus a fine, had added a considerable sum to their debt, which now totaled twenty thousand shekels. The government was demanding payment in full; otherwise, their home would be put up for sale to cover their debt.

Their first thought was that Chaim would have to take a tutoring job in the evenings instead of continuing to learn with his evening *chavrusa*, but they weren't sure this was the right course of action. They had no savings put away. Mrs. Levine was already working until noontime, when she returned home to care for her children.

Clearly they needed to make more of a *hishtadlus*, but what form should it take? Chaim thought about it overnight. The next day, he shared an idea with his wife. If she agreed, he would add another half-hour to his learning each evening. He explained to her that for a person who takes upon himself the yoke of learning Torah, Hashem takes away the yoke of *parnassah*. He felt that in the *zechus* of increasing his Torah study with *mesirus nefesh*, the problem would be sorted out. He quoted Chazal's statement, "All who toil in Torah will be successful with their property" (*Avodah Zarah* 19b).

Mrs. Levine was quite surprised but proud of her husband, and she was willing to go along with the idea. Chaim started coming home for supper at 10:30 instead of 10 o'clock.

Two days later, at 10:15 in the evening, Chaim was sitting in the *beis midrash* when an older man spotted him and exclaimed, "I've been looking for you for weeks now. At last I've found you! A while ago, I mentioned to you that I needed to rent a large apartment. I was looking for eight rooms. You said you know of a large place that is for rent, but then I couldn't find you to get the address. Do you still have the phone number of the owner?"

"Yes," Chaim answered, and he took out a pen. He wrote a few lines on a scrap of paper and handed it to the man.

"Thank you. If I take the apartment, I'll be happy to pay you the same rate that I would pay a professional real-estate agent."

Chaim wished him success and went back to his Gemara.

A week later, the same gentleman appeared in the *beis midrash* where Chaim was learning. "I went to see the apartment you told me about," he said. "It's exactly what we were looking for. In fact, we liked it so much that last night we signed a contract to buy it. At the time, it occurred to me that we have to thank you for letting us know about it in the first place. I feel that I owe you the same fee as I would have given an agent."

With that, he drew a check out of his wallet and handed it to a startled Chaim. There, in black on white, were the words "twenty thousand shekels" — the exact amount he needed to pay the tax authorities.

Chaim approached Rabbi Yitzchok Zilberstein to ask if the money was rightfully his. He also wanted to know how long he should continue with his extra half-hour's study session.

Rabbi Zilberstein assured him that he should take the money. He told him to continue with his *seder* until the end of the *zeman*.

(*Kol B'Ramah*, Vol. 298, Cheshvan 5775)

The Danger of Looking Down

THE KEY TO meriting this kind of extraordinary salvation, as Rabbi Dessler tells us, is to understand what level of *hishtadlus* is appropriate for us. Our *emunah* skills must be strong enough to fearlessly balance on the edge of the cliff. The experienced mountain climber knows that he must not look down. If he lets fear overwhelm him, he risks falling. Likewise, someone scaling the peaks of *emunah* must have the strength and courage to climb fearlessly. Otherwise, he risks a terrible fall, and he is far better off seeking a path on which he feels more secure.

The following story of Rabbi Yisrael Salanter illustrates the difference between surefooted *bitachon* and a shaky, premature venture:

The Lottery Ticket

Rabbi Yisrael Salanter delivered a powerful address on *parnassah* and *bitachon*. Shmelke, who was greatly moved by the speech, went over to Reb Yisrael and asked, "Rebbe, is it true that I can just buy a lottery ticket and trust that Hashem will send me *parnassah* by letting me win the prize?"

"True," replied Reb Yisrael with a nod. "If you really believe that your *parnassah* is from Hashem, buying a lottery ticket can be sufficient *hishtadlus*."

The next morning, Shmelke bought a ticket for the raffle scheduled for two weeks hence. He quit his job and went to the *beis midrash* to learn.

During the next two weeks, money was scarce, but Shmelke was full of hope. The day before the lottery, after Minchah, he noticed Rabbi Yisrael Salanter leaving the shul and he approached him.

"Rebbe," he exclaimed, "I did as you said. I put my *bitachon* in Hashem, gave up my job, and bought a ticket for the lottery. Tomorrow I'm going to win 40,000 rubles!"

"Really!" Reb Yisrael replied. "You know, I happen to have a substantial sum of money with me. Would you consider selling me your ticket for ten thousand rubles, right here and now?"

Shmelke paused for a second, then answered, "If the Rav would like to buy the ticket for 10,000 rubles, I would readily agree."

"If so," Reb Yisrael said gently, "then you do not really have sincere *bitachon*! A person who is absolutely certain that his ticket will win 40,000 rubles tomorrow would not agree to sell that same ticket for a quarter of its value today.

"That being the case, it would be best for you to go back to earning an honest livelihood while setting aside times to study Torah."

Another aspect of "looking down" is engaging in useless *hishtad-lus*, either by going overboard on a reasonable effort, or engaging in a futile effort out of desperation. In either case, the person is peering down into the abyss and acting out of fear of falling in. He doesn't trust that Hashem is supporting him and guiding his footsteps, and thus he slips.

This desperate thinking can affect even those whose *emunah* is strong. None other than Yosef HaTzaddik provides the Torah's primary example of too much *hishtadlus*.

Rabbi Yitzchak Dov Koppelman, the *rosh yeshivah* of Lucerne, once related in the name of Rabbi Shimon Shkop that Yosef's error was in asking Pharaoh's chief butler — not once, but twice — to advocate for him before he was released from the dungeon. "A person must do *hishtadlus*, but no more than the minimum," Rabbi Koppelman explained. Yosef was punished not only for the extra mention, but for the first mention as well, adding two years to his prison term.

Rabbi Dessler goes further, stating that Yosef did not only go overboard, but he tried an entirely desperate and useless strategy. He explains that the Egyptians were an ungrateful people, and Yosef could not have had any expectation that the chief butler would remember him. Therefore, his effort showed a lack of *emunah* — a perspective that said, "Maybe this man can help me. It's worth a try!" He counted on a person — even an extremely unworthy person — instead of relying on Hashem.

Reb Pinchas of Koritz (*Imrei Pinchas*) makes a remarkable observation regarding the Ohr HaChaim's commentary on the verse "*Vayehi mikeitz shenasayim yamim u'Pharaoh choleim* — It happened at the end of two years to the day; Pharaoh was dreaming" (*Bereishis* 41:1).

The Ohr HaChaim asks why the word *choleim*, "dream," is written in the Hebrew present tense, literally meaning "he was dreaming." He reveals that Pharaoh dreamed the same dream for two entire years, and every morning he forgot his dream. Only after two years did he vividly remember the entire dream.

This, Reb Pinchas says, indicates that Hashem had already prepared Yosef's salvation two years earlier. However, He waited for Yosef to reach his highest level *of bitachon* before he allowed Pharaoh to remember the dream and set Yosef's salvation in motion.

What does this mean to us in our effort to find the balance between *hishtadlus* and *bitachon* in our lives? It means that we must start with the premise that Hashem can do anything, and that He has even prepared the method to help us. Our major *hishtadlus* is to work incessantly on building our trust in Him so that we may merit seeing the salvation He has waiting for us.

Reducing Stress

IN MANY HOMES, a lack of *parnassah* becomes a constant source of stress. However, *bitachon* places the situation in an entirely different perspective that greatly reduces these painful emotional reactions.

A Fortune Gained and Lost

Reb Berel Cohen was a *chassidishe* Jew who lives in Kiryat Sanz, Netanya. One day, he bought a lottery ticket in a local draw. Several days later, he received the most exciting call of his life. He'd won a huge sum of money! For the Cohens, this was marvelous news. They were a family of very limited means and struggled hard to put bread on the table. Whereas some of Reb Berel's friends found it hard to "finish the month," Reb Berel often didn't know how to start it.

Husband and wife spent many wonderful hours planning how to use their winnings. Part of it would be allotted to paying off their debts; some of the money would be used for marrying off their children, and they would invest the rest and live off the profits. That night, every member of the Cohen family went to sleep dreaming of a rosy future.

A day after Reb Berel collected his money, he got another phone call, but what a different one this time!

"We are terribly sorry to be the bearer of bad news," the

caller informed him, "but there was unfortunately a mix-up in the raffle. You are not the winner of the money. The number after yours was the winning number, but we mistakenly paired it up with your phone number."

The person on the line asked Reb Berel to please return the money at once, as the real winner was demanding his prize.

The family was devastated. All their plans for the future, their beautiful castles in the air, were gone in an instant. Many heated discussions took place about how such a thing could have happened, about the unfairness of it all and whether they were even required to return the money. The only one who remained completely unruffled was Reb Berel himself. He calmly took the money, made his way back to the lottery office, and handed it over without a word of complaint.

No one could understand him.

"Aren't you upset, Tatty?" his children asked. "After all the grand plans we made, we're left with nothing! And if it clearly wasn't *bashert* for us to own that money, why did Hashem put us through all this?"

Reb Berel's answer was breathtaking.

"Sometimes there's a *gezeirah* from Heaven that a certain person has to leave this world. Occasionally, Hashem will cause this man to lose his entire fortune instead, because Chazal tell us that 'ani chashuv k'meis — a poor person is considered as dead' (*Nedarim* 64b).

"Imagine if it were destined for me to die. I am already poor, so there is no fortune to withdraw. There would be no way to retract the decree. So what did Hashem, in His tremendous kindness, do? He made me rich for a short while and then He took the money back. I went from prosperous to penniless. Now that I lost all my money, I can remain alive. So instead of being disappointed and upset, we should really all be dancing in *simchah*. I should really make a *seudas hoda'ah* to thank Hashem!"

(Be'er HaParashah, Terumah)

Rabbi Hershel Gross, former principal of Talmud Torah Belz in Tel Aviv, relates the following extraordinary episode:

The Happy Ending?

It was a week before Pesach. All over the world, Jewish housewives were busy getting their homes ready for the upcoming Yom Tov.

In the Talmud Torah of Belz in Tel Aviv, the principal was surprised to see one of the rebbis leave his classroom of boys in the middle of a lesson. The rebbi asked him if he could use the office telephone to make an urgent phone call. The principal knew that this rebbi was a very dedicated educator who was careful not to waste a moment's time. He never asked to make phone calls. Obviously this was something important. The principal readily granted permission.

After a short call, the rebbi stopped by once more to say he was returning to his classroom but needed to use the phone again in ten minutes. Indeed, a quarter of an hour later, after he finished his lesson, he was back. The second phone call ended quickly, after which the rebbi went into the principal's room to explain.

"For many years, I've been saving money. Every month, I take off a small amount of my wages and set it aside to help me marry off my children when the time comes. I put the money in the pocket of an old suit I don't wear anymore. No one knew of this hiding place, not even my wife. This morning, I suddenly remembered that she mentioned she'd be Pesach cleaning the *boidem* today, where the suit is stowed away. I asked to phone home because I wanted to warn her not to throw away the suit.

"To my dismay, she told me she'd already thrown the suit out into the garbage and had taken the bag to the trash can outside. She immediately ran out to check if it was still there, and I called her back a few minutes later to find out what happened."

"*Nu?*" the principal asked, hoping the story had a happy ending.

"It was too late. The garbage had already been removed with the suit and the four thousand dollars inside."

Four thousand dollars thirty years ago is the equivalent today of a huge sum of money!

"You know," the rebbi went on, "Rabbi Godel Eisner (a renowned and esteemed *mashpia* at Yeshivas Chiddushei HaRim in Tel Aviv) often speaks about *bitachon*. He says it's amazing to see how a *frum* Jew can learn Torah and talk about *bitachon* for years, and yet when he has one *nisayon*, he loses himself. The point of all the learning is to be able to strengthen yourself when the challenge arises.

"It's not easy to swallow the loss of such a sizable sum of money," the rebbi admitted. "But we have a Father in Heaven who knows what He's doing! I trust Him, and know that this is for the best. I refuse to get upset!"

And with that, he grabbed the principal's hands and broke out into a dance.

Kiddush Hashem and Hishtadlus

THOSE WHO SIT and learn with tremendous sacrifice face one type of stress: the test of not knowing how they will cover their expenses. Those who engage in business, a profession, or a job have another type of test that in some ways is even greater, because it is more insidious.

It's so easy for someone who works for a living to come to believe that his effort is what produces his income. Then the temptation to redouble his efforts at the expense of his *avodas Hashem* can become great. His worries multiply as his investments multiply. His honesty and integrity are constantly under siege.

Nevertheless, when such an individual works on his *emunah* and approaches life from that clear perspective, he becomes an exemplar of *kiddush Hashem*. In the story below, we see the far-reaching ripple effects set in motion by one Jew's unshakeable commitment to conducting his business with Hashem as his Chief Executive Officer:

The Dividends of a Deed

Moshe Kaufman owned a flourishing textile factory in Berlin. Originally from Kishenov, Poland, he had come to Germany with his family as a *bachur*. After he married, he opened his own business, which manufactured quilt covers and bed linen. The quality of the work was obvious, but that wasn't the only reason the business was notable. Mr. Kaufman had a reputation for honesty and exemplary business practices that spread far and wide, drawing customers from all over the country.

Herr Belgardt was one such customer. A successful businessman from Upper Silesia, Belgardt purchased linens in bulk and sold them throughout Germany. He and Mr. Kaufman shared a cordial relationship built on trust and mutual goodwill.

World War I hit Europe like an atom bomb, and when the dust finally settled four years later, people hoped to rebuild their shattered lives. It was not to be. Instead of peaceful living, the entire continent suffered the economic blow of the Great Depression, and suddenly people who had been loyal customers for many years found it difficult to make their payments to Mr. Kaufman's firm. That was why he wasn't exactly surprised when Herr Belgardt showed up at the factory one afternoon, a contrite look on his face.

Warmly welcoming him into his office, Mr. Kaufman offered the German a seat and a drink and waited to hear why he had come.

"I have bad news," Herr Belgardt said. "The economy is killing my business. Stores that used to pay me punctually owe me large sums of money. And that's in the cities and towns where people are still buying linen. Many stores have stopped selling these goods entirely. Nobody can afford new linen or quilt covers anymore. Business is dead. That's why

I came here today. I wanted to return the last consignment of merchandise that I purchased, since I don't see any way of repaying you the money that I owe you and I don't want to sink even deeper in debt."

"I am unwilling to accept the merchandise," Mr. Kaufman told the surprised German. "You have always been a loyal customer. I trust you implicitly, and I want you to hold on to everything you took from me until times improve."

"But I don't know when I'll be able to pay you back!"

"You'll pay me back whenever you're able."

Embarrassment and contrition gave way to a look of supreme gratitude.

"I won't forget this, Herr Kaufman."

"I believe you," Mr. Kaufman said.

Belgardt returned home and related the entire story to his three sons. Moved beyond words, Belgardt told his children that if they ever meet a Jew, and certainly if they ever have the opportunity to help the Kaufman family, they should do just that.

One day in September 1938, someone knocked authoritatively on the door of the Kaufman home in Berlin. One of the children peeked out from behind the curtains and almost passed out. The visitor was a tall, blond-haired man clad in the fearful uniform of the feared Nazi police.

They opened the door. One did not ignore a knock on the door by the police. Not if you wanted to stay alive. But to their immense surprise and relief, the police officer introduced himself as Otto Belgardt and told them he was a son of their father's old client.

"Recently I've been promoted to lieutenant of the police department at the Hackescher Markt," he said. This was a precinct located in a neighborhood comprised predominantly of Jews of Polish extraction who had emigrated to Germany not too long before. It was the precinct where Mr. Kaufman lived.

"My father told me what Herr Kaufman did for us fifteen years ago," he said, "and we've never forgotten his goodwill. In fact, that is why I'm here. If you ever need anything from me, don't hesitate to ask. I will do whatever I can for you."

The Kaufman family served the lieutenant coffee and cake and presented him with a beautiful set of down quilts for his family as a token of their appreciation.

Two months later, on a peaceful November afternoon, Otto Belgardt called. This time, they could hear the tension in his voice as he relayed the kind of information that could cost him his life if caught.

"There's going to be a raid on the Jewish community tomorrow morning at six," he said. "Every Polish-born Jewish male over the age of fifteen will be rounded up and sent in cattle cars over the border into Poland."

"What should we do?" Mrs. Kaufman asked the officer frantically.

"Your husband must not be at home when the raid is taking place. Tell him to hide in the hospital, which is not going to be searched."

Mr. Kaufman's first reaction when he heard this shocking piece of news was not to take care of his own safety, but to pick up the phone and begin making a round of emergency phone calls to all seventy Polish-Jewish families living in the area. He relayed the information and advised the terrified listeners where to hide. Many listened to him and followed his advice. Sadly, others didn't want to believe that the Germans would follow through on this plan and chose to remain home.

While Moshe was busy on the phone, his wife rushed their oldest son Jozy (Yosef), who was over fifteen, to the train station. He caught a Poland-bound train that evening which took him away from Germany, to what his mother hoped would be safety. Poland didn't turn out to be any safe haven for the Jews, but Jozy was able to escape to England before the Germans invaded. He was eventually reunited with his family in Gateshead, England.

That evening, Otto Belgardt knocked on the Kaufmans' door dressed in full Nazi regalia. Looking past the hated uniform and concentrating instead on the friendly face, Mrs. Kaufman informed their benefactor that her son had just been dropped off at the station, that her husband was already hiding at the hospital, and that they had followed his orders down to the tiniest detail.

"Don't worry," Belgardt told her. "Everything's going to be just fine."

"When the Nazis come to our home tomorrow," she begged him, "please include yourself in the detail of officers. Things can change for the worse at any time, and it's very important that you yourself come along with the raiding group to make sure that nothing goes wrong."

Otto Belgardt promised to do as she asked.

The next morning the streets outside the Kaufman home were filled with the shouts of "*Heil Hitler!*" as Nazi officers went from door to door searching for Polish Jews. They eventually arrived at the Kaufman home and began banging on the door.

Mrs. Kaufman opened the door. Otto Belgardt stood framed in the doorway, surrounded by Nazi officers. He did not appear friendly. Gone was the smile of yesterday or the politeness he'd shown in his dealings with them. He stood there, a Nazi in every way.

"Where is your husband?" he demanded.

Even though they knew he was pretending to hate them, the family shivered with fear. He was a very good actor, and the hatred emanating from his mouth was unnerving. The Nazis went through the house searching for Mr. Kaufman with no success. As they were leaving, Belgardt whispered to Mrs. Kaufman, "What have you done to me? There are hardly any Jews left in the entire neighborhood! Nobody is home!"

When he arrived home from the hospital, Mr. Kaufman's immediate priority was to obtain the documents necessary to get the family out of Germany. There was no time left to waste. His sons Mendel and Yitzchak Kaufman were sent to London, where the Sassover Rebbe took them into his own home, along with one other young refugee who grew up to become the *av beis din* of Yerushalayim, Rabbi Yitzchok Tuvia Weiss, *shlita*.

Countless families managed to remain intact and avoid an almost certain death sentence because of the phone call they received from the Kaufmans.

The father-in-law of the renowned *posek* Rabbi Pesach Eliyahu Falk of Gateshead, was also saved on that fateful night. Reb Farbish Steinhaus was a young man learning to be a rabbi in the Rabbiner Seminar in Berlin. Mr. Kaufman called up the head of the seminar, Rabbi Yechiel Yaakov Weinberg to warn him to hide any Polish citizens. Farbish was hiding behind the library door when the Nazis marched in and they strode right past without noticing him. He also fled the country to settle in Gateshead, where he established his esteemed family.

The Kaufman family recently decided to find out what happened to the brave Lieutenant Belgardt. They found records detailing events that occurred on the night of Kristallnacht. As Germans went from shul to shul setting fires and filling the skies with the smoke of burning Torah scrolls, Nazis arrived at the Oranienburger Strasse Synagogue — a huge ornamental building — and tried to burn it down. But they were prevented from doing so by Lieutenant Belgardt, who, at risk to his own life, held them off on the pretext that the building should be preserved as a historical site.

In addition, it was reported that Lieutenant Belgardt forged false certificates for many Jews, enabling them to flee Germany before the war broke out. Who knows how many Jews are alive today as a result of one act of *kiddush Hashem*?

A Sign of Emunah

ONE OF THE clearest signs of a person's *emunah* regarding his *parnassah* is in the way he incorporates Shabbos into his life. Does he rush home with moments to spare, taking a chance on *chas v'shalom* missing the *zeman*? Are business worries and plans constantly invading his thoughts on Shabbos? Or does he build a solid brick wall between Shabbos and his weekday concerns, and enter Shabbos as if it's an entirely different world, a world of holiness and spirituality, where money doesn't exist?

Not surprisingly, the same Moshe Kaufman who made a great

kiddush Hashem in his treatment of his customer treated Shabbos with the utmost reverence. His youngest son, Rabbi Chaim Kaufman, who became the *rosh yeshivah* of Tiferes Yaakov in Gateshead, would tell the following story:

Clients Lost and Found

Reb Moshe Kaufman would always close his business on Friday many hours before Shabbos. He liked to come home and have ample time to prepare for Shabbos and welcome in the Shabbos calmly and respectfully. One day, he had already donned his hat and coat and was about to leave the factory, when one of his major customers walked inside.

"I would like to make a large order of quilts," he announced.

Mr. Kaufman kindly requested that he come back after the weekend since he had to leave now. However, the customer informed him that it was urgent, and he could not wait until the following week. He began to inquire regarding the various types and qualities of down quilts, and Mr. Kaufman realized that this would take a long time.

"I am sorry, but I am an observant Jew and I must leave now, since I have to prepare for the holy Shabbos. I will be happy to serve you next week."

The German, a non-Jew, answered angrily, "You know that I am one of your best customers. If you don't have time for me now, then you will lose me for good!"

Mr. Kaufman looked at his watch and saw that there was still several hours before Shabbos was to begin. Should he stay for another half-hour? It was a matter of losing a substantial sum of money. *No, I am going home now,* he decided resolutely. *I will not waive a principle that I have always been careful to keep. Parnassah comes from Hashem. This customer is not the one who supports me. I will surely not lose out!*

He ordered the man to leave and locked the door of his factory amid a hail of angry threats.

That evening, when he welcomed in the Shabbos, he felt

a heavenly spirit descending upon him as never before. He would tell his children that he never experienced a more elevated Shabbos than that one, for which he had been *moser nefesh*.

Several months passed and a new customer arrived, who made a similar order to the one Reb Moshe had lost. Reb Moshe saw distinctly how he had not lost out.

Indeed, the *Chovos HaLevavos* says that one of the advantages of the *ba'al bitachon* is that he never needs to feel dependent on his employer or his customers. Although he certainly must be nice and appreciative to them, he doesn't need to flatter them or exert himself only for the purpose of finding favor in their eyes. He is free to do what is correct even if faced with opposition, since he knows that his income is determined by the Ribono shel Olam alone.

Birkas HaMazon: A Segulah for Parnassah

BIRKAS HAMAZON HAS an obvious, direct connection to the sustenance Hashem grants us. It is an expression of our gratitude, which we recite when we are already satiated, physically feeling the pleasure of the meal we have eaten. A great many sources promise that a person who recites these blessings sincerely will continue to enjoy Hashem's bounty. As the story below illustrates, this is a promise that can save one's life.

Rabbi Meir Shapiro's Secret

Reb Shimon, a regular at the Har Tzvi shul in Yerushalayim, was especially known by neighbors, friends, and fellow shul-goers for the manner in which he recited Birkas HaMazon. His was not a three-minute speedy blessing recited by heart. Instead, he enunciated each word of *bentch-*

ing slowly, with deep concentration, out of a siddur or *bentcher*.

On Succos, when the sounds of singing, *divrei Torah*, and family banter carry through the succah walls, neighbors overheard Reb Shimon's extraordinary enunciation of Birkas HaMazon. His zeal for the mitzvah piqued their curiosity, and they asked him about it. Reb Shimon related his story, a story that had started decades before. This is what he told them:

When I was eleven years old — this is going back to the 1930s — I lived in Poland. One day, our cheder was abuzz with excitement. The *gaon* Rabbi Meir Shapiro of Lublin was coming to visit to test us on our Torah knowledge.

After quizzing us, Reb Meir told us that as a reward for satisfactorily answering his questions, he would reveal a special secret.

We sat forward in our seats, hanging on to his every word. Reb Meir repeated to us the words of the *Be'er Heiteiv* (*Orach Chaim* 185), who quotes the Bach: "I have found out the reason the letter final *fei* doesn't appear in the entire Birkas HaMazon. It is because whoever recites Birkas HaMazon with due concentration, Hashem's anger and wrath (*af* and *ketzef*, both of which end with a final *fei*) will not prevail over him. The Bach quotes *Sefer HaChinuch* (430) that whoever concentrates during Birkas HaMazon, his sustenance will be provided for him in a plentiful and dignified manner."

Reb Meir went on to quote the *Ohr Chadash* (Laws of Birkas HaMazon 7), who heard it from the Bach: "One who is particular about this mitzvah should take heed not to recite it by heart, but he should recite it from a siddur or *bentcher*."

I firmly resolved from then on to always recite Birkas HaMazon with concentration, and from a siddur. My classmates would rush through their meals and rattle off the *bentching* in record time in typical kid fashion, but I sat and *bentched* with concentration. They knew that they couldn't count on me to be first in the playground. If they wanted me to play with them, they'd have to wait until I was through with my lengthy *bentching*.

My childhood was roughly cut short with the outbreak of

World War II. New words crept into our vocabulary: ghettos, starvation, *selektzias*. And the most chilling of all: Nazis.

And then one day, like so many others before us, we were shoved into cattle trucks and deported to a concentration camp. I was tall for my age, and when it was my turn for inspection I tried to make myself look even taller. Hashem was looking out for me, and mercifully I was sent to join the able-bodied group and was spared the fate of immediate death in the gas chambers.

We were ordered to line up in front of a large desk, behind which a Nazi officer was seated. The officer asked each of us our names and our qualifications. I was young and I hadn't yet had a chance to learn a trade, so I hadn't a clue what to tell him. Luckily, a Jew standing behind me whispered in my ear, "Tell him you're a cook, and I'm your assistant."

I did as he urged me, and we were both dispatched to kitchen duty. Already I saw the blessing of "his sustenance will be provided" coming to fruition, for in that place of unrelenting hunger, my kitchen job allowed me access to a little extra food.

All the time that I was imprisoned in that Gehinnom, I never once compromised on my resolve to recite Birkas HaMazon as it should be recited. When circumstances prevented me from reciting Birkas HaMazon, I didn't eat any bread — although I knew full well that there was nothing else on the menu. I went hungry rather than renege on my promise.

A few months after my internment, a Nazi officer came to inspect the camp. He marched into the kitchen, saw me looking less emaciated than my counterparts, and yelled, "I will not stand for the sight of a well-fed Jew! You think you're on vacation here? Well, you're not! Follow me — now!"

Trembling, I followed him outside, where he led me to a patch of rocky ground. From a nearby toolshed he took a small hammer and thrust it into my hands.

"I want to see a bunker hewn out of these stones within four hours," he demanded. "It must be at least two meters deep, big enough for our soldiers to take cover from enemy bombing. If you complete this job in the allotted time, back to the kitchen you go. If not — " He broke out in a sinister laugh that sent chills down my spine. Then he was gone.

I glanced down at the small hammer in my hands, the unyielding mound of rocks under my feet, and I was filled with despair. I raised my eyes heavenward and beseeched Hashem to help me. Wasn't I guaranteed that "his sustenance will be provided for him in a plentiful and dignified manner all the days of his life"? *Life.* I was determined that I would yet live to see this blessing come true once again!

I was standing there, trying to figure out where and how to begin, when an open-top truck bearing Nazi soldiers rumbled by. Seeing me, a lone Jew with a hammer in his hands, they hurled cucumbers, potatoes, carrots, and other vegetables at me, along with a slew of insults.

Already I was seeing the first part of the blessing being fulfilled: "His sustenance will be provided for him plentifully..." I'd been showered with plentiful bounty indeed.

Another few minutes passed, and another truck came rumbling by, this time carrying Polish soldiers. Seeing the heap of vegetables at my feet, they were sure I'd been appointed guard of the produce and they asked me to give them some. Thinking quickly, I told them in a stern, guard-like voice that they could have it all if they would dig me a bunker two meters deep within an hour. Delighted with the deal, the soldiers leaped out of the truck, and with their weapons and brawn dug out a bunker in thirty minutes flat. They then gathered all the produce they could and were off.

I stood there, overjoyed, giving thanks to Hashem. The blessing had been fulfilled right before my eyes! Plentifully, yes, and also, *b'chavod*, with dignity — for I did not have to lift a finger. I just had to give the command and the deed was done.

The Nazi officer was confounded when he saw the bunker. "You Jew," he snarled. "There's always someone pulling the strings for you!" But he allowed me to return to kitchen duty, where I worked until the liberation.

"After that incident," Reb Shimon told his rapt listeners, "I made a firm promise that if I was to emerge from this inferno alive, I will always cling to my resolve to recite Birkas HaMazon with utter concentration. As you see, I have kept my promise, and Hashem, too, has fulfilled His blessing many times over, providing me with all my needs in a plentiful and dignified manner."

This story is proof of the *pasuk* (*Mishlei* 10:22) that says, "It is the blessing of Hashem" — referring to Birkas HaMazon — "that enriches and one need not add toil with it." Birkas HaMazon, which is a *tefillah* that is commanded in the Torah (even *Shemoneh Esrei* is only a rabbinical mitzvah), has the power to open all the heavenly treasure stores to shower us with every blessing we wish.

As we take time out after each of our meals every day to recite Birkas HaMazon, we are winning Hashem's favor, as the Gemara (*Berachos* 20b) explains. The Gemara expounds on the verse of *Birkas Kohanim* that states, "*Yisa Hashem panav eilecha v'yaseim lecha shalom* — Hashem will lift His Countenance to you and establish peace for you" (*Bamidbar* 6:26). Regarding that verse, the angels said to Hashem, "It says in the Torah that You don't show favor (*Devarim* 10:17). Why, then, do You promise in *Birkas Kohanim*, 'Hashem will lift His Countenance toward you'?"

HaKadosh Baruch Hu responded, "How can I not show favor to the nation of Yisrael, who *bentch* after eating only a *kezayis* or *k'beitzah* (a small amount) even though I commanded them to *bentch* when they are satisfied? I will show them favor because they favor Me!"

What does this show of favor, this lifting of Hashem's Countenance toward us, do for us? The *Sifri* explains (ibid.), "He will overlook His anger, and He will turn His face toward you."

Is there a greater blessing than this? If Hashem is angry with us, He will nevertheless turn toward us and favor us. This is a promise to anyone who *bentches* with *kavannah*.

It is well known that Rabbi Yehoshua Leib Diskin would advise barren couples to be especially particular to *bentch* with *kavannah*, and they saw salvation after doing so. The Steipler Gaon was known to promise likewise. The *Ma'or VaShemesh* explains that when a person *bentches* with *kavannah*, the very food that he ate during that meal will become a medication to heal his body.

The opportunity to perform this Torah-mandated mitzvah is before us every day, several times each day. By using this opportunity to express our heartfelt thanks for all the kindnesses Hashem does for us, we will merit all the blessings we wish for, as well as tremendous reward in the World to Come.

Parashas HaMahn: Another Segulah

THE LESSON OF the *mahn* — the Heaven-sent food that the Jews ate throughout their sojourn in the Wilderness — was a vivid, demonstrable message that sustenance comes from Above. The *Mishnah Berurah* (1:13) explains that reading *Parashas Ha-Mahn* helps a person internalize this lesson. This increases a person's *bitachon* and creates a *zechus* that ensures his *parnassah*.

Without paying attention to the lesson the parashah teaches, however, the act of reciting it lacks power. The Chafetz Chaim once challenged his students with this question: "Chazal said that when the Jews ate the *mahn*, they could think about any food and the *mahn* tasted exactly like that food. What taste did it have if they didn't think about it?"

He answered, "If they didn't give it any thought, it didn't have any taste! Likewise, if one says *Parashas HaMahn* without thinking, it doesn't have any taste."

In other words, there's no point.

Hashem instructed Moshe to fill a jar with *mahn* and put it away for future generations. That is because its message is one for all time. The *mahn* is the symbol of sustenance from Heaven, which is exactly what our *parnassah* is today, although we don't see it literally dropping from Heaven.

What are the lessons to be learned from the *mahn*?

Your portion of *parnassah* is preset. Every person received the same quantity of *mahn* every day: one *omer's* worth. It didn't make a difference how hard he worked to collect it. If he thought he collected more, he came home and weighed it and he found he had exactly one *omer* like everyone else. Likewise, every person today gets the portion decreed for him on Rosh Hashanah. Working harder will not bring him a larger income, even if it seems as if it does.

No one can add or detract from your portion. Hashem delivered each person's *mahn* to him alone. No one could take from another person's portion. Likewise, no one in the world can take away what belongs to us, and we can't take what is not meant for us.

Your need for *hishtadlus* correlates to your *bitachon*. The tzaddikim merited their portion falling right on their doorstep. Less righteous people had to go further to fetch their portion. Today, too, righteous people who fully trust in Hashem will receive sustenance without having to spend their entire day earning money. Those who have less *emunah* have to make a greater *hishtadlus*.

Don't worry about tomorrow's needs today. Hashem told Moshe explicitly that no one was permitted to save one day's *mahn* for consumption tomorrow. This is one of the biggest tests in *emunah*. A person believes that in order to feel settled, he must have a substantial sum of money put away for the future. However, Hashem assures us that we need not worry about the future, for He will give us tomorrow's portion tomorrow.

Reb Menachem Mendel of Riminov explained that this day-to-day existence imposed on the Jews in the Wilderness was a test. Hashem could have rained down enough *mahn* to last for a week, a year, or even the full forty years. But He intentionally sent *mahn* every day, just enough for that day. Every night the Jews went to bed with an empty pantry and had to trust that tomorrow Hashem would feed their family again.

Hashem can easily deliver to us enough wealth for a lifetime all at once. But He wants to provide us with a means to work on our *bitachon*. When we do, Hashem sends special Divine assistance.

It's not simple, but there are so many *talmidei chachamim* and *balebatim* alike who stand up to the test. While they struggle, Hashem lovingly keeps their sacrifice in the forefront of His memory, as it says, "I remember the kindness of your youth, the love of your bridal days, when you followed Me in the Wilderness in an unsown land" (*Yirmiyah* 2:2). This refers to all the "*ochlei hamahn*": those who still, today, rely on the daily delivery of their sustenance from Above and merit living on "bread from Heaven."

Reb Yehuda Bergman is a financial consultant in Eretz Yisrael who has much experience with household budgeting for large families. He attests that there is something inexplicable about the financial status of *kollel yungeleit*. Their relatively low income doesn't begin to meet their needs, yet they manage to make ends meet in a fashion that can only be described as miraculous.

By reciting *Parashas HaMahn* with full meaning and concentration, each of us has the opportunity to enter the world of the "*ochlei hamahn*." We can shed our worries, turn our eyes toward Heaven, and wait with calm certainty for just what we need today.

Giving Tzedakah

THE TORAH PROMISES great affluence for a person who donates money generously to charity. The Gemara (*Ta'anis* 9a) relates that the son of Reish Lakish asked R' Yochanan, "What is the meaning of the *pasuk* '*Aser te'aser* — You shall tithe' (*Devarim* 14:22)?"

In other words, why is the double wording necessary?

R' Yochanan answered, "The *pasuk* is telling us, '*Aser bishvil shetisasher*' — make sure to give a tenth of your earnings to charity and you will become wealthy."

The boy asked him, "How do you know?"

"Go and try it out," was R' Yochanan's reply.

"May a person 'test' the Ribono shel Olam?" the boy asked in surprise.

R' Yochanan explained, "One may not do so with any mitzvah but the mitzvah of giving *tzedakah*, as the *pasuk* says, 'Test Me with this [i.e., *ma'aser*], said Hashem, and see if I will not throw open the windows of the heavens and pour out upon you blessing without end' (*Malachi* 3:10)."

Hashem promises us explicitly that when we give *tzedakah*, He will pay us back. Not only do we not lose out by giving *tzedakah*, but it's the biggest *segulah* for wealth. He even gives us permission to challenge Him and see if it works. Indeed, many people have "tested" this method and confirmed its power, as the following story illustrates:

Cash-back Tzedakah Deal

The present Gerrer Rebbe, Rabbi Yaakov Aryeh Alter, has set up a *tzedakah* fund to relieve chassidim of stress and anxiety brought about by the overwhelming financial demands of Pesach expenses. Any needy chassid who submits his name to the fund's *gabbaim* receives matzos, wine, eggs, fruits and vegetables, meat, fish, and even shoes and clothing for his family. This brings immeasurable relief for thousands of families.

Of course, there must be enough money coming into the fund to match the demand. That's why, six weeks before Pesach, the *gabbai tzedakah* found themselves at the home of Reb Leib,* a distinguished *talmid chacham* and *ba'al tzedakah* in England. They movingly described the community's plight and the astronomical sums of money that had to be collected.

Reb Leib was convinced that a true merit had come his way, and he signed a check for ten thousand pounds, the equivalent of fifteen thousand dollars. This was far more than he would customarily donate, but he had been saving the money to invest in a real-estate purchase and had decided that this cause was a much more worthwhile investment.

On *erev Pesach*, just as he was about to leave the house for burning his *chametz*, Reb Leib was called to the telephone. His attorney was on the line.

"I'm calling you about a certain apartment of yours, one of a pair of apartments of which you are a freeholder (a limited form of long-term ownership). Well, the leaseholder called me today and asked me to offer you the sum of ten thousand pounds for your freehold ownership of the one apartment."

Ten thousand pounds! Reb Leib knew that this was a totally exaggerated sum, quite out of proportion to the value of the purchase. His lawyer interrupted his thoughts. "Listen to me," he said. "I would advise you to sign the relevant documents immediately before he changes his mind."

Reb Leib hurried over to his fax machine, where he signed the contract and faxed it straight back before he dashed out to *sereifas chametz*. By *chatzos* the ten thousand pounds had already been transferred to his bank account.

Now he could use this windfall to purchase the property he had wanted to invest in. *If I had donated twenty thousand pounds, I would have received twenty thousand cash back*, he reflected. *Another ten thousand for the other apartment.*

Reb Leib's story is a miracle story, but on the other hand, it's simply an illustration of how Hashem runs the world. Whether we see it or not, *tzedakah* comes back to us. There are those who attest to seeing this clearly on a regular basis in their own lives.

A well-known *ba'al tzedakah* in England was asked if he could relate an experience in which he saw firsthand that giving *tzedakah* increased his wealth. He replied, "I see it all the time. I can attest that I never, *ever* felt lacking from the sums of money I gave to *tzedakah*. It always came back somehow. In fact, I can certainly attribute my entire success in business, my health, and other blessings to the *tzedakah* I have given."

Yet if we look at the wording of Chazal, "*Aser te'aser kedei shelo tischaser* — Give a tenth of your earnings to charity so that you will not be lacking" (*Yalkut, Devarim* 14:22), this seems to contradict the promise that *tzedakah* makes a person wealthy. "Not lacking" is a far cry from rich.

However, wealth on its own is not necessarily a blessing. "He who increases his possessions increases his worries," says *Pirkei Avos* (2:8). The more assets a person possesses, the more problems he has. He is concerned with so many issues that steal his time, day and night. Wealth can cause stress, and even jealousy. Certainly wealth does not equal contentment: "He who has one hundred wants two hundred" (*Koheles Rabbah* 1:34).

The Me'or Einayim clarifies that "you will not be lacking" complements the promise that one who gives *tzedakah* will receive double blessings. If a person gives *tzedakah* generously, Hashem will make that person wealthy and his wealth will be a blessing. He will feel content, not lacking.

This is not only a reward, but it is the natural consequence of the personal growth a *ba'al tzedakah* must undertake to keep his hand open for giving. It's extremely difficult to part with hard-earned money. Many philanthropists have acknowledged that what enables them to give is the constant awareness that the money isn't theirs. It has only been deposited in their account on trust, designated for performing *chesed*. But each donation is accompanied by a struggle to combat the natural inclination to keep one's earnings. A *ba'al tzedakah* is victorious in this battle time and again, but it takes great effort.

Because he strives, Hashem helps him accomplish more than he could achieve on his own. As Chazal assure us, "One who comes to purify himself, he is helped" (*Shabbos* 104a). Hashem notices the *ba'al tzedakah's* effort and helps him have complete *bitachon*, which reduces his stress in all aspects of life, bestowing contentment on him.

Hachnasas Kallah

AMONG THE MANY worthy causes to which a person can contribute *tzedakah*, marrying off a needy bride is in a class by itself. The rabbi of Antwerp, Rabbi Chaim Kreiswirth, would say that this mitzvah saved his life when he was deathly ill.

How to Annul the Decree

The doctors had informed Rabbi Kreiswirth that he had just a few more weeks to live and had thrown up their hands in defeat. But he was not prepared to give up. He went to the Steipler Gaon in Bnei Brak and pleaded that he reveal to him a way to annul the decree.

The Steipler told him, "Take upon yourself the mitzvah of *hachnasas kallah*, and this will allay the decree. This is hinted at in the *tefillah* of *Eilu Devarim* — 'These are the mitzvos whose fruits we merit to enjoy in this world while the principal reward remains intact in Olam HaBa: ...visiting the sick, providing for the bride, accompanying the deceased to their burial...' *Hachnasas kallah* makes a separation between a very sick person and his funeral."

Rabbi Kreiswirth took the Steipler's words to heart and devoted himself to marrying off hundreds of orphan boys and girls. Hashem gave him another twenty-two years of life.

Rabbi Kreiswirth's story brings to light an important point: raising money for *tzedakah* is just as effective a *zechus* as giving from one's own funds. The *Sefer Chassidim* supports this idea with an explanation of the verse from *Mishlei* that says, "*Tzedakah* saves from death." He observes that this verse is mentioned twice, once in chapter 10 and once again in Chapter 11. The first mention, he says, refers to those who have money and can give charity. The second refers to those who have little to give, but devote their time to raising money for those in need.

Giving can be difficult, but when we have a clear picture of what we are achieving when we give, we are powerfully motivated to overcome the challenge. As we have now learned, our wealth is not only protected when we give, but increased. Our worries, on the other hand, dwindle away as our *bitachon* grows. More than all of that, however, *tzedakah* is the key *segulah* for acquiring the greatest wealth of all: our very lives.

Tefillah

*P*RAYER IS *HISHTADLUS*. It's actually the most important, effective *hishtadlus* a person can do.

We tend to think that it's our obligation to do our *hishtadlus* and that prayers support our efforts. But really it's the other way around. The more we pray, the more *siyatta d'Shmaya* we are granted and the less physical effort we need to expend.

Sincere prayers for *siyatta d'Shmaya* are the source of our livelihood. But it is not only our requests that bring the *berachah*. In equal measure, prayers of thanksgiving to Hashem are a fantastic way to open the gates of abundance. A heart full of gratitude is a receptacle for Hashem's *berachos*, as the following story illustrates:

Contentment Unblocks Pipelines

A shopkeeper once came to Reb Moshe of Kobrin complaining that another Jew had opened a shop opposite his, selling exactly the same merchandise.

"Since then, no one enters my shop. The whole day I have to sit and watch how crowds of customers fill his store and come out carrying bags laden with purchases."

Reb Moshe told him, "Let me give you an excellent *segulah* that will open the gates of *parnassah* for you and cause your earnings to rise dramatically. While you observe what is going on across the road, say, 'Ribono shel Olam, blessed are You for providing livelihood for each of Your creations and for providing lavishly for this Jew opposite me.'"

"How can I do that?" the shopkeeper exclaimed. "My heart is so pained seeing the success of the Jew who is ruining my business day in and day out."

"I know," the Rebbe answered. "You feel so miserable. This is what's ruining your business! If you want to unblock the heavenly pipelines, then do as I tell you. Even though the words will be very superficial at first, it will soon come from your heart, and you will immediately see how the gates of *parnassah* open up."

Shemittah

NO DISCUSSION OF *parnassah* and *emunah* would be complete without a look at *shemittah* and those who observe it. Every seven years the farmers of Eretz Yisrael are called upon to perform this feat of tremendous *bitachon*.

The *shemittah* year is a test that no one other than Hashem could dare impose. It requires farmers to put away their tools and tractors for an entire year. They may not plant, they may not reap, nor may they tend to their land. Their entire *parnassah* is placed in a state of suspended animation.

The first question anyone would ask if their livelihood were suspended for a year — or even, for some, a week — is, "How am I supposed to survive?"

Yet with each *shemittah* cycle, more farmers answer the call of the *gedolim* to keep the halachos of *shemittah* down to their last detail rather than relying on loopholes that have been found over the years in order to avoid economic disaster. If ever anyone wanted proof in this world that Hashem is the Source of sustenance, he need look no further than the farmers who observe *shemittah*. They are known by the well-deserved title "*gibborei ko'ach* — valiant heroes" (*Tehillim* 103:20). Here are some of their miraculous stories.

Mr. Celery

The year was 1980. Rabbi Shlomo Zalman Grossman, currently *mara d'asra* in Elad, was a rabbi in the Jordan Valley at the time. After a particularly moving lecture, during which he told his audience about the mitzvah of *shemittah*, one of the listeners approached him. Identifying himself as Effie, he thanked the rabbi for his inspiring speech.

"*Kevod haRav*," said Effie, "if you promise me that all those Torah pledges you just quoted will be fulfilled, I will undertake to keep *shemittah* this year."

Well aware that most people in the Jordan Valley earn their livelihood through agriculture, Rabbi Grossman asked him what alternative job he would have during the year of *shemittah*. Effie said he'd spend his time learning and would work part-time as a secretary.

"You're the only religious person I know," he told Rabbi Grossman. "If you give me your word that the Torah's promises to those who observe *shemittah* will come true, I will keep *shemittah*."

Effie was an extremely gifted young man, and Rabbi Grossman saw that he was very serious, so he told Effie he'd have an answer for him in a couple of days. He had to consult with someone first.

Rabbi Grossman made his way to Yerushalayim to take counsel with the *posek hador*, Rabbi Yosef Shalom Elyashiv.

Rabbi Elyashiv explained that some commentaries are of the opinion that Hashem's promises were given to *Klal Yisrael* as a whole and not to individuals. He couldn't give an explicit promise to Effie.

"But you can tell him that he will surely have *siyatta d'Shmaya*, and Hashem will help him."

Effie was pleased with the response, and he began to keep *shemittah*. It was a very long and hard year. He worked as a secretary, learned Torah the rest of the time, and didn't touch his fields. His friends and neighbors thought he'd gone crazy and told him as much. Overnight, Effie turned into the laughingstock of the town. It didn't help that he refused to even lend them his tractor, forklift, or any other expensive equipment, because Rabbi Grossman had told him it was forbidden to enable people to do *aveiros*.

Effie had a very spiritual year and tried to ignore the mockery and scorn.

The year ended, Rosh Hashanah came and went, and on *motza'ei Tzom Gedaliah*, Rabbi Grossman and Effie drank a *l'chaim* that he'd managed to withstand the challenge. But the test wasn't over yet. Now that Effie was finally allowed to plant, he discovered that the agency had already distributed all the seeds and there was nothing left for him. After a lot of pleading and pulling strings, he was told that all they could give him was a large amount of faulty celery seeds, as that was the only thing they had.

With not much choice, Effie took the decaying seeds and sowed them. To everyone's amazement, the celery grew to enormous proportions. They were three times their usual size. Effie suddenly had fields and fields of waist-high celery.

The settlement's inhabitants found it hilarious, and Effie was once more the butt of their jokes. "What are you going to do with such a huge amount of celery? There's enough there to feed the entire State of Israel for several months!"

They nicknamed him "Mr. Celery." Even Rabbi Shlomo Zalman Grossman was worried. What *would* Effie do with all that celery?

On his part, Effie displayed steadfast *bitachon*. "Hashem helped me until now, and He will surely help me further."

One day Effie got a call from the man who'd given him the celery seeds. "Tell me, my friend, did you ever do anything with those problematic celery seeds?"

"Did I do anything? Are you kidding? Do you know how much celery I've got?"

"How much?"

"However much you want!"

"Really? Fantastic! You're about to become rich! You can sell it for three dollars apiece, maybe even more!" The usual price of celery was fifty cents each.

"Why?" Effie asked in surprise.

"Europe was hit with a two-week wave of frost. All their celery froze. People are staying indoors because of the cold, and they want to make hot soup, but there's no celery. Everyone is desperate for celery. Listen and do as I tell you. Get as many workers as you can to harvest the celery, and I will hire a fleet of airplanes to distribute it throughout Europe."

Rabbi Grossman got a hasty phone call from Effie, who invited him to witness the unusual scene that was about to unfold. Rabbi Grossman said afterward that he would never forget the sight. Hundreds of Jewish and Arab workers had been recruited, and they were working around the clock cutting and loading the celery. The vegetable was in such demand, in fact, that several weeks later, when Rabbi Grossman wanted to buy some for Pesach, there wasn't even a single stalk to be had.

Effie became very wealthy. He went out and bought himself a beautiful car, which he dubbed "my *shemittah* Cadillac," and an expensive Arabian steed, which he called his *shemittah* horse.

"Everyone laughed at me all year long," he explained to Rabbi Grossman. "Now I want them all to see how much profit I made from observing *shemittah*."

When Rabbi Grossman related this story in one of his lectures years later, one of the listeners said he knew Effie. He had become a *talmid chacham* in his own right and was even giving *shiurim*.

(*Emunah Sheleimah*)

The miracles that people who observe *shemittah* experience could fill an entire book. Another wondrous one took place in Beit Chilkiyah some thirty years ago. Rabbi Shlomo Pollack, the rabbi of the community, relates the story:

The Nuclear Option

It was *erev shemittah*. That year, it had rained much more than normal. The blessed downpours had yielded large amounts of wheat of a superior quality. The farmers in Beit Chilkiyah were delighted as they surveyed their crops — three times as much as usual — and they couldn't wait to sell the wheat and make enormous profits. Hashem's promise in the Torah, "*V'tzivisi es birchasi* — And I will command My blessing" (*Vayikra* 25:21), was being fulfilled once again.

But then authorities arrived and interfered. The Agricultural Ministry decided that if too much wheat flooded the market, the prices would drop, so they issued a directive that half the wheat was to be thrown into the sea.

In Beit Chilkiyah, they didn't rush to follow this arbitrary ruling. Part of the wheat was secretly transferred to *chareidi* residential centers. That still left a huge quantity of wheat stored in the yishuv's granaries.

Around that time, there was a calamity of global proportions: the atomic reactor in Chernobyl exploded. In order to extinguish the huge flames that broke out, the Russians dug a new channel from one of the large rivers, so that its waters flowed directly into the area of the reactor. The technique worked, and the fire went out, but the contaminated waters continued their flow into Turkey.

Because the waters had absorbed so much radiation, authorities forbade its use. This had far-reaching effects. The wheat-growing fields of Turkey were declared dangerous, and farmers were instructed to throw tons of contaminated wheat into the sea, leaving consumers without any flour.

The Turkish government turned to the world markets to purchase fresh, good-quality wheat for its citizens. In Beit

Chilkiyah, the farmers jumped at the opportunity and sold all the wheat in their grain stores to the Turks at full price. The money they earned, just before *shemittah* arrived, enabled them to get through the year.

Once again, keepers of *shemittah* were *zocheh* to Hashem's bountiful blessing. With awe, they witnessed firsthand how the Master of the universe coordinates worldly events, arranging a disaster in one place to bring salvation to Jews living thousands of miles away.

Conclusion: It's All Mahn

*A*S WE STRIVE to view our *parnassah* through the lens of *emunah*, we have many tools and ideas at our disposal:

- All *parnassah* comes directly from Hashem, measured out for each of us with precision every Rosh Hashanah.
- No one can deprive us of what Hashem has granted us.
- *Hishtadlus* is required, but only to the minimum degree necessary, which each person determines for himself depending on his level of *bitachon*.
- Worry is not part of *hishtadlus*. Neither is overworking ourselves or engaging in desperate, futile efforts.
- We can assist in clearing the path for our due *parnassah* to flow into our lives by using various *segulos*, which include reciting Birkas HaMazon with *kavannah*, reciting *Parashas HaMahn*, giving *tzedakah*, and *davening*.

When *parnassah* worries mount in our minds, we can think of the Jews in the Wilderness. Each day they had what they needed to get through that day. They could expect nothing more, and they received nothing less. We, too, have what we need to get through a day — often far more than that. If we think about yesterday and the day before, and every day of our lives up until now, we realize that Hashem has always delivered our *mahn*. And He always will.

Chapter 12
Emunah and Shidduchim

Finding one's fitting marriage partner is as hard as splitting the sea.

(Sanhedrin 22a)

The Best Guarantor

HE FOLLOWING STORY was related by Rabbi Yisrael Zicherman, of Kiryat Sefer, who heard the story firsthand from Mr. Oppenheim.*

Mr. Oppenheim, a wealthy Jew who lives in London, was once approached by a close friend, Mr. Goodman,* with a bold request. He wished to borrow a grand sum of close to 100,000 pounds. Mr. Oppenheim benevolently agreed to lend him the money, but understandably requested that Mr. Goodman bring two guarantors to sign the promissory note for the loan's return.

"Who on earth can commit to pay up this vast amount should I fail to repay the loan?" Mr. Goodman asked in despair. "I'll never find a guarantor!"

"Then perhaps you can get several people, each of whom will stand by a specific amount?"

Mr. Goodman remained silent. How could he explain to his friend what it felt like to be a man of means who has all of a sudden been reduced to a pauper? He had been accustomed to living a comfortable life, and now he had to think twice before he bought basic necessities. This was painful, but as long as he could hide his overdrawn bank account from friends and neighbors and avoid being regarded with pity, he could at least retain his dignity. To be compelled to reveal his plight to several people and plead with them to be his guarantors would be absolute torture!

"I really don't want to disclose to so many people that I've fallen on hard times," he stammered. "I really don't want it to go public."

Mr. Oppenheim nodded sympathetically. He understood in an instant. Of course, he didn't want Mr. Goodman to be subject to humiliation, but how could he lend him this significant sum without any guarantee that he would get it back? He tried to come up with some other way to help out his friend. Suddenly he hit upon an idea.

"I know what!" he said. "I'll appoint the Ribono shel Olam to be your Guarantor!"

With that, he drew up a contract, specifying the date by which the loan was to be repaid, and handed his friend a check.

The specified date came and went, but the money didn't. Another month passed, and then another, but the loan was not repaid. Mr. Oppenheim started getting a little nervous. When he pressed Mr. Goodman for the repayment, Mr. Goodman mumbled a vague explanation that his business was still going through some rough patches, and it would take a little more time for his investments to yield a profit.

Realizing that the chances of him getting the money back were very slim, Mr. Oppenheim turned to the Guarantor of the loan: the Ribono shel Olam. But instead of asking for the return of the one hundred thousand pounds, Mr. Oppenheim had a different request.

"Ribono shel Olam," he said, "I am prepared to be *mevater* on the money, because You have blessed me with plenty. But what I do desperately need is a *shidduch* for my daughter, who is turning thirty and still hasn't found her *bashert*. Please, could You arrange a suitable match for her in lieu of the loan's repayment?"

The Ribono shel Olam, indeed the best Guarantor, was

quick to act, and within a month Mr. Oppenheim's daughter was engaged to a wonderful boy. Shortly after that, Mr. Goodman's business recovered from its slump, and he was able to return his loan in full. But when he came to repay the money, Mr. Oppenheim refused to accept it.

"My dear friend," he said, "your Guarantor has already paid up the debt, and you have no need to pay me again!"

He explained to the baffled Mr. Goodman all that had occurred since the due date of the loan's repayment.

"But how am I now to repay the loan to my Guarantor?" asked Mr. Goodman. "I want to make good on my debt!"

After some discussion, the two friends came up with the perfect compromise. Since that year, 2001, was a *shemittah* year in Eretz Yisrael, Mr. Goodman would donate money to farmers who kept *shemittah* with *mesirus nefesh* and incurred financial loss in the process.

Mr. Oppenheim was grateful to his *Shadchan*, Who had seemingly not been impressed by his wealth or *yichus* or any other external factor, but had been moved by his deed of compassion and sincere faith.

Indeed, prayer and good deeds can move a *shidduch*, as the above story demonstrates.

Like Splitting the Sea

*C*HAZAL SAY, "FINDING one's fitting marriage partner is as hard as splitting the sea" (*Sanhedrin* 22a). For whom is it hard? For Hashem? For Him matchmaking is as easy as splitting the sea. For us it's as hard as splitting the sea. Just as we know we can't split the sea, we have to understand that we are not determining any match — even if it looks as if we are.

Anyone who has been in *shidduchim* for a lengthy period will attest that neither money nor talent nor the most professional *shadchan* with the best power of persuasion — absolutely nothing—can move a *shidduch* if it's not meant to be. Our hands are tied behind our backs even though it seems as if we are doing, choosing, and deciding. We are all puppets in the hands of the One above. He is pulling the strings, and we are just waiting patiently until the *zivug* that He has chosen "falls from Heaven" at the appropriate time.

Let's look into the story behind the marriage of two of our *Imahos*: the mothers of *Klal Yisrael*.

It was the talk of the town in Charan that Yitzchak had twin sons, Yaakov and Esav. The older one, Esav, would be a suitable match for Leah, the older daughter of Lavan. Yaakov would surely marry Rachel, the younger sister.

Leah heard the gossip, and when visitors came from Be'er Sheva, she inquired about Esav. She was horrified to learn that Esav was terribly wicked, while Yaakov was righteous. She began to pray that she should merit marrying the tzaddik instead of Esav and that she should merit having righteous children. She cried so hard that her eyes became red and swollen, and her eyelashes fell out.

What transpired in the end?

She ended up marrying Yaakov, and she married him before Rachel did. With her *tefillos*, she succeeded in changing the *zivug* destined for her. *Tefillos* can enable us to merit a much better *zivug* than we originally deserved.

This is not all she merited. The *pasuk* says, "*Vayar Hashem ki senuah Leah vayiftach es rachmah*— Hashem saw that Leah was hated, so He opened her womb" (*Bereishis* 29:31). The Midrash comments that the *pasuk* means that "Esav, whose deeds were hateful, was designated to Leah" (*Midrash Rabbah, Bereishis* 71:2). The Kedushas Levi explains that Hashem saw all of Leah's *tefillos* and the tears that she had shed since she was a young girl. He heard her *tefillos* that she should be able to marry Yaakov and build *Klal Yisrael*—and He opened her womb.

Leah was the only one of the *Imahos* who was not barren. She gave birth to six of the holy *shevatim*, three times as many as Rachel. She was the mother of Levi, from whom descended the *Kohanim* and Levi'im who served in the Beis HaMikdash. She was the mother of Yehudah, who was the forefather of David HaMelech and the dynasty of *Malchus Beis David*.

Her *tefillos* for her *zivug hagun* saved her the pain and suffering of waiting many years for children and gave her the merit to become the mother of these distinguished families of *Klal Yisrael*.

Rachel, Leah's sister, never had to *daven* for her *zivug*. She knew that she would marry Yaakov. On her wedding day, she sacrificed her chance to marry the tzaddik and become the mother of *Am Yisrael* in order to save her sister from being shamed.

After her postponed wedding, she was shocked to discover that she was unable to conceive. According to the laws of nature she would never have children. Then the *pasuk* states, "*Vayizkor Elokim es Rachel*—And Hashem remembered Rachel" (*Bereishis* 30:22).

Rashi there quotes the *Midrash Rabbah*, which explains that "He remembered how she had saved her sister from shame." Rachel had many merits, but it was this merit that tipped the scale in her favor and resulted in the miraculous birth of two of the tribes. Had she not sacrificed her opportunity to be Yaakov's first wife, she would not have merited any children. The extra seven years of waiting saved her years of inconceivable misery.

It's extremely trying to remain single and be in *shidduchim* for an extended period, but this *pekel* is definitely instead of other, perhaps, heavier *pekelach*. We have to trust our Father that He truly loves us; He has not forgotten us. Each day that passes is a precisely measured dose of *mesirus nefesh* that is giving us exactly what we need. The grief of a "no" from the other party spares us from much bigger aggravation.

A person may think Hashem is not answering his *tefillos*. It is just the opposite. Since Hashem is so kind and wants the best for him, He knows that after waiting a little longer, that person will deserve the best *shidduch*. Every good *kabbalah* and all the extra *tefillos* and mitzvos that the person accumulates during this trying time leads him to merit a much better marriage, and righteous children that he wouldn't have deserved previously.

It is written, "I will redeem them, but they spoke lies about Me... I gave them tribulations to strengthen their arms, yet they think badly of Me" (*Hoshea* 7:13–15).

The Gemara explains: Hashem gives us tribulations as a kindness in exchange for much harsher suffering or to enable us to receive special gifts of which we were previously unworthy. Meanwhile, we think that Hashem has forsaken us, and we begin to "think badly of Him"! (*Avodah Zarah* 4a).

It's a promise that every person has his *zivug* chosen for him forty days before he is born (*Sotah* 2a). The Chafetz Chaim explains that a person may begin to wonder, "Perhaps I am suffering because I sinned, and I no longer deserve what Hashem wanted to give me." He explains at length in his *sefer Shemiras HaLashon*, on *Parashas Shelach*, that this was the line of thinking that led to the sin of the spies. They began to doubt that they were worthy of entering Eretz Yisrael and conquering the Land, even though Hashem had promised them they would. He states that this is the way that the *yetzer hara* depresses many people today, and it is totally false. Hashem will always give a person what He designated for him, even if he is unworthy, so long as he has not deliberately rebelled.

Nothing and no one can take away anyone's *zivug hagun*. We just need to feel hopeful and thank Hashem for every setback, trusting that He is doing what is best and that the disappointment of the moment will bring the right one more quickly.

Waiting for the Moment to Arrive

The Right Girl, at the Right Time

"Sorry, she says it's just not the right *shidduch* for her daughter," the *shadchan* told me. The other party had only gotten the resumé a day earlier. I wondered, had they even called one reference? Did they have any interest in finding out who my son was, other than his detour from the well-trodden path of a *yeshivah bachur*?

I was disappointed, because this girl seemed so suitable. She was a little "out of the box" herself, and she had a number of interests in common with my son Yosef.* But this certainly wasn't the first time we had gotten such an immediate negative response. In some ways, I didn't blame the girls' parents. They didn't feel comfortable about their daughters meeting him.

Yosef's teen years had been a long, frightening journey for my family. He had never been a great student, but he had always been an extremely giving, well-intentioned boy. He was knocked down a lot. Doors were closed to him, and he ended up in a yeshivah with other boys who had faced closed doors. There he picked up a lot of habits that took him in the wrong direction. We eventually sent him abroad to a very small, intense program led by a rabbi who focused on hearts and *neshamos* before Gemara and *Rashi*.

Now Yosef was home, working hard in a local business and eager to build his own life. He had done a lot of thinking and growing. He had forged his own path in *avodas Hashem* that didn't quite conform to any one group. He wore black velvet yarmulkes and large white knit ones as well. His *peyos* were a bit long. His clothes were casual. But he was rock solid in his commitment to be at three minyanim a day, to learn a little every day, and to keep the mitzvos according to halachah.

His rebel days were behind him, and he wanted a wife who would help him create a solid Jewish home on a firm foundation. We cast our net wide, contacting friends and *shadchanim* locally in the New York area, and in many other cities throughout the country. No one could make heads or tails out of Yosef, and there had not been one date in nearly two years.

I looked at him and my heart sank. All he wanted was to live a good life! Why was this door also closed to him? I cried to Hashem every day, begging Him to inspire someone, somewhere, to take a chance on my dear son. His older siblings' *shidduchim* had all gone quickly. It was hard to see him struggling also in this area.

Knowing how he must feel inside, I just kept encouraging him, telling him, "Yosef, you're one in a million, and Hashem has someone so special picked out for you. You just have to find each other."

I said it and I believed it, but I couldn't for the life of me figure out how it was going to happen.

It was January 5773/2013 when my son left for Eretz Yisrael to attend his friend's wedding. He had taken off two weeks from work and had arranged to stay with his former roommate, Dovid,* who lived with his wife and baby outside Yerushalayim.

Dovid's wife, Tamar,* was eager to help Yosef find his *bashert*. When she heard he was coming, she began making inquiries. In Eretz Yisrael there were more possibilities. The categories were not as clearly defined in their American-Israeli circles. She put together a list of three possibilities for Yosef, and for the first time in his life, he had the privilege of going out on *shidduch* dates. He took each date very seriously, trying to look past superficial traits and discover the person within. But for various reasons, none of Tamar's suggestions worked out.

I was fully expecting Yosef to call me sometime during his visit and ask me to change his ticket so that he could stay in Eretz Yisrael longer. I knew he was happy there among his many friends, and he was not looking forward to resuming his life at home. But he hadn't made that request.

The day came for his return, and I arrived home from some errands to find my answering machine loaded with calls. They were all from Yosef.

"I need to talk to you, Ma. Please call me as soon as you can."

I called him immediately. "I'm at the airport," he said. "But I didn't check in yet. I want to stay another two weeks. I just feel like I can't get on that plane, like there's still something for me to do here."

I agreed to make the change, and he got a lift back to Dovid and Tamar's apartment. It was Thursday. On Friday, they were expecting another guest, Yitzy,* a nineteen-year-old friend of Dovid who was in the army and coming to spend Shabbos with them. Dovid was eager for Yitzy and Yosef to meet. He felt that they had very similar personalities, almost as if they were brothers.

Sure enough, Yitzy and Yosef hit it off. They spent a pleasant Shabbos together, and after making Havdalah, Yitzy got ready to return to his base.

"Wait!" Tamar told him. "Everyone sit down right here in this living room. We're going to think of a *shidduch* for Yosef."

After a brief silence, Yitzy piped up. "I've got it. She's a girl my older sister works with. She's been around our house, and she seems perfect for Yosef. And I should know, since we're so much alike!"

Tamar set up the date with Naama. She was from a small Sephardic community in another part of the country. Her parents were *ba'alei teshuvah*, but both her father and brother were accomplished *talmidei chachamim*. She herself had strong *hashkafos* and wanted a husband who was also committed to living a life of *avodas Hashem*.

Naama and Yosef met. To her, his casual attire and long *peyos* meant nothing at all. She didn't grow up with any awareness of what various types of clothing signified, and so none of it was an issue. They spent several hours together getting to know each other. They met every day that week, and by the next week, there was a *l'chaim*. My husband and I didn't meet our new daughter-in-law in person until we came to Eretz Yisrael for the wedding a few months later.

As we got to know her over the past few years, we've discovered what a true *tzaddeikes* Hashem chose for Yosef. She is gracious and grateful, supportive and strong. She is a wonderful mother, a hard worker, and, most of all, she appreciates Yosef for all his talents, gifts, and goodness. Yosef also benefited by becoming part of her wonderful family in Eretz Yisrael, where he feels loved and accepted.

When I look back on this story, I can only marvel at the *hashgachah pratis*. We literally did not see where our salvation might come from. But the *pasuk* (*Tehillim* 121:2) gave us the answer: "*Ezri me'im Hashem oseh shamayim va'aretz* — My help is from Hashem, Maker of heaven and earth." Only our Creator could have arranged that the lives of these two very different people from very different worlds should intersect.

He used many agents: Tamar, who cared so much about Yosef's happiness; Yitzy, who thought of the *shidduch*; and even me, who got to the telephone just in time to change the ticket. Now Yosef and Naama have a beautiful *bayis ne'eman* in Yerushalayim, two precious daughters, and a bright future together. I can't think of them without my heart overflowing with gratitude to Hashem for a clear and open miracle.

It might be hard to really believe that all is for the best and that every aggravation is actually a *chesed*, but this is the real truth. The situation might look like the exact opposite of *chesed*, but the fact that it is kindness is certainly true, even if it seems farfetched.

Waiting and enduring while being in *shidduchim* is a favor to us from Hashem. We must believe it and feel grateful. With this frame of mind, we can *daven* with a happy heart that the right one should come quickly. Surely in the merit of our faith and gratitude despite the trying situation, Hashem will answer our *tefillos*.

Strengthening our *bitachon* and feeling hopeful, accompanied by good deeds and prayers that Hashem lead us the right way, is certainly the quickest route to the right *shidduch*.

Epilogue

> *R. Simlai said: Six hundred and thirteen mitz-*
> *vahs were told to Moshe, three hundred and*
> *sixty-five negative mitzvahs, corresponding to*
> *the number of solar days [in the year], and*
> *two hundred and forty-eight positive mitz-*
> *vahs, corresponding to the number of the or-*
> *gans of man's body...*
>
> *David came and condensed them to eleven*
> *[principles]...*
>
> *Yeshayah came and condensed them to six...*
> *Michah came and condensed them to three...*
>
> *Again came Yeshayah and condensed them*
> *to two...*
>
> *But it was Chabakkuk who came and con-*
> *densed them all into one [principle], as it says,*
> *"But the tzaddik shall live by his emunah"*
> *(Chabakkuk 2:4).*
>
> *Talmud, Makkos 24a*

JUST ONE PRINCIPLE, and just one word, which encapsulates all of Hashem's Torah — *emunah*. In this book, we've taken a journey through the world of *emunah*. We've found the principles that it's based on. We've discovered many techniques to help us incorporate *emunah* into every aspect of our lives. And we have read the stories, so many stories, true narratives of people who faced their challenges with courage and with *emunah*. We've explored the power of *hakaras hatov* and of *tefillah*, examined how *hishtadlus* and *emunah* can coexist peacefully, and discovered the benefits of *emunah* in all aspects of our lives.

Let us take the tools, and the inspiration, with us further, as we journey toward deeper, more authentic *emunah*.

And may the time come soon, when we will not need to grope in the darkness to find Hashem's closeness and kindness. The entire Jewish nation will witness the bright light of Hashem's *Shechinah*, as the verse says, וְאָמַר בַּיּוֹם הַהוּא הִנֵּה אֱלֹקֵינוּ זֶה קִוִּינוּ לוֹ וְיוֹשִׁיעֵנוּ זֶה ה׳ קִוִּינוּ לוֹ נָגִילָה וְנִשְׂמְחָה בִּישׁוּעָתוֹ, "And on that day it will be said: 'Behold, this is our G-d — we hoped to Him that He would save us, this is Hashem to Whom we hoped. Let us rejoice and be glad in His salvation'" (*Yeshayah* 25:9).

Appendix

Living Examples of Emunah

Hashem does not test the wicked. Why? Because they will not be able to withstand it. Whom does He test? The righteous, as it says, "Hashem tests the righteous."
(Midrash Tehillim 11:5)

THE FOLLOWING ARE additional interviews with several *ba'alei emunah* whose life circumstances have placed them in a battlefield where their faith, strength, and courage are constantly called upon. They are true soldiers who have earned their skills the hard way and have graciously agreed to share their insights.

May their stories inspire us all to envision the great heights of *emunah* toward which a Jew can strive.

Real Life Emunah
Never Give Up Hope
An interview with
Rabbi Aharon Margalit,
author of As Long as I Live

Two-and-a-half-year-old Ahrele was traumatized when a tractor racing at top speed almost plowed into him. A heavy stutter plagued him from that moment on, until the age of fifteen.

Shortly after this incident, he contracted a severe case of polio. Though his life was spared, he was left severely disabled. He spent years recuperating in a convalescent home alone, far away from friends and relatives. He finally reunited with his family, arriving home in a wheelchair.

He continued to suffer emotional abuse from his classmates, until he matured and overcame his stutter and his handicap with intense physiotherapy.

He married and contracted cancer — once and twice. Having emerged intact from all these challenges, aside from other personal tragedies, he is today a source of inspiration and a popular lecturer across the globe.

Did you ever wonder, *Why me?* You went through so much hardship as a child, enough to last a lifetime. So when you received major blows again and again, recurring illness and the murder of your son, did you ever ask yourself, *Why me again? Why do others seem to sail through life while I always have to confront new challenges?*

No, never. My parents instilled in us children a simple and

pure *emunah*: to accept whatever Hashem sends our way and not to question or probe why this or that had to happen. Even as a very young child, I never viewed my situation negatively. I used to think, *These are my circumstances. What is the best way to deal with them?* There was no bitterness, no complaining, no anger.

How did you dare hope, after the doctors gave you a few days to live, that you would see miracles? Don't many righteous people have bitachon and yet they don't see miracles? Why did you believe you would?

It wasn't that I hoped for a miracle. I didn't think of a full recovery in terms of a "miracle." It's just that I knew that Hashem can and does help so many people in so many situations, and I hoped He would help me, too.

What I absolutely refused to do was believe, even in my heart of hearts, the doctors' pessimistic prognosis for my illness. I said to myself numerous times, *Doctors were given the right to cure, but no more than that. There is only One Who can determine what will be, and that One is Hashem.*

I never felt that I deserve more than righteous people. They are of a different caliber, and I can't compare myself to them. I simply believed, and still believe with a complete faith, that there is nothing Hashem is unable to do.

You have an amazingly positive outlook and a strong willpower. What would you tell others who are not as strong by nature and feel that they can't cope?

I always tell people that it doesn't make a difference what a person is going through. It's his own decision whether he will be happy or miserable. Our challenges are chosen for us from Above, but to be a "*nebbach*" is not a decree from Heaven. Every person has the ability to handle his problems, if only he wants to.

What advice do you offer to people to help them cope?

Being optimistic is not always an inborn trait, but it can always be developed.

There is one tremendous gift that Hashem gave us that we can use to create optimism and combat depression, and that is the power of imagery. This wonderful tool can help us feel positive by painting pictures in our mind. The more vivid and positive the pictures we create, the more we will be convinced that Hashem will truly help us.

It also enables us to reach our goals and aspirations without feeling overwhelmed by the obstacles in our way. For example, let's say a person wishes to organize a *siyum ha-Shas* or set up a *chesed* organization. He should concentrate on his goal and imagine how things will look when he succeeds. Once he is full of enthusiasm, Hashem will help him surmount all the obstacles.

Did you imagine that you would recover from your grim diagnosis and be a source of encouragement for Jews all over the globe who suffer illness, emotional ailments, or other serious problems?

No! I did not dream that would happen. But when I was told of the diagnosis, I did pace up and down the room in thought, asking Hashem to help me discover what good could possibly come out of my condition. I finally decided that being in the hospital ward would be an opportunity to cheer up other patients and fill them with hope and put a smile on their faces. This is what I busied myself with in the hospital instead of feeling sad.

Wow! Look how Hashem takes a person's good intentions and actions and expands them magnificently until they shine on the whole world! How do you reconcile acceptance versus never giving up? How far does hishtadlus go in a seemingly hopeless situation?

Hishtadlus varies from person to person. I just wanted to live! So I did anything that would help me live. A person should do all he can that he believes is logical.

But along with his efforts, he must humbly accept Hashem's will and not try to fight reality. He should use his strength to try to grow from the situation he is in, and not waste energy on living in denial and refusing to accept his challenge.

This is a commonly asked question: What happens when a person had strong emunah, for example, believing that a relative would be cured, yet this didn't happen?

Emunah is not a means to an end. It is an end in itself. If *emunah* would be a means to an end, then when someone with stark faith sees that things did not work out like he imagined, he could become a *kofer*! It could lead to not wanting to believe anymore.

Emunah is a mitzvah in itself. Even if a person had strong faith that his relative would be cured and the relative passed away, his *emunah* was not in vain. He performed the mitzvah of having faith, and this mitzvah remains with him regardless of the outcome.

Hashem decides what the outcome will be. He has *cheshbonos* beyond our comprehension, and our job is to have *emunah* regardless of the outcome. If things do not work out, we still get tremendous reward for our *emunah*, and our faith was definitely not in vain.

What final message would you like to convey to others?

Never, ever give up. I would like to share several pointers that form my "*emunah* kit," which I designed for myself on the night I was informed of my illness. I have reviewed these steps over and over again in my head thousands of times:

- *Hashem is "kol yachol" — He can do anything and everything.*

- *The purpose of creation was so that Hashem could give to His beloved creations.*

- *I am a child of Avraham, Yitzchak, and Yaakov, which means that Hashem wants to be kind to me, too.*

- *Now that I strongly believe that Hashem wishes to deal kindly with me, He will surely do so!*

- *Tzaddikim say that emunah widens the pipelines through which blessings pour down from above. The more we increase our emunah, the more we increase and expand the flow of blessings upon ourselves. Now that I wholeheartedly believe that Hashem will send me yeshuos and chasadim, He will certainly do so.*

Real Life Emunah
In Touch with Hashem

Mrs. Nechumelle Jacobs, age thirty, was born with cerebral palsy, a condition that affects the brain signals that control body movement. Nechumelle has limited mobility and little use of her left hand. In her own words:

I have cerebral palsy, which means that the signals my brain sends to my muscles get mixed up along the way so they can't make out what they have to do. Cerebral palsy is caused by injuries or abnormalities of the brain. It usually develops before birth, but it can happen at any time during the first two years of life, while the baby's brain is still developing. In my case, it probably happened at birth, when at some point my brain was deprived of oxygen. *B'chasdei Hashem*, CP only affected my motor control, not my breathing, speech, or intellect.

I have all the classic symptoms of a specific type of CP: spastic cerebral palsy. I can't walk unaided and I often feel that my muscles are taut, but when I tell them to stretch, they won't listen to me. The muscles in my left hand are exceptionally stiff.

When I was growing up, I used fantasy as a coping mechanism. I have a very good imagination, and I love to read. In my mind I would transport myself to other places where I could walk, run, draw, brush my hair, and do all the things I couldn't do in real life.

As a young girl, I visited Rabbi Yehuda Zev Segal, the Manchester *Rosh Yeshivah*, several times. I was too young to remember this (he was *niftar* when I was about eight years old), but my mother told me that on one occasion, after I had met with him, I said to her, "After I get married, I want to come live in Manchester to be near the *Rosh Yeshivah!*" Young as I was, I felt that he cared.

I was the youngest of a large family, and my parents did everything they could to give me a regular childhood. Of course I needed a lot of help, and I had to do special exercises, but otherwise, I was just like any other child.

I was lucky to attend a school that was very accommodating of my needs. The administration ensured that my classroom was wheelchair accessible, and the teachers were sensitive about my feelings. For example, when I took part in the school production, my teachers made sure that other girls in that scene were also seated.

My classmates, too, were very supportive. My friends used to take me for walks and on trips in my wheelchair. They treated me as a regular girl who happened to need help in some areas. Before tests, they let me use their notes since I had difficulty with speed writing during lessons.

There is no *eiruv* in my neighborhood so I couldn't go out in my wheelchair on Shabbos, but my friends came to visit every Shabbos afternoon. There is no way I can describe all the help my friends gave me. They could have patronized me and made me feel disabled, but instead, I was treated as their equal.

When I was fourteen years old, I underwent surgery that was supposed to help me walk. The surgery did not help me walk; instead, it left me with chronic pain. I consulted countless doctors and was treated with numerous therapies — conventional and unconventional — to combat the constant pain that plagued me over many years.

I once heard a *vort* which aptly reflects my difficult experience: Why is there a double expression in the words "*Refa'einu Hashem v'neirafei* — Heal us, Hashem, and we will be healed" (*Shemoneh Esrei*)? Because it is only when Hashem heals us that we can be fully healed. Doctors can try from today until the next millennium. They can prescribe all kinds of medications, but there's no guarantee for success. I can vouch for that. After nine long years of experimenting with innumerable healers and remedies, years in which I constantly pleaded with Hashem to send the right healer, Hashem decided it was time.

The right *shaliach* came in the form of a doctor who gave me an injection that greatly reduced the pain. Seeing that it helped, he gave me this injection every three months, keeping the pain under control. Last year, my situation further improved when a compassionate and capable physiotherapist felt my leg during a therapy session and said, "You're having spasms. You need Botox to relax your muscles." My doctor followed up on her recommendation, and he now administers both injections at every three-month visit. With this course of treatment, my pain has all but disappeared.

One of my big disappointments during my teen years was that I would not be able to attend the out-of-town seminary that my sisters had attended. In hindsight, I can see that I had many positive experiences at the local seminary. I was privileged to hear Rabbi Ezriel Tauber speak at a two-day seminar. I established a close connection with one of my seminary teachers. And I experienced the highlight: a tour of Europe. Our seminary visited Prague, Poland, and many *mekomos kedoshim*.

As I got older, I started writing poetry, which helped me tremendously, allowing me to vent my pain and frustration on paper. To this day, I write poetry when I feel I need a boost.

When I was nineteen years old, I underwent minor surgery. Unexpectedly, some complications set in, and my hospital stay was extended to ten long weeks. It was a difficult time, but I have fond memories of family and friends who showed their concern during that period. Rabbi Tauber was in England at the time, and he came to visit me in the hospital to give me much-needed *chizuk*. Specifically, he quoted the *pasuk* "*Imo anochi v'tzarah* — I am with you in your pain" (*Tehillim* 91:15), saying that when we are in pain, Hashem is there for us more than ever.

My experience with CP as a *frum* Jew is very different from that of nonreligious CP sufferers. I feel that I am respected by my family and friends despite the fact that I am disabled, because Jews respect internal values rather than externals.

On one of my hospital visits, I overheard a young boy express his fear of going to school with crutches; he was afraid he would be bullied. I felt sorry for him and grateful that this, at least, had never been one of my worries.

For many years, I went through the pain of being single, longing to find my true *bashert*. I cried many tears and beseeched Hashem over and over again to help me find a *shidduch*. Once again, I saw that when the time came, Hashem came to the rescue. When I was twenty-nine, I got engaged and married. My husband comes from a completely different family background from mine: he's the oldest, I'm the youngest; he's Lubavitch, I'm *litvish* (not to mention that he's eleven years older than me.), but we are perfectly suited for each other. When I think about all the qualities that I *davened* that my spouse should have, I feel so grateful that Hashem fulfilled each of my requests.

My husband and I encourage and support each other through our respective struggles. I need help with my daily tasks, but the upside is that in some areas life can be very simple. All it takes is a phone call to Hotline (a nonprofit organization) to have a nutritious supper supplied every day of the week!

As someone who has had a fair share of challenges in life, people often ask me to give them advice on how to cope with their challenges. My answer is that I can't advise others. First of all, because I cannot claim to have all the answers. I am only human, and I still find it hard to embrace everything I go through with complete acceptance. I do still cry, and I do still complain (or, as my friend puts it, I'm not complaining, I'm just explaining). Second, every individual is unique, and even for those of us with disabilities, there are so many different types out there, and so many varying levels of tolerance levels and personality factors, that there is no one blanket answer for all.

What I can do, though, is share a number of *divrei Torah* that I have heard and written down over the years that have strengthened my *emunah* in trying times:

It may seem to us that after the sin of the *eitz hada'as*, the one who had been the catalyst for the *aveirah* got off with the most lenient punishment. The snake, who encouraged Chavah to eat from the forbidden fruit, was punished with the curse that everything would taste like earth. What's wrong with that? It's so convenient to have food wherever you go.

But in truth, it's the worst punishment, because the snake never needs to ask Hashem for anything. Hashem wanted to cut off ties with him, so he gave him all he could ever wish for and said goodbye. As for us, Hashem gives us afflictions because He seeks a connection with us.

Because of everything I have gone through, I feel a very close connection with Hashem. I am always "in touch" with Him.

My husband told me the following special *vort* the day we got engaged:

It says, "*Harofei lishvurei lev* — [Hashem] is the healer of the brokenhearted" (*Tehillim* 147:3). The *roshei teivos* (acronym) of these words is *Hallel*, and the *gematria* of the *sofei teivos* (last letter of each word) is 13. When we say *Hallel* with a broken heart, when we thank Hashem even though we are in pain, we can bring down the thirteen Divine attributes of mercy.

My friend once told me this *vort*:

Avraham managed to bring Yitzchak to the *Akeidah*, the ultimate *nisayon*. Yet Sarah, when she merely heard about it, died. It was too much for her to bear. How could this be? They were both on a very high spiritual level.

The answer is that Hashem only tests us with what we can bear. Hashem tested Avraham with the *nisayon* of the *Akeidah* because he could withstand this test, but since it was not Sarah's *nisayon*, she did not have the strength to bear it.

A chassid once told the Gerrer Rebbe, the Imrei Emes, about a difficult situation he was experiencing. The Rebbe said to him: "If you say '*Ana Hashem*' with *kavannah*, you will see your salvation."

After the Rebbe was *niftar*, the chassid complained to his son and successor, the Lev Simcha, "I say '*Ana Hashem*' with so much *kavannah*, but I have not yet seen my salvation."

The Rebbe's son answered, "My father did not mean that you should have *kavannah* when you say in *Hallel*, '*Ana Hashem hoshiah na*' and '*Ana Hashem hatzlichah na*'— Please, Hashem, help us; please, Hashem, grant us success. My father intended that you have *kavannah* at the words '*Ana Hashem ki ani avdecha* — Please, Hashem, for I am Your servant' (*Tehillim* 116:16). Help us, Hashem, for we are Your servants and we submit entirely to Your will."

If we accept Hashem's will, we are satisfied with our lot in life.

Finally, Mrs. Mandel, my seminary teacher, once told me: The English word "life" is built around the word "if." Nonbelievers live their lives thinking, *If only this would happen, if only I could do this, etc.* But the word for "life" in *lashon ha-kodesh*, *chaim*, is built around two *yuds*: Hashem's Name. As *ba'alei emunah*, believers, we live our lives knowing that Hashem orchestrates everything, and therefore all is good.

Nechumelle's husband, Mr. Yisrael Jacobs, speaks:

My experiences have taught me that only Hashem is the true Healer. It isn't the cream or the pill that cures us, although it may sometimes seem like it. When a doctor prescribes medication for me, I always say a *tefillah* before taking it, for I know it is only He Who can make this work.

I have also learned to always try making other people happy, because that brings the ultimate happiness. If I would always focus inward, on what I must endure right now, I would be miserable! So I focus outward: What does this other person need? What will make him happy? And that brings me true contentment.

Nechumelle's mother, Mrs. Miriam Berger, speaks:

When people ask me how I manage to sustain my *emunah* in trying circumstances, I tell them: Because I have no choice. *Emunah* is the only way I can keep going. Without it, I would have despaired and been unable to continue a long time ago.

Hashem gives us two *berachos*: we don't know what's ahead of us, and we don't get to choose our challenges. When raising Nechumelle, we took each day as it came and left the rest in Hashem's hands. We knew that this was what was meant to be, and was the best that could be. We didn't blame anyone — not the doctors, circumstances, or ourselves — but accepted everything as Hashem's will. There were no recriminations such as "If only —" "We could have —" "We should have —" "Why did he/she —" We knew that everything was meant to be, had to be, and was the best that could be.

May we have the *zechus* to realize that everything that happens to us is for the best and experience true *emunah* in our lives.